SCM STUDYGUIDE TO CATHOLIC LITURGY

SCM STUDYGUIDE TO CATHOLIC LITURGY

Edited by
Martin Foster
and
Peter McGrail

scm press

© Catholic Bishops' Conference of England and Wales 2018

Published in 2018 by SCM Press
Editorial office
3rd Floor, Invicta House,
108–114 Golden Lane,
London EC1Y 0TG, UK
www.scmpress.co.uk

SCM Press is an imprint of Hymns Ancient & Modern Ltd (a registered charity)

Hymns Ancient & Modern® is a registered trademark of Hymns Ancient & Modern Ltd
13A Hellesdon Park Road, Norwich,
Norfolk NR6 5DR, UK

British Library Cataloguing in Publication data

A catalogue record for this book is available
from the British Library

978 0 334 05662 1

Typeset by Regent Typesetting
Printed and bound by
Ashford Colour Press

Contents

Abbreviations

AG	*Ad Gentes*
AAS	*Acta Apostolis Sedes*
CCC	Catechism of the Catholic Church
CDW	Congregation for Divine Worship and the Disciple of the Sacraments
CFW	*Consecrated for Worship*
CIGI	*Christian Initiation, General Introduction*
CTM	*Celebrating the Mass*
DS	Denzinger
ESV	English Standard Version
GILH	*General Instruction on the Liturgy of the Hours*
GIRM	*General Instruction of the Roman Missal*
ICEL	International Commission on English in the Liturgy
JB	*Jerusalem Bible*
LG	*Lumen Gentium*
MD	*Mediator Dei*
NRSV	New Revised Standard Version
OC	*Order of Confirmation*
OCF	*Order of Christian Funerals*
OCIA	*Order of Christian Initiation of Adults*
OCM	*Order of Celebrating Matrimony*
ODPB	*Ordination of Deacons, Priests and Bishops*
OM	Order of Mass
PCS	*Pastoral Care of the Sick*
RBC	*Rite of Baptism for Children*
RCIA	*Rite of Christian Initiation of Adults*
RM	*Roman Missal*

RP	*Rite of Penance*
RSV	Revised Standard Version
SacCar	*Sacramentum Caritatis*
SC	*Sacrosanctum Concilium*
UNLYC	*Universal Norms for the Liturgical Year and Calendar*

The Contributors

This book has been written by a group of laypeople and clergy who make up the Liturgical Formation Sub-Committee of the Liturgy Committee of the Bishops' Conference of England and Wales. They include parish priests, pastoral advisers to different dioceses, and nationally based officials and academics, and they bring to the task of exploring and explaining the liturgy of the Catholic Church a range of experiences, perspectives and expertises. They are:

Richard Conrad OP, who teaches at Blackfriars, the Dominican House of Studies in Oxford, and at Maryvale.

Stephen Dean, composer and publisher of liturgical music, former diocesan director of music for the diocese of East Anglia.

Caroline Dollard, Marriage and Family Life Adviser for the Catholic Bishops' Conference of England and Wales, and a member of the *RCIA* Network Executive. Former chair of the Society of St Gregory.

Andrew Downie, parish priest in Hexham and Newcastle diocese and chaplain to Durham University. Secretary of the Catholic Theological Association.

Martin Foster, Director of the Liturgy Office and Assistant Secretary to the Department for Christian Life and Worship of the Catholic Bishops' Conference of England and Wales. Choral Director at St Mary's University, Twickenham.

Jonathan How, parish priest in Arundel and Brighton. Former Director of Studies at St John's Seminary, Wonersh.

Peter McGrail, priest of the archdiocese of Liverpool. Associate Professor in Christian Theology and Head of Theology, Philosophy and Religious Studies at Liverpool Hope University.

Foreword

The celebration of the liturgy is at the heart of the life of the Church. Liturgies that are celebrated with solemnity and care not only give praise and thanksgiving, but also raise the hearts and minds of all who participate. It is important that those who have a role in the liturgical celebration carry out their ministry with due skill and understanding.

I am very grateful to the Liturgical Formation Sub-Committee of the Department for Christian Life and Worship for their work in preparing and writing this *Studyguide to Catholic Liturgy*. I hope that it will encourage and support the formation of ordained and lay liturgical ministers.

Bishop Alan Hopes
Chairman, Liturgy Committee
Catholic Bishops' Conference of England and Wales

Introduction

Let us consider three snapshots of the Roman Catholic (henceforth, 'Catholic')[1] community at prayer across the course of an ordinary Sunday. We start with the main morning service in a town centre parish. To the outside observer what goes on there may appear a curious blend of the formal and the informal. At the start of the service the youngest children may be shepherded out from the church – perhaps forming an enthusiastic but untidy procession. The music might be led by a choir gathered in an upstairs gallery accompanied by an organ, or perhaps by an oddly assorted instrumental group located at the front or side of the church; in either case, the congregational singing would probably range from the downright hesitant to the mildly enthusiastic. Various people would come forward from the congregation to perform different liturgical functions – reading, presenting the gifts of bread and wine, assisting in the administration of Holy Communion – yet the service as a whole never lapses into chaos, and the rites at the altar would be performed with precision and intense care.

We move forward to the late afternoon, and find ourselves in the cathedral for the celebration of Evening Prayer. As the robed choir sings an elaborate musical setting of the Canticle of the Virgin Mary, the ministers solemnly move to the altar and then circle it slowly, wafting clouds of incense. The congregation, meanwhile, make the sign of the cross on their bodies as the song begins and then stand still in respectful silence.

Finally, we move forward once again to the small hours of the night, to a hospital ward, where a priest stands alone beside the bed of an unconscious person, and in an almost inaudible murmur anoints the forehead and hands of that person with olive oil.

Three very different scenes, three very different contexts: what do they have in common? For Catholics they all form part of a rich tapestry of activities that fall under the title of 'liturgy'. The three liturgical snapshots were first of the celebration of the Eucharist, which most Catholics would refer to as the 'Mass', then of the formal Prayer of the Church (sometimes called 'The Divine Office' or the 'Liturgy of the Hours'), and finally of the Anointing of the Sick. However, there are many other activities to which the word is applied. Most conspicuously among those activities are the other rituals that Catholics understand to be sacraments: Baptism, Confirmation, Marriage, Ordination and Penance (Reconciliation). But liturgies, too, are the rituals that mark stages in the way along complex processes – such as funeral rites, or the paths of decision and conversion that individuals travel as they make their way towards membership of the Church or commitment to life as a member of a religious order. The word 'liturgy' covers events that can border on the spectacular, such as an evening Vigil celebrated by the Pope with thousands of young people, or the quiet midweek Mass in a parish celebrated by a single priest and a congregation of two or three. Liturgy, too, figures in countless, practically private, blessings of people, places and objects – and, indeed, in the extremely discreet performance of rituals of exorcism.

In short, the liturgy is a key dimension of how the Catholic Church prays, how it ministers, and how it invites its members to structure their lives. The centrality of liturgy was underlined in the teaching of the Second Vatican Council (1962–65), which stated that it is 'the summit toward which the activity of the Church is directed; it is also the source from which all her power flows'.[2] That is a bold statement, and the purpose of this book is to explore what it means in practice in the lives of Catholics today.

How to Use this Book

This book has been prepared to guide its readers through each of the main liturgical events celebrated by the Catholic Church – the Mass, the processes of initiation, the liturgies associated with ministry, marriage, the daily round of prayer, the liturgies of healing and those liturgies associated with Christian death. These are all presented in Parts 2 and 3 of the book, and if you are looking for specific information on one of these liturgies you can refer directly to the chapter in which it is discussed. There you will find details on the theology that underlines each liturgy, some historical details where necessary, and a detailed discussion of the liturgy's structure and of its pastoral application.

In order to help readers to understand what is specifically 'Catholic' about Catholic liturgy, three general chapters have been provided in Part 1. The first sets in place the general background, by establishing what exactly it is we are dealing with when we speak of the 'Roman' liturgy, and sketching in the essential historical background. The second chapter explores in detail the umbrella concept of 'liturgy' in a Catholic context. In particular, it leads the reader step by step through the theology of liturgy that was set out by the Second Vatican Council. The third chapter then relates that theology to practicalities, and explores the relationship between the texts found in the various liturgical books and the act of celebration that is a key characteristic of Catholic liturgy. Taken together, these three chapters present the 'DNA' of Catholic liturgy – both in its self-understanding and in its practical enactment.

In Part 2 this 'DNA' is uncoiled through a detailed consideration of the various different liturgical rites of the seven sacraments recognized by the Catholic Church. The first chapter in this section of the book provides an overview of the Catholic Church's theology of sacraments; this will help you to become familiar with some of the concepts and words that crop up in the following chapters. We then proceed to consider the 'Sacraments of Christian Initiation' – Baptism, Confirmation and the Eucharist – viewed as the ritual processes through which the Catholic Church forms and inducts its new members. The Catholic Church has developed discrete liturgical patterns that it uses for the initiation of adults and of children; you will find both of these patterns treated in detail. Because of the centrality of the Eucharist in Catholic worship, two chapters are assigned to its discussion; the first of these considers its structure and the meaning of its various parts, the second examines it theologically. The section then moves through the remainder of the major sacramental rites – those at the service of the communion of the Church (Marriage and Ordination) and the sacraments of healing (Penance and the Anointing of the Sick).

Part 3 moves beyond the category of sacraments, and explores some of the broader aspects of the idea of liturgy. This takes us into a consideration of the way in which the Catholic Church uses the liturgy to express the passage of time: the end of the earthly life celebrated in funerals and the patterns of daily, weekly and yearly prayer and liturgy.

Close to the start of each section in Parts 2 and 3 is a summary of the publication of the relevant liturgical book and a list of its key contents. A subsequent box provides the structure of one of the main liturgical celebrations of the rite.

In addition to the printed book, there is a dedicated section on the website of the Liturgy Office of Catholic Bishops' Conference of England and Wales that provides access to the various Church documents mentioned in the text and further supplementary resources (www.liturgyoffice.org.uk/Resources/StudyGuide).

Notes

1 Titles – and their abbreviations – almost inevitably raise issues of ecumenical sensitivity. While acknowledging such sensitivities, the authors have chosen to reflect the language used by the Roman Rite.

2 Second Vatican Council, 1963, Constitution on the Sacred Liturgy, *Sacrosanctum Concilium* (*SC*), 10.

Part 1

Principles of Catholic Liturgy

1

The Roman Rite

PETER MCGRAIL

The Roman Rite

This book is about the Roman Rite. That statement begs a question, as the word 'rite' can be used in three different ways in discussions of the liturgy:

1   In the title of some of the books that contain parts of the liturgy, such as 'The Rite of Christian Initiation of Adults'; in other words, a collection of related liturgical activities. This use of the word 'rite' will gradually disappear as it is replaced by the word 'order' in new translations of the liturgy into English.
2   To indicate a discrete sequence of events within a broader liturgical celebration – for example, 'the Introductory Rites', which form the opening section of the Mass.
3   In the expression 'the Roman Rite'. This use of the word 'rite' indicates in the broadest terms the way in which those dioceses whose bishops are in communion with the Bishop of Rome celebrate the liturgy.

The first two meanings are self-explanatory and will crop up across the book. The third meaning, however, needs a little more exploration. Instead of using the word 'rite' here, we could say, 'the Roman way of celebrating liturgy'. An understanding of that 'way of celebrating' touches not only upon the official texts of the liturgies as we now find them, but also on the centuries of tradition and development that lie behind them. Those developments take us back to the early history of Christianity when the papal liturgy of the city of Rome emerged alongside other local 'ways of celebrating' liturgy. In the West those local liturgical traditions developed most notably in the north Italian city of Milan (often called the 'Ambrosian' Rite); in Spain (the 'Hispanic' or 'Visigothic' Rite); in France (the 'Gallican' Rite); in Ireland; and Latin-speaking North Africa. Today only the Ambrosian and Hispanic Rites continue, albeit in a geographically restricted and Romanized form.

Further east there were even more local rites. Distinctive 'ways of celebrating' were formed in modern-day Syria and the Holy Land (the 'West-Syrian' Rite); in modern Iraq and eastwards to India (the 'East Syrian' Rite); and in Egypt (the 'Coptic' Rite). The political and cultural importance of the imperial capital city of Constantinople during this period is reflected in the broad geographical spread of its own distinctive way of celebrating the liturgy (the 'Byzantine' Rite). To further complicate the picture, in later centuries some Christians who followed the various Eastern Rites united with the Bishop of Rome. Their descendants today form part of the Catholic Church, yet they have retained their ancestors' distinctive ways of celebrating the liturgy. These 'Eastern Rite' Catholics would include, for example, the Greek Catholic Church of the Ukraine and the Syro-Malabar Catholic Church of India. A consideration of their liturgical traditions, however, lies beyond the scope of this book.

The 'Genius' of the Roman Rite

So, what is distinctive about the Roman way of celebrating the liturgy? A summary response was coined over a century ago by the English liturgical historian Edmund Bishop. He wrote that, 'the genius of the native Roman Rite is marked by simplicity, practicality, a great sobriety and self-control, gravity and dignity'.[1] In many ways the Roman Rite reflects the way that the Latin language works. Latin can express complex ideas in very few words; the ancient prayers of the Roman Rite do the same. Yet the shortness of these prayers can mask the richness of their inner content: when we examine in detail the sparse words of the classic texts, we often find that just two or three Latin words have expressed complex theological ideas. All of this presents a challenge when it comes to translating the Roman Rite into languages built upon very different grammatical principles to those that underpin Latin.

Another key feature of the Roman Rite is the way in which it constructs its liturgies by bringing together two different building blocks. The first we can describe as 'fixed'. These are those parts of a liturgy that are always the same whenever the liturgy is celebrated. So, the Mass will always contain several set dialogues between priest and people (for example, 'Lift up your hearts' – 'We lift them up to the Lord'). The second building block is made up of 'changeable' elements – these differ depending on the season or the context in which the liturgy is celebrated. For example, the funeral rites contain a range of prayers to be said by the minister that reflect the age of the deceased person, or the circumstances in which they had lived or died. This combination of fixed and changeable elements does two things: it sets up a familiar pattern that helps participants to feel 'at home' in the liturgy, and it allows for each celebration of the liturgy to be shaped to the feast, season, or event. All this made the Roman Rite easy to use – and this straightforward practicality helps to account for its spread during the first millennium beyond the boundaries of the diocese of Rome itself.

The Roman Rite Today: The Historical Context

The liturgy celebrated in most Catholic churches today is the result of a long historical development. It contains many very ancient elements but has changed along the course of its history. It is not the purpose of this book to provide a full account of that history – you will find some indications of where to look for that in the 'Further Reading' section. Our focus is the liturgies of the Roman Rite celebrated in most Catholic churches across the world now. These came into their current form during the second half of the twentieth century and were the result of a wholesale revision of the liturgy set in motion by the Constitution on the Sacred Liturgy of the Second Vatican Council, *Sacrosanctum Concilium*.

Sacrosanctum Concilium

The Second Vatican Council (1962–65) produced 16 documents that have substantially shaped the thought and life of the Catholic community. The first of these to be agreed by the Council was the Constitution on the Sacred Liturgy (1963), usually known by its Latin title taken from its opening words, 'Sacrosanctum Concilium'. This document set out the underlying principles that governed the revision of the Roman liturgy. While it is not, technically, a doctrinal document, its opening section provides a succinct theology of the liturgy that enjoys authoritative status within the Catholic Church.

Nonetheless a little history is important. The Constitution, and the reforms that flowed from it, did not happen in a vacuum. Behind them lay a century of liturgical scholarship and experimentation that is generally known as the 'Liturgical Movement'. Without an understanding of this long gestation the rationale behind today's liturgy cannot be understood. Scholars generally trace the origins of the Liturgical Movement to the foundation in 1833 of the French Benedictine monastery of Solesmes by Prosper Gueranger. The Movement is usually regarded as closing with the promulgation of *Sacrosanctum Concilium*. However, the truth is more complex on two fronts. First, the Liturgical Movement had a long pre-history as it built upon foundations laid from the seventeenth century onwards by scholars who studied and published the early liturgical texts that they discovered in libraries across Europe. Second, the Liturgical Movement itself fell into two broad phases.

The Liturgical Movement: Phase One

The first phase continued and intensified the historical liturgical research that had been carried out by earlier generations of scholars and was largely carried out in Benedictine monasteries – at Gueranger's Solesmes, but also at Beuron and Maria-Laach in Germany and Mont-César (Keizerberg) in Belgium. The monks engaged on this work sought out ancient liturgical texts, published academic editions of early manuscripts, and analysed those texts in detail. Crucially, Gueranger and others also communicated those scholarly findings to a broader audience beyond a monastic setting through intelligent but popular publications such as the multi-volume *The Liturgical Year*.[2] However, the leaders of the first phase of the Liturgical Movement were not interested in revising the texts of the various liturgical rites. It was not until the twentieth century that liturgical scholarship and the encouragement of liturgical devotional practice began to converge with other currents within the Church and to lead, cautiously at first, towards a revision of the actual liturgical texts themselves.

The Liturgical Movement: Phase Two

The starting pistol for the second phase was sounded in 1903 by the Papal Instruction *Tra le Sollecitudini* on sacred music.[3] This was the first in a series of liturgical reforms carried out under Pope St Pius X (1835–1914; Pope from 1903). *Tra le Sollecitudini* introduced into the liturgical vocabulary a concept that became a key principle for the second phase of the Liturgical Movement. This was the notion that the 'active participation' in the liturgy was the 'foremost and indispensable source' of the true Christian spirit.[4] It took six years for the expression to be taken up as the rallying call it became, but in 1909 Dom Lambert Beauduin (1873–1960), a monk of Mont César, made it a cornerstone of his address to the 1909 National Congress of Catholic Works in Malines. Beauduin emphasized the need to open the riches of the liturgy to the laity, and so highlighted a paradox. On the one hand, the Catholic Church emphasized the centrality of its sacramental system and held attendance at Sunday Mass to be the touchstone of Catholic identity. Yet, on the other hand, in practice it was not the liturgy that nurtured the spiritual life of most Catholics. Their spirituality, instead, was built upon a rich tapestry of extra-liturgical devotional activities addressed to Christ, to the Virgin Mary, and to the saints that were largely independent of the formal liturgy. Significantly, these devotions were generally performed in the vernacular languages, rather than in Latin. This ease of access, together with the emotive content of many devotions, contributed towards their popularity. Beauduin's strong desire was that participation in the liturgy itself – rather than the popular devotions – should inform and shape the inner spirituality of Catholics. The emphasis on participation raised, of course, the question of language because Latin remained the only language in which the Roman Rite was celebrated. Therefore, the production of bilingual Mass books that allowed the congregation to follow the prayers and rituals in their own languages was regarded across the first part of the twentieth century as the primary tool for opening the riches of the liturgy to the people.

Questions for Reflection

- What might be the chief features of a liturgically formed spirituality?
- How might it differ from other popular forms of spirituality?

As the century progressed, liturgical scholarship intensified and liturgical experimentation began. A place where these went together was the abbey of Maria-Laach. From 1917 onwards, an experimental Mass was celebrated each week there, at which the priest faced the congregation across the altar, intercessory prayer was made after the readings, and the bread and wine were processed to the altar by members of the congregation. At the same time, the scholar Odo Casel (1886–1948), himself a monk of Maria-Laach, developed his 'Mystery Theology' which, while controversial in its time, paved the way for one of the key motifs of *Sacrosanctum Concilium*, the Paschal Mystery.

The Liturgical Initiatives of Pope Pius XII

As the century progressed, the question was more insistently asked as to whether further official revision of the rites themselves was needed if the ideal of active participation was to be achieved. Concrete steps in that direction were taken under Pope Pius XII (1876–1958; Pope from 1939). Pius XII took things forward in two directions. First, in 1947 he published an Encyclical Letter on the Sacred Liturgy, *Mediator Dei*.[5] This document set out for the first time an official and authoritative systematic theology of liturgy. The document was simultaneously defensive and progressive – it opposed certain approaches to liturgical renewal (almost certainly, but not directly, Casel's Mystery Theology) while taking forward the Church's understanding of what was going on when its members gathered in prayer. It is impossible to overestimate the significance of this document in the lead-up to the discussion of the liturgy at the Second Vatican Council. Many ideas found in *Mediator Dei* lie behind the text of *Sacrosanctum Concilium*'s theological section – although the complete absence of footnote references to recent papal teaching in the final text of the Constitution rather masks its closeness to the encyclical.

The second direction in which Pope Pius XII took the Roman liturgy was the resumption of the revision of the rites themselves that had begun under Pope Pius X. To the average Catholic layperson, the impact of the accelerating process of revision during Pope Pius XII's long pontificate was felt in a relaxation in the regulations governing the fast to be observed before reception of Holy Communion, and in permission for Masses to be celebrated in the evening. Greater latitude was also given for the celebration of some of the rituals in the language of the people, rather than in Latin. The most radical revisions were carried out by a small commission that Pope Pius established, and which is normally named after him – the 'Pian' Commission – which met from 1948 to 1962, and which was tasked with preparing a general reform of the liturgy. The work of this Commission culminated in the revision in 1951 and 1955 of the liturgies celebrated between Palm Sunday and Easter, which foreshadowed the reforms undertaken after the Council.

The Second Vatican Council and Liturgical Renewal

The work of the Pian Commission was wound up shortly before the start of the Second Vatican Council, and responsibility for taking forward the general liturgical reform passed to the Council. After the final text of *Sacrosanctum Concilium* had been agreed and the Constitution promulgated on 4 December 1963, a new body was set up to bring its ideas into practice. This was the '*Consilium* for the Implementation of the Constitution on the Sacred Liturgy' (henceforth, '*Consilium*').

The *Consilium* (February 1964–August 1969)

The *Consilium* was an international body of bishops and liturgical experts that was responsible for the revision of the liturgical books of the Catholic Church. It carried out its work through a number of study groups, each of which was tasked with the revision of a particular book or aspect of the liturgy. The revision of the rites was substantially completed by the *Consilium's* successor body, the Sacred Congregation for Divine Worship (1969–83).

Translation

All the liturgical books prepared by the *Consilium* were written in Latin. However, one of the most obvious impacts of the post-Vatican II revision of the liturgy has been its translation into the vernacular – that is, into the ordinary, everyday languages of people across the world. The Roman Rite had traditionally been celebrated in Latin – and particularly in the turmoil of the Reformation, the liturgy was understood to serve a vital function in conserving and transmitting the faith of the Catholic Church. For centuries, the universal use of Latin was regarded as a sign of both unity and orthodoxy. By the eve of the Second Vatican Council, however, permission was increasingly being granted for the vernacular celebration of substantial sections of various rituals (for example, of Baptism). The extension of this faculty to the entire Roman liturgy was triggered by article 36 of *Sacrosanctum Concilium*, which strikes a carefully balanced note, reflecting the intensity of the debate on translation at the Council. Latin was to be preserved in the Latin (Roman) Rite, but the use of the vernacular was to be extended – cautiously, and always under the oversight of the local bishops. In practice, however, the use of the vernacular very quickly extended to all the rites of the Church. The new Latin texts produced by the *Consilium* serve as definitive 'Typical Editions' upon which the translations into different languages are based.

The principles underpinning those translations have changed across the period since the Council. The *Consilium* set out the initial ground rules in 1969 with a formal Instruction, generally known by its French title, *Comme le prévoit*. This Instruction established that a literal word-for-word translation of the Latin texts was not required. Instead, there should be a relationship of 'dynamic equivalence' between the Latin and vernacular texts. The language of the people should express the key content of the original; the words and ideas used, however, should reflect the structures and grammatical characteristics of the modern language. The strength of this approach was that it opened the way for the liturgy to be prayed in a natural and fluid manner. The weakness was that the results were at times rather loose and sometimes imprecise. In 2001 a revised set of translation guidelines was published in the form of the Instruction *Liturgiam Authenticam*.[6] Rather than the 'dynamic equivalence' preferred by its predecessor Instruction, the 2001 Instruction insisted on a very close relationship between the Latin original and the translations. Technically, this approach of 'formal equivalence' results in translations that are far closer to the Latin originals, and which are more formal than the everyday language of the people.

The International Commission on English in the Liturgy (ICEL)

English translations of the Roman Rite are prepared by an international commission of bishops who represent the national Bishops' Conferences of 11 English-speaking countries. Their work is supported by a secretariat based in Washington DC. ICEL was first established in 1963, and its current statutes were approved by Rome in 2003. ICEL does not publish liturgical books – the task of approving and eventually publishing a translation for use in each territory is the responsibility of the local Bishops' Conference. Before that can happen, however, the Vatican Congregation for Divine Worship and the Discipline of the Sacraments needs to confirm the authenticity of the translation. In 2017 Pope Francis issued a document, *Magnum Principium*, that places the weight of the decision of approval with the Bishops' Conference.

'Ordinary' and 'Extraordinary' Forms of the Roman Rite

For many commentators, the promulgation of *Sacrosanctum Concilium* and the subsequent work of the *Consilium* mark the point at which the Liturgical Movement passed definitively into the mainstream of the Church and lost its distinctive identity. In the eyes of a small but vocal minority of Catholics, however, the post-Vatican II reforms are regarded as a divergence from the original intentions of the Liturgical Movement. As a pastoral response, some limited use of the pre-Vatican II forms had been permitted by the Vatican during the years after the Council. In 2007, Benedict XVI (1927–; Pope 2005–13) issued the Apostolic Letter *Summorum Pontificum*, in which he considerably broadened out the circumstances in which the older forms may be celebrated.[7] Importantly, he distinguished between two forms of the Roman liturgy. The 'Ordinary' form is that adopted after the Second Vatican Council; the 'Extraordinary' form is the Roman Rite as it stood on the eve of the Council. The liturgy encountered in most Catholic settings is the 'Ordinary' form, but it is possible to find oneself at celebrations that use the pre-1963 rites. However, a detailed consideration of the 'Extraordinary' form lies beyond the scope of this book.

Notes

1 'The Genius of the Roman Rite', in *Liturgica Historica: Papers on the Liturgical and Religious Life of the Western Church* (Oxford: Clarendon Press, 1918, 1962), pp. 1–19, at 12.

2 This substantial work has been printed many times in several languages, and remains in print today.

3 Pope St Pius X, 1903, *Motu Proprio* on Sacred Music, *Tra le Sollecitudini.*

4 The quoted passage is taken from the Preamble to the document.

5 Pope Pius XII, 1947, Encyclical Letter on the Sacred Liturgy, *Mediator Dei (MD).*

6 Congregation for Divine Worship and the Discipline of the Sacraments, 2001, Instruction on the Use of Vernacular Liturgies in the Publication of the Books of the Roman Liturgy, *Liturgiam Authenticam* (Rome: 2001).

7 Pope Benedict XVI, 2007, *Motu Proprio* on the Use of the Roman Liturgy prior to the Reform of 1970, *Summorum Pontificum.*

2

Catholic Theology of the Liturgy

PETER MCGRAIL

Until the twentieth century the Catholic Church lacked an 'official' theology of the liturgy. Detailed theologies of the sacraments had, of course, been in place for centuries – and Chapter 4 of this book will lead the reader into these. However, an all-embracing understanding of what was happening in theological terms when the Church gathered to worship had never been agreed. Yet the rites that were revised after the Second Vatican Council were informed by a rich theology of liturgy developed across the century. This chapter explores that theological vision, and begins by posing a basic question: what, exactly, does the word 'liturgy' mean?

The Word 'Liturgy'

The English word 'liturgy' translates the Greek word '*leitourgia*'. This is formed from two other Greek words: '*laos*', meaning 'the people', and '*ergon*', meaning a work or an action. So *leitourgia* is frequently translated as 'the Work of the People' – which can suggest that liturgy is primarily a human activity. However, a better translation would be 'something done on behalf of the people'. In the ancient world, the word '*leitourgia*' frequently described a public service carried out by a citizen – such as serving as a civil magistrate. The boundaries between civil and religious roles were fluid, so it is not surprising to find the word used to describe a religious role in the Greek translation of the Hebrew Scriptures and in the New Testament: the worship carried out by the Temple priests. However, to map that Old Testament understanding on to the worshipping Church of today would provide an incomplete definition. Simply to state that the liturgy is public worship carried out on behalf of the people by ordained ministers fails to give adequate attention to the person and role of Christ. Therefore, the Catholic theology of the liturgy takes as its starting point neither the assembly of the faithful nor the activity of the ministers, but the work of Christ.

Christ, the Great High Priest

Drawing substantially on Pope Pius XII's *Mediator Dei*, *Sacrosanctum Concilium* asserts that the person, first and foremost, who is at work on behalf of the people in the liturgy is Christ himself.[1] This response is founded on three theological principles.

The Content of Christ's Worship: The Paschal Mystery

The Gospels relate that during his lifetime Christ prayed to the Father, gave thanks to the Father, blessed the Father – all activities that we would describe as worship. The New Testament letters and the Book of Revelation also speak of the risen and ascended Christ offering prayer and intercession for the Church in an act of heavenly worship. However, to understand Christ's priesthood more fully we must ask what his interior motivation is for these activities. Let us stand back for a moment from the events of Jesus' earthly life, and shift our focus to the admittedly perplexing question of the Holy Trinity. A helpful way of engaging with the notion of the Trinity is to focus on how its members relate to one another – Father to Son, Son to Spirit, Spirit to Father. The Father eternally gives himself to the Son, and the Son glorifies the Father in giving himself fully to the Father in return. In other words, everything that the Son is and does constitutes a gift of himself to the Father. Theologically, this is the origin and foundation of Christian worship.

How this relates to the liturgy becomes clear when we consider the incarnation – the entrance of the Son into time and space to share in human nature.

The incarnation introduces the further dimensions of worship and of sacrifice into the relationship between Son and Father. The New Testament understands the birth of the Son as an act of self-emptying ('*kenosis*') – again in obedience to the Father. St Paul reminded the Christians of Philippi that they should have the same mind as Christ who, 'though he was in the form of God, did not regard equality with God as something to be exploited, but emptied himself, taking the form of a slave, being born in human likeness'.[2] Through the incarnation the Son's devoted pouring out of himself in submission across eternity finds expression in time and space as worship, when he experiences humanity in its fullness, in its frailties and in its mortality. *Mediator Dei* drew upon chapter 10 of the letter to the Hebrews to draw out the link between the incarnation and Christ as worshipper:

> No sooner, in fact, is 'the Word made flesh' than he shows himself to the world vested with a priestly office, making to the Eternal Father an act of submission which will continue uninterruptedly as long as he lives: 'When he came into the world he said . . . "Behold I come to do your Will".'[3]

All of Christ's earthly ministry can be understood in terms of his self-emptying – summed up in his declaration that he came 'not to be served but to serve and to give his life a ransom for many'.[4] The last point emphasizes the essential unity between the incarnation and the cross. Indeed, *Mediator Dei* understood all the events of Christ's earthly life and ministry as directed towards this sacrificial end.[5] However, if we look closely at the passage taken from the letter to the Philippians that was cited above, we find that while Paul, too, passes directly from the incarnation to the cross, he completes the sequence of events by speaking of Christ's glorification:

> And being found in human form, he humbled himself by becoming obedient to the point of death, even death on a cross. Therefore God has highly exalted him and bestowed on him the name that is above every name.[6]

For St Paul, therefore, the crucifixion and exaltation of Christ form an essential unity; to speak of Christ's redemptive work only in terms of the cross provides an incomplete account. *Sacrosanctum Concilium* developed this theme by introducing into the formal teaching of the Church the necessary vocabulary to describe that unity. Christ's death, resurrection and ascension are collectively described as constituting the 'Paschal Mystery'.[7] This terminology recurs across the document, and it expresses one of the key themes of *SC* and of the subsequent liturgical revision.

The word 'Paschal' relates to the Latin word for Easter, but also looks back to the Jewish Passover tradition, with all its sacrificial and redemptive overtones. 'Paschal' speaks of both Good Friday and of Easter Sunday, of the cross and of the resurrection. It points more effectively, therefore, to the rich set of ideas found in the letter to the Philippians than would the apparently more straightforward term 'Easter Mystery'. As for the word 'Mystery', the letters to the Ephesians and Colossians speak of the 'mystery' of God's plan for human salvation – hidden since the creation of the world but now revealed in Christ.[8] The 'Paschal Mystery' is, therefore, the heart of the good news.

Three key ideas converge in the Paschal Mystery. First, Christ on the cross places all he is and has into the hands of the Father in obedience to the divine plan. The cross, therefore, is the place where the relationship between the Son's obedience and his incarnate worship is most clearly expressed. Christ obediently ascends the cross as the cosmic High Priest. The second idea flows from the first: he also hangs there as sacrificial victim. The cross marks the culmination of a life that is sacrificial from beginning to end. It is Christ's total and unqualified gift of himself that brings about human salvation. Sinful humanity has never been capable of the pure gift of self to God that is right and proper. God sends his Son to implant in humanity his eternal gift of himself to the Father, so that by clinging to him as his Body, humanity can now at last be in right-relation to God. Through the Paschal Mystery Christ, therefore, simultaneously glorifies God and redeems humanity.[9] The third idea flows from *SC*'s insistence that the Paschal Mystery draws the cross, the resurrection and the ascension into a unified whole. The resurrection of the human body of Jesus begins the transformation of the entire created order. The 'normal' pattern of fallen existence is that life inevitably succumbs to death, but Christ's rising initiated a new pattern, throwing the inevitable march from life to death into reverse. He is the 'first fruits' of the new creation[10] in which it will be life rather than death that will have the final word, renewal and not decay, hope and not despair.

What are the implications of all this in the life of the worshipper? The first is to understand the entire Christian life as an ongoing identification with the glorified humanity of Jesus. St Paul explored this in the letter to the Romans by associating Christian baptism with the Paschal Mystery:

Do you not know that all of us who have been baptised into Christ Jesus were baptised into his death? We were buried therefore with him by baptism into death, in order that, just as Christ was raised from the dead by the glory of the Father, we too might walk in newness of life.[11]

The Christian life that follows Baptism is characterized for Paul by an ongoing identification of the believer with the Paschal Mystery; indeed, Paul invented words to express this: Christians are 'co-buried' with Christ, 'co-risen', and so on.[12] The Christian life is, therefore, one of progressive transformation, and all the various rites of the Catholic Church have as their central content the progressive working out of the consequences of participating in Christ's Paschal Mystery in the life of the believer.

The second implication relates to the destiny of the material universe, and to the role of elements taken from the natural order in the liturgy. The dramatic reversal of the destiny of death that is set in motion by the Paschal Mystery extends beyond the renewal of humanity – it is the whole of creation that has been set on course to a new destiny by Christ's rising from the dead. Again, in writing to the Romans, Paul describes the whole of creation as being set free from the cycle of decay, groaning in the birth-pangs of what is to come.[13] As we shall see in Part 2 of this book, this final point is crucial to an understanding of Catholic liturgy that makes great use of elements drawn from the natural order – bread, wine, oil, water, material signs, images and symbols.

Christ and the Church

If the Paschal Mystery forms the content of Christ's worship, how does that relate to the liturgy that is celebrated by the Church today? More specifically, returning to an earlier point, in what way does it help us to understand Christ as the primary actor in the Church's liturgy? The response given by Catholic liturgical theology is rooted in the biblical image of the Church and Christ as forming a single body. In the New Testament, this image is most fully expressed in St Paul's first letter to the Corinthians in which he urges a very divided congregation to recognize that the disputes that have arisen among them are utterly contrary to their nature as Christians.[14] Through Baptism they have been called to something greater. The Church is not merely a collection of like-minded individuals, each relating to Christ on a one-to-one basis. Rather, it forms an organic whole, centred on Christ who does not stand apart from it but is himself part of the complex entity Christ-and-Church.

The liturgical implications of this notion are profound. If Christ and the Church are so closely linked as to form a 'corporate personality', then the Church is drawn into the worship that the incarnate Son offers to the Father. Similarly, the Church cannot offer worship in time and space without involving its Head – the cosmic dimension of worship penetrates the earthly, the spiritual and the material. All this found its clearest expression in *Mediator Dei*, which framed its definition of the liturgy in terms of the corporate unity between Christ and the Church:

> The sacred liturgy is . . . the public worship which our Redeemer as Head of the Church renders to the Father, as well as the worship which the community of the faithful renders to its Founder, and through Him to the heavenly Father. It is, in short, the worship rendered by the Mystical Body of Christ in the entirety of its Head and members.[15]

The liturgy, therefore, is essentially collective, and liturgical services can never be private functions. At the same time, the utter incongruence of any note of liturgical individualism is obvious. The impact of any liturgical celebration will always extend beyond the immediate set of worshippers, and the liturgy requires that any congregation understands what it is doing within a broader framework than its own context or particular set of needs. Each and every liturgy brings into focus the nature both of the Church and of its mission in the world.[16] Therefore, *SC* states that the liturgy 'manifests' the Church,[17] as 'a sign lifted up among the nations'.[18]

The Presence of Christ in the Liturgy

The intense association of Christ with the Church carries a further liturgical implication: as the Church celebrates the liturgy, Christ is present and active in the liturgical action. *Mediator Dei* offered a list of four ways in which Christ is present in the liturgy.[19] This list was taken up by *SC*, which added a scriptural dimension:

Christ's Presence in the Liturgy (*Sacrosanctum Concilium*, 7)

1 In the person of the minister at Mass.
2 (Especially) in the Eucharistic species.
3 In the sacraments – 'when a man baptizes it is really Christ himself who baptizes'.
4 In the Scriptures – 'it is he himself who speaks when the holy scriptures are read in Church'.
5 In the liturgical assembly as it sings and prays – 'for he promised, "Where two or three are gathered in my name, there am I in the midst of them"' (Matt. 18.20).

This emphasis placed by both documents on the multi-faceted idea of Christ's presence indicates the pivotal role it plays in the Catholic understanding of liturgy. It also offers a response to the earlier question regarding the principal agent in the liturgy. It is Christ – present and active in the celebrations of his Body, the Church. What this means in practice will be explored for each different type of liturgical celebration in the chapters of Part 2 of this book. However, before that we need to ask how it is possible to speak of Christ as present in the liturgy.

The Holy Spirit and the Liturgy

A constant criticism of the Western tradition made by the Eastern Churches has been the tendency of the West to focus on the person and action of Christ in the liturgy while failing to pay due regard to the role played there by the Holy Spirit. SC went some way to redressing this imbalance. It argues that the Spirit played a key role in the mission of Christ[20] and of the Apostles,[21] and continues to be active in the liturgical prayer of the Church.[22] The Son's emptying of himself in the incarnation, therefore, on which the twin liturgical themes of worship and salvation are grounded, is presented as an event of the Spirit. The mission of the Church, manifested in the liturgy, is driven forward by the presence of the Spirit in the Church. The whole prayer and worship offered by the Church in the liturgy is animated by the Spirit.

The Holy Spirit and the Mystical Body of Christ

These various strands come together in the notion that the liturgy is an activity of the Body of Christ. The intense union of Head and members implied by the image begs a question: how is it possible to speak of this corporate personality in the first place? If the concept is to have true meaning at the deepest level, then that unity requires an undergirding principle that extends into the depths of both Head and members and draws them into the most intense unity. The Second Vatican Council identified that principle with the Holy Spirit. Its detailed response is not, however, to be found in *SC*. The relationship between the Holy Spirit, the Mystical Body of Christ, and the liturgy was taken up and developed more fully in the Dogmatic Constitution on the Church, *Lumen Gentium,* which was promulgated in 1964. There we read that Christ constitutes the Mystical Body by communicating his Spirit to his followers.[23] The same Spirit, therefore, is in the Head and members, and 'unifies and moves the whole body'.[24] It is by virtue of the presence and activity of the Spirit, therefore, that one can even speak of the liturgy in terms of 'the full public worship . . . performed by the Mystical Body of Christ, Head and members'.[25]

The Holy Spirit, liturgy and time

The presence and action of the Spirit introduces a further dimension to the Catholic understanding of liturgy; because of the Spirit's engagement in the liturgy something strange happens there to time. We tend to think of time as passing along a straight line; we live from one present moment to the next. As each event occurs, it immediately leaves the present and becomes part of the past. In a similar way, ahead of us lies a vast future that is unshaped and uncertain. Of course, memory and imagination can both recall the past and creatively anticipate the future, and the memory of past events can impact on life in the present – just as the future can be eagerly anticipated or dreaded. However, any relationship between past, present and future goes on at a purely psychological level; neither memory nor imagination can take us either backwards or forwards in time – they cannot restore a past event to the present nor can they make the future happen here and now.

Yet, these principles break down when confronted with a Holy Spirit which is not constrained by the dimensions of time or space. The presence and activity in the liturgy of that Spirit carries two significant repercussions – one relating to the past, the other to the future. During the liturgy there is a constant reference back to the events of the history of salvation through the proclamation of the Scriptures. This finds its clearest expression in the Eucharist, celebrated in response to Jesus' command, 'Do this in memory of me'. The presence and action of the Spirit in the liturgy makes this remembering more than the casting of a collective mind back to historically remote biblical events. Rather, as the Mystical Body which is constituted by the Spirit recalls God's saving action in the past, then the inner dynamism of those past events becomes present and effective here and now.

The implications of this for the Eucharist will be discussed in Chapter 8, where the rich biblical idea of memorial – or 'anamnesis' – will be considered. There is, however, a more general application of the principle that extends across the whole liturgical field. As we have noted, the core content of Christ's worship is the Paschal Mystery in the full sense expressed above, remembering that Mystery forms a part of every liturgy. That constant 'calling to mind' in a context animated by the Holy Spirit means that the liturgy is a constant making present in time of Christ and his saving work. The answer, therefore, to the question at the close of the previous section is that Christ is present in the liturgy through the free movement of the Spirit across the barriers of time and space.

To focus solely on the past, however, would result in an incomplete perspective. There is a second liturgical consequence of the Spirit's transcendence of temporal boundaries, this time touching on the relationship between the present and the future. The liturgy is not only the place where the historically past realities of the Paschal Mystery become present and effective; it is also the place where the future – and, specifically, the end of time – is anticipated. The Christ who is present by the power of the Spirit is the glorified risen Lord. *SC* expresses this extraordinary notion when it refers to the liturgical assembly as the place where the end of time breaks into the present: 'In the earthly liturgy we take part in a foretaste of the heavenly liturgy which is celebrated in the Holy City of Jerusalem toward which we journey as pilgrims, where Christ is sitting at the right hand of God, Minister of the holies and of the true tabernacle.'[26]

This passage requires us to think carefully about the idea of 'heaven'. Is it a sort of parallel universe that exists alongside the one that is accessible to the human senses? Underpinning that perception there can easily lie an unspoken assumption that heaven is outside space and time. However, the Scriptures describe the Spirit as the gift of the last days, and Jesus says that the Spirit will reveal 'the things that are to come'.[27] The liturgy, therefore, speaks not of a heaven outside time, but as the very consummation of time. This way of looking at things can sometimes presume that heaven is another point in space and time to our own, but 'heaven' must surely be more than a parallel state or universe: it is the definitive reign of God. The liturgy gives its participants a foretaste of the end of the world, and so sets up a tension between the now and the not yet; it expresses a longing for and a hope of the final drawing together of all the threads of cosmic history in Christ:

> With all the warriors of the heavenly army we sing a hymn of glory to the Lord; venerating the memory of the saints, we hope for some part and fellowship with them; we eagerly await the Saviour, Our Lord Jesus Christ, until he our life shall appear and we too will appear with him in glory.[28]

Participation in the Liturgy

So, finally, we turn to the participants and their experience of the liturgy. The notion of liturgical participation is a key and recurrent theme in *SC*, and was a key driver for the programme of liturgical revision mapped out by the Constitution: 'In the restoration and promotion of the sacred liturgy the full and active participation by all the people is the aim to be considered before all else, for it is the primary and indispensable source from which the faithful are to derive the true Christian spirit.'[29]

During the years since the Council, the notion of participation has become one of the most contentious and acrimoniously debated liturgical issues in the Catholic Church. As questions of participation will emerge again and again across the length of this book, it is useful to clarify at the outset how this surprisingly complex notion is to be understood. We shall begin by looking at the expression itself and especially at the Latin word that is normally translated as 'active'. We then consider the relationship between 'internal participation' – what is going on inside a person during the liturgy – and its 'exterior' counterpart.

'Full, active, conscious participation'

As was noted in the previous chapter, the concept of participation emerged with *Tra le Sollecitudini*; in *SC* it is described as 'full, conscious and active participation'. Of the three adjectives, the one that most constantly appears is the word generally translated as 'active'.[30] The frequency of its use, the considerable weight placed upon it in *SC*, and the very force of the word itself, undoubtedly contributed to a widespread popular sense that liturgical participation equated to people 'doing things' during the liturgy. One corollary of this understanding could be an approach that regards an individual's participation to be in some way diminished or impaired if they lack an 'active' part to play, a role that is specific to them in the celebration.

The Latin word that is generally translated as 'active' is not the straightforward '*activa*', but '*actuosa*' – for which there is no direct English equivalent. The word does, certainly, convey the notion of action, but it implies a quality of action – an action that is sustained by a particular conviction, orientation, or drive. It points, therefore, to those actions that manifest and are underpinned by something that is going on within the person who performs them. Use of the expression '*participatio actuosa*', therefore, suggests that the liturgical participant is engaged on two levels. As they take part in the liturgy an internal process is going on related to the meaning of what is being celebrated. At the same time, they engage with their bodies in the liturgical action – through physical movement, song, acclamation, use of symbols, bodily posture, and even stillness and silence. The internal and external dimensions inform each other; it is not a case of choosing between either interior or exterior participation, but of recognizing that the two necessarily operate interactively.

Sacrosanctum Concilium makes only the briefest mention of 'interior' and 'exterior' participation.[31] Such a mention was, however, made by *Mediator Dei*, and when, during the course of the Council, a number of bishops asked that a fuller exposition should be inserted into the text, the Commission responsible for steering the liturgical constitution through the Council replied that all this was clearly set out in the encyclical, and that therefore there was no need to provide again a complete exposition of the ideas.[32] What follows, therefore, is informed by that encyclical.

Exterior liturgical participation

Put simply, human beings have bodies – they touch, they taste, they see, they move; they interact in space and time with other human bodies. This is as true of how they engage in liturgical worship as it is of any other field of human activity. The liturgical rites, therefore, both communicate to each participant the doctrinal content of what is being celebrated and also enable the participants to express their response to it. Moreover, in the context of liturgy this engagement with the physical takes on two further layers of meaning. First, it expresses the social nature of worship: Christians participate not as individuals but as members of the Mystical Body. The liturgy 'reveals and emphasizes the unity' of that Body.[33] Hence, we return to the theme developed in SC that the liturgy manifests the Church. Second, the physical engagement with the material symbols that lie at the heart of the sacraments is itself the means by which participants are drawn into the Paschal Mystery. The baptismal water, the oil of anointing, the bread and wine in the Eucharist, point of themselves to the renewal of the created order inaugurated in Christ's rising from the dead. The liturgical use of these physical signs not only points to the Paschal Mystery, but conveys its effects: '[The liturgy] involves the presentation of man's sanctification under the guise of signs perceptible by the senses and its accomplishment in ways appropriate to each of these signs.'[34]

Here we encounter a fundamental principle of Catholic sacramental theology. Just as, in the incarnation of Christ, the divine became present and active in a physical body, so too in the liturgy human beings – spirit and matter – are drawn deeper into the life of God through their engagement with elements drawn from the material universe.

Interior liturgical participation

The effectiveness of an individual's exterior participation in the liturgy rests on several factors, some of which are exterior – for example, the care taken in preparing the liturgical environment, the quality and appropriateness of the music, vestments and sacred vessels. Even the lighting, the heating and the effectiveness of the amplification system can affect the degree to which a person engages with a liturgical celebration. However, what is going on inside the individual worshipper, too, considerably influences their participation in the liturgy. First of all, their emotional state of mind, immediate preoccupations and even their general health can factor into the way they approach a liturgical event. However, both *Mediator Dei* and *Sacrosanctum Concilium* focus particularly on the spiritual disposition of the worshipper.[35] Put simply, the depth and quality of participation is ultimately not governed by the emotional energy experienced in a liturgical celebration, nor by the intellectual stimulation given by a sermon. It is, rather, governed by the fundamental patterns of an individual's internal world – the priorities that determine the choices they make, the motives that feed into their actions, the extent to which the worship of God forms a constant background to their lives – and by the coherence of these internal factors with the external celebration.

As with so much else regarding the liturgy, all this may be best understood in relation to the Paschal Mystery. In this way, the core question becomes one of the extent to which the life of the individual Christian is gradually becoming patterned after the example of Christ's own self-emptying in loving service. This is, of course, a lifelong process that takes place both inside and outside the Liturgy. It is dependent upon a personal life of prayer,[36] and can draw fruitfully from forms of popular religious expression beyond the liturgy.[37] The Catholic Church's understanding is that a virtuous circle can be established between an individual's interior life and the liturgy. A developing personal alignment to Christ's Paschal Mystery feeds into an exterior participation in the liturgy. In turn, that exterior participation reinforces, sometimes challenges, and carries forward into mission what is happening within the person. Liturgical participation, in short, is concerned with conversion of heart and transformation of life. Pope Benedict wrote:

> A heart reconciled to God makes genuine participation possible. The faithful need to be reminded that there can be no *actuosa participatio* in the sacred mysteries without an accompanying effort to participate actively in the life of the Church as a whole, including a missionary commitment to bring Christ's love into the life of society.[38]

Notes

1 *Sacrosanctum Concilium* (*SC*), 7; see *Mediator Dei* (*MD*), 20.
2 Phil 2.6–7.
3 *MD*, 17. See Heb. 10.5–7.
4 Mark 10.45.
5 Mark 10.45. See also Heb. 5.7.
6 Phil. 2.7–9.
7 *SC*, 5, paragraph 2.
8 Eph. 3.9, 11; Col. 1.26–27.
9 *MD*, 17; *SC*, 7, paragraph 2.
10 1 Cor. 15.20, 23.
11 Rom. 6.3–4.
12 See, for example, Rom. 6.5–11.
13 Rom. 8.19–23.
14 1 Cor. 12.12–27; see also Eph. 4.15–16.
15 *MD*, 20; this idea is take up by *SC*, 7.
16 See *SC*, 26.
17 *SC*, 26.
18 *SC*, 2.
19 *MD*, 20.
20 *SC*, 5.
21 *SC*, 6.
22 *SC*, 6.
23 Second Vatican Council, 1964, Dogmatic Constitution on the Church, *Lumen Gentium* (*LG*), 7, paragraph 1.
24 *LG*, 7, paragraph 7; see also Rom. 8.9–11.
25 *SC*, 7, paragraph 3.
26 *SC*, 8.
27 John 16.13.
28 *SC*, 8.
29 *SC*, 14, paragraph 2.
30 *SC*, 11; 14, paragraphs 1 and 2; 21, paragraph 1; 27, paragraph 1; 30; 41, paragraph 2; 48; 50, paragraph 1. Note that the expression is not immediately evident in nos. 11 and 48 of the standard English translation (Austin Flannery, Vatican Council II: Basic 16 Documents (Dublin: Dominican Publications, 1988)) which somewhat paraphrases the Latin original.
31 *SC*, 19.
32 Presentation of Bishop Joseph Martin (19 November 1962) *AAS* I/3, pp. 702–7.
33 *MD*, 23.
34 *SC*, 7, paragraph 3.
35 *MD*, 24; *SC*, 11.
36 *SC*, 12.
37 *SC*, 13.
38 Pope Benedict, 2007, Apostolic Exhortation, *Sacramentum Caritatis* (*SacCar*) (London: Catholic Truth Society), 55.

3

Fundamentals of Liturgy

MARTIN FOSTER

Initial Reflection

- Recall a recent liturgy you attended for which there was a special service booklet or leaflet (if possible you may wish to compare a number of leaflets).
- Does the leaflet contain everything you need to participate in the liturgy?
- What is included, what is missing?
- Is the leaflet for someone who will be familiar with the liturgy or is it for those who might be less familiar?
- What different contexts would affect both the content of the leaflet (e.g. Sunday Mass or Wedding) and the amount of text it contains (regular parishioners or mostly unchurched)?
- What will help participation, what will hinder it?

In This Chapter

One definition of the liturgy is the public formal worship of the Church, as found in its official liturgical books. Yet, the relationship between worship and liturgical text varies widely across Christian denominations. Some, such as the Quakers, may have no books of services at all: Quaker worship is marked by shared silence, spontaneous contributions without an appointed leadership. Nonconformists may have an official Worship book, but it is not obligatory to use it and the service may be the creation of the minister, although it will often follow a familiar pattern. For the Catholic Church, the formal worship of the Church is enshrined in a number of liturgical books, which is a very concrete sign of unity. Yet surprisingly, this does not necessarily result in uniformity of performance. Moreover, the formal liturgies of the Church, such as the Mass and other sacraments, do not exhaust the public prayer of the Church. Indeed, whereas all liturgy is prayer, not all prayer is liturgy. Formal liturgies will have approved texts for prayers and will be governed by rubric (in this context, the rules for celebration) and liturgical law. Less formal liturgies or prayers might include devotions, a holy hour, or prayer in a catechetical context. These are less formal, not necessarily in their performance, but in the fact they have fewer official texts and they are structured by liturgical principles rather than law.

This chapter will look first at the liturgical books, examining how they are arranged and overviewing their contents. The second half of the chapter will look at the non-verbal elements that are the performative aspects of a liturgical celebration. All the various elements will give the reader building blocks to appreciate the chapters on the specific liturgical rites.

Revising the Rites

The first revised rite to be published after the Second Vatican Council was the *Rite of Baptism for Children (RBC)* in 1969, and the last was *Exorcisms and Related Supplications* in 2000. The texts are issued in Latin, and this definitive text is known as an *editio typica* (typical edition). Since their initial publication, some books have been further revised. This revision may have been carried out in the light of other rites – the second edition of the Lectionary includes readings from rites that were published subsequent to the initial edition. It can also reflect changing circumstances – the second edition of Marriage includes a new chapter to provide for the celebration of Marriage before an assisting layperson.

As each rite was issued in Latin, translations were prepared for use in the vernacular. In English for the majority of rites this work has been done in common by the International Commission on English in the Liturgy (ICEL). Similar Commissions exist for other languages such as French and German. Preparing an English translation can also involve further local adaptations of the rite – the *Order of Christian Funerals* (henceforth *OCF*) for England and Wales includes rites for use at a crematorium which are not found in the Latin text.

A Library of Books

The books of the Roman Rite are grouped together in four main collections: the *Roman Missal*, the Roman Office, the Roman Pontifical and the Roman Ritual. The *Roman Missal* is concerned with the celebration of Mass; the Roman Office provides the Liturgy of the Hours – the prayers said at different times of the day, sometimes referred to as the breviary. The Roman Pontifical is for the liturgies normally celebrated by the bishop; the Roman Ritual – the sacraments and other rites normally celebrated by a priest. The following table gives the major liturgical books contained in each collection:

Roman Missal	Roman Office	Roman Pontifical	Roman Ritual
Missal. Lectionary.	Liturgy of the Hours.	Confirmation. Ordination of Bishop, Priests and Deacons. Dedication of a Church and an Altar.	Christian Initiation of Adults. Baptism of Children. Penance. Pastoral Care of the Sick. Marriage. Funerals.

A feature of the revised books is that although the structure of the individual rites is often simplified they also include a greater variety of liturgies for different circumstances and a wider range of texts. For this reason they are often published as individual rites, rather than as a single Roman Ritual for example.

A Typical Liturgical Book

How a book is presented and structured can tell you a lot about the contents of the book and its authority:

Title page

The title page of a liturgical book of course gives the title of a 'rite', but also states the authority that underpins it. For example, the title page of the *Order of Celebrating Matrimony* (henceforth, *OCM*) begins by stating which family of books it belongs to – for example, 'The Roman Ritual' – then gives the authority for the edition, mentioning the Second Vatican Council, Pope Paul VI and Pope John Paul II. The title is given followed by the particular information – currently, 'Second' edition and finally the date of the translation.

THE ROMAN RITUAL

Renewed by Decree of the Most Holy Second Ecumenical
Council of the Vatican,
Promulgated by Authority of Pope Paul VI
and Revised at the Direction of Pope John Paul II

THE ORDER OF CELEBRATING MATRIMONY

English Translation According to the Second Typical Edition

MMXIII

Contents

Liturgical rites have a common structure:

- Decrees.
- Introductory material.
- Liturgical texts.
- Appendices.

The Decrees give legal force to the rite and there is usually one for each Latin edition and the English edition. It will state when the rite was published, when the text may be used in the liturgy, and when its use is mandatory.

Introductory material

For the sacraments there is first a papal document, an Apostolic Constitution. This highlights the main theological points of the rite and explains exactly how the revision has followed the mandate of *Sacrosanctum Concilium*. It also states the Sacramental Form (see Chapter 4) which is necessary for the validity of the sacrament.

> The Sacrament of Confirmation is conferred through the anointing with Chrism on the forehead, which is done by the laying on of the hand, and through the words: *Accipe signaculum Doni Spiritus Sancti*. (N. be sealed with the Gift of the Holy Spirit.)[1]

The Introductions – frequently referred to by their Latin name of '*Praenotanda*' – are a significant development in the renewed liturgy. The term '*Praenotanda*' is translated as General Instruction or Introduction depending on the rite; it usually has the following elements:

- Theological overview of the rite.
- Description of the various liturgies in the rite.
- Guidance on questions such as who is the minister of the rite.
- Adaptations to the liturgy.

The theological introduction will indicate some of the principles that have both underpinned the revision of the rite and direct its celebration. For example *OCF* states that the purpose of the funeral rites is threefold:

- Proclamation of the Paschal Mystery by which we are saved.
- Prayer for the deceased that God will be merciful.
- Comfort for those who mourn.[2]

The description of the various liturgies provides an explanation of the elements that make up the rite. As well as being informative this offers guidance on the celebration of the liturgy. For example, the *General Instruction of the Roman Missal* (henceforth, *GIRM*)[3] offers the following explanation of the role played by the Lord's Prayer during the Eucharist:

> In the Lord's Prayer a petition is made for daily bread, which for Christians means principally the Eucharistic Bread, and entreating also purification from sin, so that what is holy may in truth be given to the holy. The Priest pronounces the invitation to the prayer, and all the faithful say the prayer with him; then the Priest alone adds the embolism, which the people conclude by means of the doxology. The embolism, developing the last petition of the Lord's Prayer itself, asks for deliverance from the power of evil for the whole community of the faithful.

> The invitation, the Prayer itself, the embolism, and the doxology by which the people conclude these things are sung or are said aloud. (*GIRM*, 81)

An 'embolism' is a text inserted between two texts which were once continuous. The doxology is a text of praise, here 'For the kingdom . . .'.

SC (37–40) was clear that rites may need to be **adapted**. The final section of many of the Introductions is a guide to the possible adaptations that may be mandated by national Bishops' Conferences. For example, the General Introduction to the *Rite of Christian Initiation of Adults* (henceforth, *RCIA*) offers the following possible adaptation:

Each conference of bishops has discretionary power to make the following decisions: to decide that in the same rite the tracing of the sign of the cross upon the forehead be replaced by making that sign in front of the forehead, in regions where the act of touching may not seem proper. (*RCIA* 33)

The reference here is to the Rite of Acceptance into the Catechumenate, where enquirers are signed with the cross (see Chapter 5). Here it allows the bishops to make an amendment based on cultural sensibility. The General Introduction can also outline the adaptations which an individual bishop may make for his diocese, and what the minister can do locally.

Liturgical law

The Introductions to the liturgical books have the status of liturgical law, setting out underlying principles and offering guidance on how the rites are to be celebrated. The Church's liturgical law is not organized within one book, but is distributed across a number of documents, which can have different relative weight and importance. The document on church buildings *Consecrated for Worship* (*CFW*) offers a useful summary of the status of various documents, their relative weight and the type of information they contain.

The liturgical law of the Church is given in a variety of different documents:

- Conciliar, most recently those of the Second Vatican Council.
- Papal.
- Curial; in the field of liturgy particularly those of the Congregation for Divine Worship and the Discipline of the Sacraments.
- Local, originating from a diocesan bishop or from the Bishops' Conference.

The documents will be one of the following:

- *Theological* (examples include the Constitution on the Sacred Liturgy, *Sacrosanctum Concilium*).
- *Legislative* (examples include the Code of Canon Law, the liturgical rites and their Introductions).
- *Executive* These seek to clarify the law and recommend an approach to be followed in implementation. Examples include Instructions issued by the

Congregation for Divine Worship and the Discipline of the Sacraments, such as *Redemptionis Sacramentum*, and instruction for local implementation published by Bishops' Conferences – such as the aforementioned *Consecrated for Worship*.[4]

An instruction that the priest should not change anything in *GIRM* 24 is preceded by the following text:

In order that such a celebration may correspond more fully to the prescriptions and spirit of the Sacred Liturgy, and also in order that its pastoral effectiveness be enhanced, certain accommodations and adaptations are set out in this General Instruction and in the Order of Mass.

These adaptations consist, for the most part, in the choice of certain rites or texts, that is, of the chants, readings, prayers, explanatory interventions, and gestures capable of responding better to the needs, the preparation, and the culture of the participants and which are entrusted to the Priest Celebrant. (*GIRM*, 23–4)

A feature of the revised rites is the range of options and alternatives that they provide. One of the responsibilities of the priest and those involved in preparing the liturgy is to make choices. This is chiefly to facilitate the provision of appropriate pastoral care. For example, *OCF* offers a wide range of prayers that reflect different circumstances of death: children, old age, after a long illness or a sudden tragedy; it also includes prayers for those who have taken their own lives.

The act of making a liturgical choice implies both a knowledge of the options available in the rite and the circumstances of the celebration. In determining which liturgical texts to use, not only should the priest put the needs of the people before his own, but should also be aware of the participants' life situations and formation in the life of the Church:

The pastoral effectiveness of a celebration will be greatly increased if the texts of the readings, the prayers and the liturgical chants correspond as aptly as possible to the needs, the preparation and the culture of the participants. This will be achieved by appropriate use of the many possibilities of choice described below.

Hence, in arranging the celebration of Mass, the Priest should be attentive rather to the common spiritual good of the People of God than to his own inclinations. He should also remember that choices of this kind are to be made in harmony with those who exercise some part in the celebration, including the faithful, as regards the parts that more directly pertain to them. (*GIRM*, 352)

Liturgical rites

The rites make up the bulk of the liturgical books. They can be ordered in one of three broad ways:

- In chronological order: either by following the liturgical year or by setting out in sequence the stages of a rite (for example, *RCIA* or *OCF*).
- For some rites (for example, *OC* and *OCM*) the first chapter sets out the normative or model form, and the later chapters will set out adaptations according to various circumstances.
- According to the number of persons involved, for example, the forms of the rite differ depending on the number of subjects (for example, infants to be baptized or candidates for Ordination to the Priesthood).

Liturgical Texts

Before turning to liturgy as performance, consideration is here given to the contents of the liturgical books and to how they provide the material for the liturgical celebration. We will first look at the texts of the liturgy, starting with those found in the liturgical books, and examining the distinction between those passages intended to be proclaimed out loud and those that convey information to the participants. Then we will consider the texts that are sung or said in the liturgy but that are not found in the official texts.

Informative texts

In any liturgical text some of the words on the paper are not intended to be spoken. They contain information about the rite and how it is to be celebrated. These include the titles of the various rites and any headings that indicate the structure of the rite. Some liturgical books give an outline of each rite which can indicate the relative weight of each part.

Informative texts – rubrics

Rubrics – named after the red ink with which they are written and which distinguishes them from spoken text on the page – provide information about how the rite is celebrated. Rubrics can give guidance, provide an introduction to a section, indicate the content, and present the possible options available. They can instruct on posture and gesture, and whether the text is spoken or sung, as can be seen in these rubrics from *OCM*:

> *Homily*
> 57. After the reading of the Gospel, the Priest in the homily uses the sacred text to expound the mystery of Christian Marriage, the dignity of conjugal love, the grace of the Sacrament, and the responsibilities of married people, keeping in mind, however, the various circumstances of individuals.

> *The Celebration of Marriage*
> 59. With all standing, including the couple and the witnesses, who are positioned near them, the Priest addresses the couple in these or similar words:

Rubrics can convey exact information that is to be acted upon: in *OCM* 59 all are told to stand. Rubrics also provide guidance and implied information: in *OCM* 59 the couple and witnesses should be standing close together; however, the rubric here does not say where the priest is standing but directs him to address the couple. We can, therefore, presume he is standing near them, and that he may have moved from where the homily took place. They also provide guidance. Thus, the rubric on the homily (*OCM*, 57) not only suggests possible content but also reminds the priest to be aware of the pastoral situation.

Texts to be spoken

Much of the liturgy is taken up with spoken words. These are made up of different forms and styles of text which help create the warp and weft of the liturgy. Many of these words can be sung but first we consider liturgical texts that are not normally sung.

Texts to be spoken quietly

At various points in the Order of Mass there are texts that the priest prays quietly, asking that he may exercise his ministry with greater attention and devotion (*GIRM*, 33):

- Before the Gospel.
- Preparation of Gifts.
- Before Communion.

Texts to be spoken out loud

In the rubrics and in the norms that follow, words such as 'say' and 'proclaim' are to be understood either of singing or of reciting (*GIRM*, 38). The majority of liturgical texts are intended, in the renewed liturgy, to be spoken out loud. To help differentiate between the forms of texts, we arrange them by who speaks or sings them.

Texts spoken by one minister

The presidential prayers are texts that are proper to the presider or priest celebrant. At Mass they include the Collect, Prayer over the Offerings and Prayer after Communion. They also include the Eucharistic Prayer and Preface. More details about these texts will be found in Chapter 8 on the Celebration of the Eucharist.

Presidential prayers are almost without exception addressed to God the Father, and the priest says them on behalf of the people. The 'Amen' that they add to these prayers is an assenting statement that they associate their prayer with his. The texts, particularly on Solemnities, can express some of the theology of the celebration. Other texts spoken or sung by an individual minister include the Exsultet and the Blessing of Water at the Easter Vigil and the Prayers and Blessings in the celebration of the sacraments. Also falling within this category are the readings in the Liturgy of the Word.

Texts spoken in dialogue

Many times during the liturgy the bishop, priest or deacon speaks a short sentence, to which the assembly respond. These include Greetings, Dialogues, Blessings and Dismissals. A further example would be the second and third forms of the Penitential Act and the Kyrie. Through an expression of relationship and invitation, these dialogues draw people into a unified body with a common purpose. Each statement is generally short, and the response is so familiar to the majority in the assembly that they know it by heart.

Texts spoken by all

Some texts are sung or said by all together. These include the Gloria, the Creed, the Sanctus and the Lord's Prayer during the celebration of the Eucharist. These texts are unchanging, which aids memory and participation. Two texts are also sung or said by the congregation alone, without the priest: the Memorial Acclamation and the Acclamation after the Lord's Prayer ('For the kingdom. . .').

Questions for Reflection

When the priest receives the bread and wine at the Preparation of Gifts he may say the prayer that begins *Blessed are you, Lord God of all creation* . . . to which people respond *Blessed be God for ever*. The Order of Mass offers three ways this might be done:

1 If there is singing, *Blessed are you* . . . is said quietly by the priest.
2 *Blessed are you* . . . is said out loud with all responding.
3 The congregation is silent and *Blessed are you* . . . is said quietly.

- Which of these options do you prefer and why?
- What different contexts might suggest the use of each one of the options?

Texts to be sung

One of the features of the 2010 *Roman Missal* was that it contained more music in the Order of Mass, frequently providing the musical setting of a text first, and only then the text without music. This increase in the sung content is a reminder that the normative form of the Roman liturgy is that it should be sung. This is for a mixture of practical and theological reasons. In large buildings, such as churches, song can travel further and be more easily heard than speech – especially in an age before amplification. Music can also be an aid for memory. Turning to the theological motivations for singing: as it sings, a group of people can form one voice – which is a sign of the unity of the Body of Christ. This is further developed when the image of the heavenly liturgy as involving a great chorus of voices is brought into the equation.[5] This musical image finds its way into the closing section of the Preface at each celebration of the Eucharist, which typically concludes, 'And so, with Angels and Archangels, with Thrones and Dominions, and with all the Hosts and Powers of heaven, we sing the hymn of your glory, as without end we acclaim.' The earthly liturgy connects with and seeks to imitate that liturgy. The sung texts in the *Missal* can also be distinguished according to who sings them: a minister alone, a minister in dialogue with all, or sung by all together.

Model texts – which can be replaced

For some texts in a rite, particularly Introductions, a model text may be given, with the suggestion that the priest may use 'these or similar words'. The model text will indicate what might be included, but recognizes that different circumstances may require changes of emphasis. An example might be the Introductions in the Celebration of Marriage.

Other texts that might be thought of as particular to a celebration may have models within the rite. The third form of the Penitential Act has model invocations – for example, 'You were sent to heal the contrite of heart' – but these may be replaced by ones prepared locally. (They should follow the model in being invocations of the merciful Christ.) In a similar way there is in the *Roman Missal* an appendix of model intercessions. In some rites (for example, Ordinations) a model homily is offered.

Another example would be the Entrance or Communion antiphons which are often replaced by a liturgical hymn or song. Sometimes they will share the same text or themes but often they will focus on another aspect of the celebration.

Texts not in the rite

A thanksgiving hymn after Communion is mentioned in the rite as an option – as also is a period of silence. However, unlike the Communion antiphon, a model text for such a hymn is neither given nor suggested.

Within any celebration of Mass the priest or deacon may also use words that are not provided by the *Missal*, but can be thought of as filling in various gaps during the celebration. These words could take the form of instructions, invitations or information. The most straightforward example of such words is the parish notices given at the end of Mass. However, they might also include lines spoken during the liturgy, such as an invitation before the Creed, 'let us stand to proclaim our faith'. Even more significantly, such words may seek to invite participation through description: 'we baptize baby Louise in water which is a sign of God's cleansing love'. However, the risk in this last instance is the danger of reducing a sense of people's engagement through their senses and imaginations. Filling in the gaps in the liturgical text is generally not necessary, and the tools of the liturgy should be used instead. So, at the beginning of the Creed people can be invited to stand by a simple gesture from the priest who then begins by singing or saying the text.

Fixed texts and choices

This chapter began by noting that Catholic liturgy is laid down within liturgical books, but has gone on to explore how in practice it involves a number of levels of choices. For example, some texts are prescribed – only the text of the 'Holy, Holy' may be used after the Preface. At other points, a text may be selected from a fixed range – for example, the Eucharistic Prayer may be selected from among the ten found in the *Missal*. Other aspects of the liturgy, such as a hymn or song to accompany the Communion process, may be more freely chosen. The parameters governing choice are both practical (Do people know it? Can they sing it?) and textual (Is it suitable for this part of the Mass or for this liturgical season?).

Put together

It may be helpful to put these various categories together and look at a common Sunday experience. The following chart sets out the range of texts found in the Introductory Rites:

Table of Introductory Rites

Part	Who	Type of text	Source
Entrance Hymn	All	Free choice	Hymnbook
Sign of the Cross	Priest	Fixed	*Missal*
Greeting	Priest and All	Fixed – range of choices	*Missal*
Introduction	Priest	Free	Priest
Penitential Act 1	Priest and All	Fixed – range of choices	*Missal*
Kyrie	Cantor and All	Fixed	*Missal* (or Musical Setting)
Gloria	Cantor, Choir and All	Fixed	*Missal* (or Musical Setting)
Collect	Priest and All	Fixed	*Missal*

Scripture and liturgy

Before moving on from our examination of texts, it is important to review the use of scripture in the liturgy. Scripture is primarily heard in the Liturgy of the Word, which presents readings from the Old and New Testaments as found in the Lectionary. In terms of the main 'collections' it is part of the *Roman Missal*, though it includes texts for all liturgical celebrations, with the exception of the Liturgy of the Hours. The readings and the Lectionary are considered in more detail in Chapter 7, the Celebration of the Eucharist.

The readings are not the only place in which Scripture can be found within the liturgy. The Bible is also the primary source for the antiphons. These are usually short biblical texts intended to be sung, and are found in the *Missal* and in other rites. They are found in the Hours, where they are used at the beginning and end of the psalms and the canticles (psalm-like texts from the Old and New Testament). Antiphons are interpretative texts that provide a way of understanding the surrounding context. In the Hours they offer a focused viewpoint from which the psalm text can be understood. In particular they link the Old Testament psalm text to the New Testament Mystery of Christ. This is especially true in the liturgical seasons, when the antiphons can draw out resonances in a psalm text to the Paschal Mystery. The antiphons at Mass are intended to be sung as part of a procession – so at Communion the antiphon accompanies the procession to Communion. The antiphon can either interpret the action of going to Communion or be interpreted by it.

As well as containing direct biblical quotations, liturgical prayers can also make use of scriptural allusions. Such echoes can be found throughout the liturgy. One example would be the invitation to Communion, 'Lord, I am not worthy that you should enter under my roof, but only say the word and my soul shall be healed.' The allusion is to Matthew 8.8, when Jesus is approached by a Roman officer who seeks healing for his servant.

Longer liturgical texts can be a particularly rich source of scriptural images and allusions. The Blessing of Water at the Easter Vigil presents a series of images of water from Old and New Testaments (the text can be found in Chapter 5, p. 95 – *RCIA*). Two features of such use of Scripture can be noted. First, the texts are often set in close proximity, in a series of images – what is presented is a juxtaposition of themes, rather than exegesis. Second, use is made of Old Testament 'types' or 'typology'. This is where an Old Testament figure or action is understood to prefigure in some ways either the life of Christ or the action of the liturgy. So the crossing of the Red Sea, by which the people of Israel were saved from slavery in Egypt through water, is used as an image of baptism.

Liturgy as performance

Introduction

There is a risk that those who engage in the study of liturgy can become so engaged with the books and the texts that they forget that the liturgy is primarily an action, something that is done. The playwright Tom Stoppard has noted that 'a play is a script of an event which has not yet happened'. The same could be said of the liturgy – a ritual book, no matter how fascinating in itself, needs to be enacted or done so that it can be fruitful. Words are just one of the elements or fundamentals which make up a celebration of the liturgy. Other elements will include people, the space and the movement within it, music and silence, time and symbol. Liturgy is an embodied action, all of the elements engage the physical body and its senses. In recent years liturgists have learnt from and contributed to the area of Ritual Studies, which offers tools and insights into how people worship. Ritual Studies recognizes worship as part of what it means to be human. One aspect of ritual is about the formation and passing on of identity. At a simple level that is what is happening when we go to Mass in an unfamiliar parish, and through the experience of the liturgy have a perspective of the parish's identity.

Another reason for considering these elements is that they become building blocks for the preparation of liturgy and prayer. A celebration where everyone sits all the way through or everything is said, where one person does everything or too many people do something, misses out on dimensions that help enrich the prayer and participation.

People

Assembly

The liturgy is a manifestation of the Church: it always takes place within a gathering of the baptized. Christ promised that 'where two or three are gathered in my name, there am I among them' (Matt. 18.20). So when the Church gathers in the liturgy, Christ is present. He is present in the praying and singing of the assembly; indeed the assembly becomes the presence of Christ, but also through the action of the Holy Spirit the assembly participate in Christ who offers prayer and thanksgiving to the Father (see Chapter 2).

The assembly is not a uniform body. A Mass celebrated with a small group of 20 who know each other well may be a different experience to celebration with a large group of 200 who may not have met before. Increasingly, many who attend weddings, baptisms and funerals may never have attended Catholic worship before. Paradoxically, where there is some stability – and therefore the possibility of priest and other ministers knowing the assembly well – it will actually be the liturgy that forms the community rather than the reverse. In that sense, the liturgy can be both a form of pastoral care and a place of formation.

Liturgical ministry

Catholic liturgy is not congregational. It requires a priest and other ministers to assist in the offering of the liturgy so that praise and worship can be offered to God. The Latin root of ministry is from *ministrare*, to serve, and those who minister share baptismally in the priesthood of Christ who came to serve, not to be served. Ministry is done for the sake of others so it can be seen that ministry has a two-fold purpose: to offer worship to God and to enable the participation of the assembly. A reader, for example, will, in proclaiming the readings, tell of the mighty deeds of God but also, through clarity of delivery and understanding, will help others to hear and receive the word.

Ordained ministry

From the New Testament the foundation of a three-fold ordained ministry of bishop, priest and deacon can be discerned. Though each fulfils his ministry in different ways it is particularly in the celebration of the liturgy that that ministry is exercised (see Chapter 10). Within Catholic liturgy there is an expectation that it will be led or presided over by a single person. This is true even at a celebration of Evening Prayer, where the priest might only sing the Introduction, pray the Collect, and give the blessing at the end. In practice he 'does' relatively little, yet there is a sense that he has held the whole celebration together.

Catholic liturgy is also hierarchical. Pride of place is given to the celebration of Mass by the bishop with his priests and people because such celebrations manifest the local church, which is the diocese. Some sacraments and liturgical actions (for example, Ordination) are reserved to the bishop; only a bishop or priest may celebrate Mass. When a deacon is present there are parts of the liturgy, in particular the instructions and invitations, that fall properly to him.

Lay liturgical ministry

One of the marks of the liturgical reform is the growth in lay ministry, which is now seen as a regular part of the liturgy. In parishes across the country men and women assist the liturgy in the roles of reader, cantor, server, etc. In Chapter 2, the inadequacy of a viewpoint that understood liturgical participation merely as people 'doing things' was noted. Similarly, it is inadequate to regard ministry as giving people things to do in church. Ministry ought not to be regarded as offering a sign of approval, nor as providing a way to involve people in the liturgy. The primary ministry of the baptized Christian is to be an ordinary member of the liturgical assembly.

However, ministers should have an aptitude for the role they are invited to fulfil and should be willing to participate in formation so that they can act with skill and understanding. For example, the Introduction to the Lectionary proposes the formation of readers as three-fold:

- *Technical* – to proclaim the text with clarity and appropriate pace, to comprehend the amplification system, to appreciate the place of silence in the liturgy.
- *Liturgical* – to understand the structure and place of the Liturgy of the Word within the Mass and the purpose and context of the individual readings, to know how to approach the ambo (the lectern), and other aspects of liturgical movement within a particular space.
- *Spiritual* – to reflect on the readings and make connections with the other texts and with the reader's faith, to communicate what has been reflected on in how the reading is proclaimed.

This three-fold division could easily serve as the basis for other ministerial formation – for example, with musicians or leaders of the Liturgy of the Word with children.

Finally, formation should not be seen as a one-off event. Parishes should offer ministers opportunities to deepen their understanding and to come together in prayer and reflection.

Liturgical space

A church building is a space for the celebration of liturgy. It can have other functions as well: a church is frequently a place of prayer and devotion, a place of memory and identity, a place of history and beauty. Later chapters will look at specific objects: the altar, the ambo, etc. A church will have a place for the assembly and a sanctuary where are placed the altar, ambo and chair for the priest. The liturgical documents describe ideal buildings, but churches are constructed in a variety of ways and are shaped by many factors including different understandings of liturgy, money, available land. There are broadly three different historical models of liturgical space that we find in England and Wales:

- *Liturgy as mystery* – this model draws on the model of many medieval churches. It is divided into two distinct spaces: the nave (where the people are) and the sanctuary (where the priest and altar are). These are often separated by a screen. The liturgical action is understood to happen at one end, to be distant. There can be a strong sense of an axis moving from nave to sanctuary to heaven itself;
- *Preaching space* – these buildings would be characterized by their wide naves from which all have good sight lines of the sanctuary. Often they would also have prominent pulpits for preaching situated in their naves. The design is based on Roman seventeenth-century models that were developed by Jesuits and Oratorians. This approach to church design developed in the nineteenth century to a related model, which might be call '*places of devotion*'. The overall plan still followed the longitudinal plan of nave and sanctuary, but the focus of the entire space had become the tabernacle and space was frequently shaped in order best to accommodate the liturgy that most eloquently

expressed popular Eucharistic devotion – the Exposition and Benediction of the Blessed Sacrament.

- *Liturgy for the gathered people of God* – through the influence of the Liturgical Movement the altar became placed more centrally, with the space for the assembly often having a semi-circular basis where more people are closer to the altar but also can see other members of the assembly. Such designs can have less of a sense of direction as the focus pulls in a number of ways. The danger is that it can be seen as a closed circle rather than an open space.

Questions for Reflection

- Which of these models best describes the place where you regularly worship?
- What would you regard as the most visible items?
- Are you familiar with another church that has a different model? What do you see as the advantages and disadvantages of celebrating the liturgy in each building?

It might be observed that a church building and how it is arranged express both a model of church and a model of liturgy. Another way of considering this is to look at where the baptismal font is placed within the building. The different places express (and form) different understandings of baptism. When the font is placed near the door it connects with baptism as entry into the Church. How it is used will make connections with other liturgies. A font near the door may also be used expressively in the funeral rites or serve as the place from which people bless themselves with Holy Water. When it is placed near the altar there is a link being made between Baptism and Eucharist. It also may facilitate the baptism of children during Sunday Mass as it will be in a more visible space. Some fonts will allow for the baptism of children and adults by either pouring water or by immersion – the presence of such a font in a church would generally suggest that this was a parish that had engaged with adult initiation.

The body in worship

One of the comments that non-Catholics make when they first attend Mass is to note the long periods of standing. Within the liturgy there are four main postures: standing, sitting, kneeling and bowing. These postures are shared, we make them in common. We attach meaning to each position and connect them with various parts of the liturgy.

> There is a common understanding of the significance of the postures of standing, sitting, and kneeling within our culture.
>
> We rise to greet people, to honour someone important, to express readiness for action, or when seized with excitement. In Christian liturgical tradition, standing is the basic posture of an Easter people lifted up to greet its risen Lord. The assembly stands at Mass, for example, during the proclamation of the Gospel reading.
>
> We kneel as a human gesture of submission. In Christian tradition, kneeling is an acknowledgement of one's creatureliness before God. It can signify penitence for sin, humility, reverence, and adoration.
>
> We sit to listen, to rest, to watch. At Mass it is appropriate, for example, to sit during the Homily and at the Preparation of the Gifts. (*CTM*, 57–60).

It is worth considering when preparing even a simple prayer service what differences in posture there might be. Not only do we attach meaning to what we do but that meaning shapes our understanding. So if the Gospel is proclaimed we should stand both as a sign of respect but also to help us to listen. A recognition of the changes in posture may also be necessary where a number of unchurched people might be attending a funeral, for example. It can be helpful to consider the different ways that people can be informed about the change, especially those that are non-verbal – either from a gesture or clear leadership of the priest, or as part of the ministry of a regular congregation to those who mourn.

Music, flow and silence

The flow of the liturgy is not just a question of the overall length and timing of a celebration, but rather of how the whole celebration holds together. Each liturgy has its highpoints – and so it also contains periods of time that either lead up to or away from these highpoints.[6] To understand that the liturgy has a dynamic movement rather than being just a series of discrete events is important – not just theologically but also for those who prepare and evaluate liturgical celebrations.

Music is one of the ways that the liturgy is given texture or warp and weft. Many of the texts that can be said in the liturgy can also be sung and they may be considered as texts sung by all, texts sung in dialogue, texts sung by a single minister. Another way of considering music within the liturgy is by the context within which it happens. Music is either sung to accompany another liturgical action, such as a procession, or it forms a liturgical act in itself, as does the Gloria. Music that is tied to action should allow people to be involved in that action: to sing and see the Breaking of Bread at the Lamb of God; to sing and process to Communion. This might either suggest the use of music that is well known so that people can sing without needing to look at a text too much, or uses refrains that can be easily picked up.

Music offers a further structural function in that the parts of a liturgy that are sung almost inevitably become more prominent than the spoken text around them. This calls for special care to ensure that in a predominantly spoken liturgy, those sections that genuinely form liturgical highpoints are sung. In a celebration of Mass, the liturgical highpoints would be the Proclamation of the Gospel and the Eucharistic Prayer; the priorities for singing, therefore, would be the Gospel Acclamation and those Acclamations (Holy, Memorial Acclamation, Amen) in the Eucharistic Prayer that are sung by all. Paradoxically, in a liturgy where a great deal is sung it can be harder to give a shape to the whole.

A key element in the flow of a celebration is the place of silence. Silence is used in different ways in the liturgy. It can be held during an extended period of communal reflection as is stipulated following the homily and after the distribution of Holy Communion. It may be a moment of recollection and prayer as is intended for before the Collect or as part of the intercessions. Silence can be the context for participation through seeing or listening as a minister proclaims the word, etc. There can also be short pauses or breaks as a way of pacing and articulating the structure of the liturgy, such as following the Amen at the end of the Eucharistic Prayer so that all are ready to stand and pray the Lord's Prayer.

Time and calendar

Part of the structure of the Roman liturgy extends to time. The liturgy follows a cycle of liturgical seasons each year, and a calendar of saints' days. These will be explored in greater detail in Chapter 12, especially the pre-eminence of Sunday as the day of the Lord's resurrection. When thinking of preparing liturgical celebrations there should be an awareness of the liturgical seasons. It may be that the choice of day means that the importance of the celebration attached to the day has precedence over what is planned. For example, a Confirmation planned for 29 June would use the readings for St Peter and Paul. There may also be a question of authenticity – how do the natural cycles of light and dark affect liturgical celebrations? Does it make sense to decorate a church with many candles when the sun is blazing through the windows?

Symbol

The integrity and authenticity of the things we use in liturgy help to shed light on the symbols and their use which is fundamental to liturgical celebration. 'Symbol' is a word that has a number of nuances. It can suggest something that is not wholly true and the meaning has been added on – the symbolic meaning of something. Within the liturgy symbols have authenticity and integrity – they are what they are and they mean what they mean. A candle is not a 'symbolic light' but is something that tangibly lightens the darkness. At the Easter Vigil a single candle can bring light into a church. But a candle also points to another reality that is at the same time true. Jesus tells us that he is the Light of the world and so in the candlelight Christ is glimpsed.

- In the liturgy symbols work as verbs. It is in the lighting of the candle, the burning down of its wax, the sharing of light from one candle to another, that the symbol speaks.

- The symbols in the liturgy are natural – they are simple, and drawn from the natural world.
- Symbols have an ambiguity – they offer a range of images, not all of which may be positive. Water gives life and cleanses but it can also drown you.

Typically in the liturgy primary symbols such as water are placed within a complex of other (secondary) symbols which help interpret the liturgical action. For example, at the Baptism of children the primary symbol is water, or – more precisely – it is water poured over the baby or in which the baby is immersed. This symbolic action is preceded by the blessing of water in which a series of images of water is invoked, and it is followed by a series of illustrative (explanatory) rituals that further interpret what has taken place through the use of secondary symbols: the anointing of the baby with the oil of Chrism, the lighting of a candle, the clothing in a white garment. In this way, the liturgy builds up a network of symbols which make connections and deepen the potential meanings.

It is a liturgical cliché to say that symbols should be used abundantly as a sign of the abundant life that they offer. That the waters of baptism should be more than a few drops, that the oil should be generous and not a mere dab. This is true but there is also a need to reflect on how sacramental rites are celebrated so that the various elements work together to bring forth new life.

Notes

1 *Order of Confirmation* (*OC*) (London: Catholic Truth Society, 2016), 14.

2 *Order of Christian Funerals* (*OCF*) (London: Geoffrey Chapman, 1990), 1–7.

3 *Roman Missal*, 2010, *General Instruction of the Roman Missal* (*GIRM*) (London: Catholic Truth Society).

4 Catholic Bishops' Conference of England and Wales, 2006, *Consecrated for Worship: A Directory on Church Building* (*CFW*) (London: Catholic Truth Society).

5 Lectionary for Mass, 1981, *Introduction* (London: Collins, Geoffrey Chapman). Cf. 55.

6 Catholic Bishops' Conference of England and Wales, 2005, *Celebrating the Mass* (*CTM*) (London: Catholic Truth Society), 57–60.

Part 2

The Sacraments

4

Catholic Sacramental Theology

RICHARD CONRAD, OP

Having considered the nature of liturgy, and some 'mechanics' of liturgical study and practice, we turn to the sacraments. It is not recorded that Jesus gave his disciples a definition such as 'sacraments are outward signs of inward grace ordained by me'. Rather, the Church celebrated the sacraments he gave her, and only after 1,000 years or so systematically asked, 'Which of our rites are sacraments possessing divine authority, and how do they work?' The Middle Ages developed a sacramental theology that is part of the Church's heritage, and since then it has been usual to study 'sacraments in general' before examining each individual rite. This has the advantage of bringing out the value of sacraments, and revealing recurring features, but runs the risk of encouraging people to apply general concepts to each sacrament in too rigid a way, forgetting that *each* sacrament has its own *unique* dynamic.

The most influential of the medieval theologians, St Thomas Aquinas (1225–74) developed a carefully thought-through approach to understanding the sacraments that has informed Catholic theology ever since. In this chapter we shall integrate Aquinas' approach with some modern insights and concerns. After outlining his basic perspective, we shall note the main sources of Catholic sacramental theology, then explore in more detail how the sacraments communicate God's saving work; indeed, they communicate the Triune God to humanity. This will help us appreciate their power, and how they enmesh humanity into the unfolding of God's saving work, to the extent that men and women, as sharers in Christ's Priesthood, and as his Body in the world, are made, themselves, sacramental.

The Seven Sacraments of the Catholic Church

Sacraments of Christian Initiation
  Baptism
  Confirmation
  The Holy Eucharist

Sacraments of Healing
  Penance (Reconciliation)
  The Anointing of the Sick

Sacraments at the Service of Communion
  Orders
  Marriage

Note 1: The first reception of the Holy Eucharist completes a Christian's initiation into Christ's Body, hence the Eucharist is listed as a Sacrament of Initiation. But it is much more than that.
Note 2: Orders and Marriage commission and empower Christians to serve others in ways that are especially important for the Christian community, hence they are listed as 'sacraments at the Service of Communion'. But each sacrament, in its own way, commissions and empowers Christians to serve others.

Basic Perspective: Sacraments as a Channel of Revelation

Aquinas presented the sacraments as, basically, signs – sacred signs that reveal what God is doing for human salvation. This meant he could see the rituals God inspired people to celebrate in ancient times, and the ones God prescribed for the Jewish people, as true sacraments. Besides being a good form of worship, they were *signs* of what Christ would in the future do, though they did not have the same power as the sacraments he was to give. Seeing sacraments as *signs* helped Aquinas to show how closely they suit human nature, for he said it is natural to us to learn through the senses. So the sacraments – like Scripture – are means of communication. Both bring God's Word to us – his personal Word, Jesus Christ.

Human communication and consolidation by word, gesture and deed

It is natural to human beings to communicate by our creative, open-ended language. We use language not only to teach, but to affect each other in many ways, building up (or breaking down) relationships. A shared language is often a component of a shared culture, even though there are countries in which many languages are spoken.

We communicate not only by words but also by *gestures*, 'spontaneous' gestures such as a hug, and 'considered' ones such as giving a present. Gestures can bond. Certain *acts* have a similar or greater 'symbolic weight', such as feeding family or guests, or making love, or bathing a baby. Acts that do not count as 'gestures' can also have meaning: actions speak louder than words. Public 'ritual' acts, like the State Opening of Parliament, Presidential inaugurations, the Festival of Remembrance, and street parties, express and cement social cohesion. Citizens are 'inculturated' by learning to appreciate them, rather as ancient cities cherished the customs given them by their founders. (By inculturation is meant the process by which, as children grow up in a place, or when immigrants take a citizenship course in their new country, they take on the culture, character and norms of a group or country.) They come to understand the history and meaning of the public rituals they witness or participate in – and these rituals often have a subconscious formative influence.

God's communication by deed, gesture and word to found and heal

God has founded, and is crafting and creating, a city to which we belong by hope (Heb. 11.10). For Aquinas, 'Grace does not abolish nature but perfects it':

the Creator builds up humanity's relationship with him by means that suit us: by language, by gestures, by deeds, and by providing a 'Constitution', laws, and customs that inculturate men and women into his City. He gives:

- The Scriptures as a 'foundation document', which includes expressions we use to speak to or about God.
- In them, a record of the mighty deeds by which he has saved and established his people.
- The sacraments as his gestures towards men and women, and as the customs that inculturate them.
- The Old Law and the New Law as the way of life. Note that the various New Testament authors agree that while the *moral* component of the Old Law remains valid, the *ceremonial* component has been superseded.

God does this in a fallen world that needs healing. If the human mind had not been weakened by the Fall, each created thing would speak of God's Beauty and Wisdom, but as it is God must remind us that he exists, and sacraments serve this purpose by using material things and so prompting us to see all things as pointing to God. Human relationships have been distorted by sin; but, because sacraments employ human contact, they proclaim the healing of relationships. Note that we cannot administer sacraments to ourselves; they remind us that we need one another. (As often, the Eucharist is a bit different, and the priest who consecrates does give himself Holy Communion.) On the journey back to God, each one of us, and in a way the whole cosmos, must pass through death to resurrection; the sacraments point back to Jesus' own passing-over to be humanity's way home, and point forward to the coming Kingdom.

Scripture and sacraments do not only remind us that God exists, and through them he does not only say, 'I am healing you'. Rather, as we say special things to special friends, so as to express friendship, so God says something really wonderful to us. He performed saving deeds, and gives his people the Scriptures and a precise number of sacraments, to say what human beings could never work out for themselves: he is not only the Creator who has given us *our* selves; he is the Friend who wants to give us his Self, and will do so in an unimaginably close way in the coming Kingdom.

Jesus as primordial sacrament, the Word who echoes throughout history

Yet, it is not really Scripture that is the Church's 'foundation document' or the 'Constitution' of God's City. This is Jesus himself. He is the Word of God, eternally uttered by the Father who puts all that he is, and all that he plans, into his Son, his perfect Image. God the Father spoke his Word into the midst of this world's history, when 'the Word became flesh and pitched his tent amongst us' (cf. John 1.14). Jesus' whole life and ministry, his death and resurrection, are God the Father speaking as clearly as possible both what he is and what he wants for humanity, as a friend would share with a friend her understanding of herself and her hopes. Jesus is the Foundation into whom we are built, just as he is the Vine and the Head of whom we are branches and members (Eph. 1.20; 1 Pet. 2.4–6; John 15.1–8; Col. 1.18). He is our New Law, our identity into whom we have to be inculturated. God in Christ is the City's Founder. Jesus – above all, in his Sacrifice – is God the Father's deed that speaks louder than any words. Jesus is the Father's great gesture towards us, his Eternal Covenant, his irrevocable pledge of loyalty.

God's personal Word was spoken into the world at one place and one time; hence, if people are to receive him in their own place and time, he must 'echo' across the years. He was glimpsed before he came by those who witnessed the mighty deeds, heard the prophetic words, and celebrated the rituals that spoke of his future sacrifice. The same Word meets us in the Scriptures and sacraments that have been handed down by the body of his Disciples. In the sacraments, men and women in each age hear, feel, taste and see the Word spoken into the world 2,000 years ago. No celebration of a Christian sacrament is a *new* message from God. It is the Message spoken once and fully as Jesus Christ, being brought home to us.

So Jesus himself is the most fundamental sacrament; in all particular sacraments he extends, through his ministers, his role of effectively revealing his Father and his Father's plan.

Sacraments and Scripture as reinforcing and validating each other

We should be wary of the suspicion that Protestants prefer Scripture while Catholics prefer sacraments. Despite differences of theology, 'classical' Protestants celebrate sacraments devoutly; the Catholic liturgy cherishes Scripture. We need not appeal to Scripture to validate sacraments; it would be better to say it is the liturgy, especially the Eucharist, that validates Scripture! Some Old Testament texts grew up in the context of liturgy; some New Testament texts were composed to be read in the assembly at the Breaking of Bread, and by the time they were composed Christians had been baptizing, laying on hands, and anointing the sick for some decades. It is in the liturgy that Scripture still 'comes alive' and its great richness unfolds.

Really, sacraments and Scripture confirm each other: both are *channels of God's personal self-revelation*, and in complementary ways bring us into contact with God's One Word, Jesus Christ.

When refuting the Gnostics, who transferred selected scriptural images into a body of non-Christian myths, St Irenaeus wrote:

> He also who retains unchangeable in his heart the rule of the truth which he received by means of baptism, will doubtless recognise the names, the expressions, and the parables taken from the Scriptures [by the Gnostics], but will by no means acknowledge the blasphemous use which these men make of them . . . The Church, though dispersed through the whole world, even to the ends of the earth, has received from the apostles and their disciples this faith: [She believes] in one God, the Father Almighty, Maker of heaven, and earth, & the sea, & all things that are in them; and in one Christ Jesus, the Son of God, who became incarnate for our salvation; and in the Holy Spirit, who proclaimed through the prophets the dispensations of God. (*Adversus Haereses*, Book 1, ix, 4–x, 1)

Irenaeus pointed people back to the questions they answered when standing in the font. These constitute a 'rule of truth' and grew into the Creeds. This faith has come down in the Tradition; it is held by the Catholic Church – which, St Irenaeus goes on to say, is led by accredited teacher-bishops (notably the Bishop of Rome) who can trace their authority back to the Apostles. This suggests that

Sacraments/Liturgy, Scripture, Creeds, Tradition, and Church/Magisterium form a 'five-fold cord' linking us to Jesus, each strand of which safeguards and illuminates the others. No Christian has authority to invent a new Church, functioning on different principles, nourished by alternative 'scriptures' and ad hoc 'sacraments'. The Church is formed by what it has received through the Apostles, who are the Church's personal foundations (Eph. 2.20; Rev. 21.14).

Sources of Sacramental Doctrine and Theology

Look at the rites themselves – including their 'settings' and history

Students of Scripture and other great texts often read introductory books and articles for orientation and background, but can be tempted to neglect the primary texts. When studying sacraments, it is essential to read, carefully, the actual words of the sacraments; to be sensitive to the material things, gestures, and experience of the enacted rituals! This means the *whole* ritual. Aquinas identified a 'core gesture' and 'key words' for each sacrament – its 'matter' and 'form' (we might say, its 'flesh' and 'soul'). This reminds us how word and gesture confirm each other. It hints at how the Divine Word *became flesh*. But Aquinas relegated the 'liturgical context' to a set of supporting and explanatory rites. The Liturgical Movement redressed this by reminding us to explore *the dynamic and meaning of the whole*. So, for example, the Blessing of Baptismal Water (see Chapter 5) can be dispensed with in an emergency. But it is a rich expression of doctrine, doctrine that is taken as read in an emergency.

Jesus as Founder, in his Jewish context

It is Catholic doctrine that Jesus instituted the seven sacraments. When we investigate this, we must acknowledge the critical issues, and the dearth of data from the Church's earliest period. Aquinas showed some awareness of this: he recognized that Jesus did not explicitly prescribe Confirmation, and suggested he instituted it by promising the gift of the Holy Spirit that this sacrament imparts.

It seems to me that we can be more confident of Jesus' foundational role than some scholars allow; also that theology stands to quarry fuller interpretations of the sacraments from the Old Testament and Jewish background to the Christian sacraments.

The Magisterium

Part II of The Catechism of the Catholic Church[1] provides a synthetic doctrine of the sacraments, including recent developments in sacramental theology. The Catechism offers many references to magisterial texts that can be followed up for further details, as well as to Scripture and the Church Fathers.

What and Whom Do the Sacraments Reveal?

If sacraments are basically channels of revelation, we can ask how their symbolism works, and what they show us. They do not merely teach us truths; by them the Triune God communicates with us personally. This section will therefore begin to explore their power as 'channels of grace'.

How does sacramental symbolism work?

Aquinas had one Latin word, *signum*, which can mean both 'sign' and 'symbol'. Modern English catechists often distinguish the two concepts. Signs are 'pointers', either obvious, like a road-sign saying 'Norwich' or a large shoe outside a cobbler's shop, or conventional, like a red traffic light which means 'stop'. By contrast, a *symbol* is a reality in its own right, such as light, darkness, water, bread, embrace or gift, that represents a deeper and greater reality. In the right context it will be experienced as making present and embodying such a reality, without encapsulating it fully.

The sacraments employ *symbols*, eloquent realities such as washing some-one, applying a perfumed 'cosmetic', eating bread and drinking wine together, expressing an apology, applying ointment, commissioning someone, and getting married. The water of baptism, for example, naturally speaks of cleansing, birth, life, refreshment and death. In the Jewish context it speaks also of creation, the Flood, the journey to freedom through the Red Sea and, under Joshua (whose name is a form of Jesus), through the Jordan, as well as transition to a new state. The sacraments rely on an agile receptivity to subtle and multivalent symbolism. Jesus could take openness to such symbolism for granted in his time. Perhaps the 'icons' on our computer screens mean that, once again, we can accept 'allusive' (even elusive) symbolism.

Revealing past, present and future

One of Aquinas' antiphons for Corpus Christi runs:

O sacred Banquet, in which Christ is received;
the **memory of His Passion** is renewed;
the **mind** is filled with **grace**;
and a **pledge of future glory** is given us, alleluia.

This text expresses Aquinas' teaching that the Eucharist, and all the sacraments, show us God's saving work in all its dimensions, past, present and future. They symbolize what Jesus did and suffered in the past. We need to add more explic-itly than Aquinas did that they show us many aspects of Jesus' ministry, and his resurrection, as well as his passion. The sacraments show us what God is doing in and for us now, both individually and as a Church. They also show us what God will do for us in the coming Kingdom: they are sacraments of hope, in which we receive the Holy Spirit as the 'down-payment' on eternal life (2 Cor. 5.5; Eph. 1.14).

Revealing and veiling

The Gospels describe a number of encounters between Jesus and his disciples after the resurrection. One of these tells of him walking with two disciples to Emmaus (Luke 24.28). Jesus – whom initially they did not recognize – explained the Scriptures to them. He seemed to need to walk further, and they pressed him to stay with them; but as soon as they recognized him in the Breaking of the Bread he vanished from their sight – as he had to, since just as human beings cannot for the present see God as he is, so neither can they cope with Jesus' humanity in its full risen glory. He has gone ahead as Pioneer (Heb. 2.10), and until we catch up with him we 'walk by faith, not by sight' (2 Cor. 5.7). Like the disciples at Emmaus, people recognize him in the Breaking of the Bread, since, to suit our pilgrim state, the Triune God, and the Son's saving humanity, are revealed by the words and imagery of Scripture, and by the sacraments, in a way that at the same time veils. The sacraments will have done their job when God gives himself to be known, loved, possessed and enjoyed 'face to face'. Until then, they empower the journey and provide a way of laying hold of the Goal.

The Holy Trinity's Self-communication

When we speak, we sometimes merely 'convey information'. But conveying information about ourselves can become self-communication. God's revelation is always self-communication. Aquinas explained that each of Father, Son and Spirit wants to abide in men and women now, as the Known in the knower and the Beloved in the lover, and to give himself to them perfectly in the coming Kingdom. The twentieth-century theologian Karl Rahner insisted that the Triune God's self-giving is *the* fundamental reality. The sacraments are 'channels' of the self-communication, the 'unfolding to us', of the Holy Trinity. The revision of the rites after the Second Vatican Council brought out this dimension of the sacraments more fully, and for the Catechism of the Catholic Church presents the liturgy as the work of the Holy Trinity. If we examine the way that God self-communicates in the sacraments, we can recognize three Trinitarian 'patterns':

In the sacraments, the Revealing Word comes home to us

In the eternal life of the Holy Trinity, the Father begets the Son as his Image and Word, his perfect 'self-expression'. The Father 'spoke himself' into the world by sending his Son to take flesh and be born of Mary; Jesus expressed his 'personal character' as Word and Image by revealing his Father. He did this most clearly by his Sacrifice, which is the Father's irrevocable pledge of loyalty. The sacraments are a kind of extension of the incarnation. They symbolize Christ's ministry, Sacrifice and resurrection, so that, through them, the Father's purpose is revealed, his loyal care expressed.

In the sacraments, the Spirit brings Christ to us

The Father breathes forth the Holy Spirit with and through the Son as their Impulse and Bond of Love. So in the eternal life of the Holy Trinity, the Spirit is from the Son, not vice versa. But when the Divine Persons 'go forth into the world', their relationships are 'projected' into a complex history. So, in the course of time, *the Spirit brought the Son* into the world: Jesus was conceived by the power of the Holy Spirit. This has its own beauty, because the Father and the Son eternally love humanity in the Holy Spirit, the Divine Love, and since the Son's coming into the world expresses this love and puts it into effect, it is itself the work of this Love.

The Spirit who crafted the Divine Word's human nature crafts the sacraments that bring home to us the Word Incarnate. So the Catechism of the Catholic Church 1091 presents the Holy Spirit in the Liturgy as 'the Artisan of God's masterpieces'. He is invoked in many rites; from the fourth century onwards the Eastern Churches began calling him down to make the bread and wine become Christ's Body and Blood, and the Western Church does this explicitly in Eucharistic Prayers II, III and IV.

In the sacraments, the power of Christ's Sacrifice brings the Spirit to us

In God's eternity, the Spirit is from the Father through the Son. Hence in his humanity, Jesus was filled with the Holy Spirit: '[he] dwelt among us, . . . full of grace and truth. For from his fullness we have all received' (John 1.14, 16). The great act of the Trinity's self-communication is Jesus' Sacrifice. Having fully revealed his Father's love Jesus could impart his Father's personal love. 'He bowed his head and 'he handed over the Spirit' (cf. John 19.30). The Spirit, who is eternally from the Father through the Son, was given into the world by the Father through the Son's Sacrifice. He was in fact given to people of every stage of human history, though Pentecost disclosed in a spectacular way what had been achieved at Calvary.

The Blood-and-Water, the Living Water, that John saw flow from Jesus' side, symbolized both the gift of the Holy Spirit, and the Eucharist and Baptism that build up the Church, Christ's Bride, who is animated by the Spirit. Hence we should expect the sacraments to exhibit and enact the pattern of Jesus' Sacrifice, the core event that echoes throughout all space and time. In all the sacraments, the Father gives us the Holy Spirit through the power of Christ's Sacrifice. Hence each is a new Pentecost.

We can see this in the formula of absolution, pronounced by the priest during the Sacrament of Reconciliation. In the revision of the liturgy after the Second Vatican Council, this was expanded to begin: 'God the Father of mercies, through the Death and Resurrection of his Son, has reconciled the world to himself, and sent the Holy Spirit among us for the forgiveness of sins.'

Similarly, the Prayer for consecrating Chrism asks the Father: 'Pour into it the strength of the Holy Spirit, by the cooperating power of your Christ, from whose holy Name this Chrism takes its name.'

The Power of the Sacraments

By seeing sacraments as means of communication we have begun to explore their power. Human words, deeds and gestures can build up relationships; the sacraments are God's 'gestures'. Citizens are inculturated by certain public rituals; Christians are inculturated into a world of sacramental meaning – sacramental rituals have power to form Christians. Certain stuffs such as bread and wine, and certain actions like bathing or feeding someone, are naturally laden with significance. If God comes to men and women through such 'media', then of course his gestures will have power – or, better, the natural power of the media he chooses makes them *apt channels of his divine power*.

The sacraments bring home to people, in their own time and place, God's great act of self-communication, the Paschal Mystery of Christ's Sacrifice and resurrection with its outcome, Pentecost. In the sacraments, Christ gives the Holy Spirit; in turn the Spirit brings Christ. The presence of the Word and the Spirit of course has power to re-form believers. The Spirit, who is Love, pours a divine love into them, 'charity', which makes them God's friends. We tend to share a friend's outlook, hence the Spirit makes the People of God truly wise, imparting a 'wisdom from above' (James 3.17) by which they share God's perspective, and are conformed to Christ the Divine Wisdom. By Wisdom and Love they embrace the Father and become like him, so as to be sharers in the Divine Nature (2 Pet. 1.4). The Fathers of the Church, and the liturgy, celebrate this gift of being divinized. Catholic theology calls it 'sanctifying grace' – except that the Latin *gratia gratum faciens* really means 'the gift that makes us gracious, [morally] graceful and grateful, pleasing to God'. This grace, imparted by the sacraments, is an objective reality in the Christian. Although it grounds his or her personal relationship with the Trinity, it cannot be 'merely subjective' – people cannot be in a relationship with the Creator without the Spirit transforming them in the depths of their being!

The power of God's Word and Gesture

The Old Testament presents God's Word as having power to accomplish what it says; see Psalms 33.6 and 9, 107.20, 148.5; Isaiah 55.11. When God says, 'Let there be light', light is. Jesus is God's Word. If his passion, death and resurrection are God's great gesture, then of course they have a divine power to accomplish their meaning. Jesus' death and resurrection have power to turn men and women from sin and to enliven them by imparting the Holy Spirit. If the sacraments extend to humanity the Word and Gesture that is Jesus, then of course they have the power to 'effect what they signify', as Aquinas put it. Herbert McCabe expressed it: 'In the sacraments God shows us what he does and does what he shows us.'[2] The sacraments reveal Christ's sacrifice, and apply its power to those who receive them, so as to impart the Holy Spirit who makes men and women alive in Christ, and guides them so that the life of grace may securely grow into the life of glory.

Sacraments as 'channels of grace'

Just as no celebration of a sacrament is a new message from God, so its power is not independent of Jesus' Sacrifice. Aquinas expressed this using the concept of 'instrumental causality'. A modern adaptation of his example will make this clear: When I want to write on a white board, I use my hand to grasp a dry-wipe marker. Only a human being can write, not a hand or a pen by itself; but by far the best 'tools' for a human being to use are the hand and the pen. Likewise, only God can save and divinize. But to bring his transforming grace to the human beings he has made, God 'channels' his grace through Jesus' life, death and resurrection and, thence, through the sacraments. Jesus' humanity, with all that he did and suffered, are like the hand in the analogy – they are joined to God in the incarnation. The sacraments are like the dry-wipe marker, devised and taken up by God to bring his purpose home to us; sacraments apply to us the power of Jesus' own death and resurrection.

More powerful than magic – yet we can resist!

If sacraments have an objective, divine power to effect what they signify, are they a kind of magic? No; they are quite the opposite. In magic, exact performance of the ritual is said to be essential, and the powers said to be at work belong to the performer and the materials. If a spell is done correctly, the effect automatically happens to the victim. In reality, even if magic did work, it could not have the power directly to influence someone's mind and will. In a sacrament, the reverent performance of the rite is of course very important – but if the priest is irreverent or clumsy it does not affect the power of the sacrament. Provided the meaning gets through – God's meaning – the sacrament works. The power does not belong to the minister nor to the material, but to God. The power – being divine – can and does work within the recipient's mind and will, building up Faith and Love.

The sacraments are much more precious than magic. Putting a spell on someone to make them love you is not very satisfying. Working at building up a friendship by communication and co-operation may be more demanding, but it is more precious, and ultimately more effective; *this* is the analogy for sacraments. God builds up friendship between humanity and himself, by a self-communication that involves the recipient, and involves the Church in the person of her minister.

One person can make a friendly overture that another person rejects. Likewise the power of the sacraments can be resisted, just as people can resist the power of Christ's cross. But God, precisely as God, is the Highest Cause, and therefore he reaches deepest. As and when he wills, he can reach into the depths of the human mind and will so as to attract, gently and powerfully, our welcoming of him. He does not over-rule, but *enlarges*, human freedom. Infant Baptism is a sign of this. God imparts grace and the abilities to believe and love, so that later on the child can consciously welcome them. Even here, God does not typically bypass natural human dynamics (though he can when he will): children are brought to Baptism by their parents and godparents, and the Christian community's representative ministers the sacrament to them, rather as in the human and personal interaction between parents and infants the initiative lies with the parents, and through them the child receives values and society's language, which he or she will increasingly own and use.

Both objective power and personal receptivity

In the third century, some people who had been baptized outside the Catholic Church wanted to become Catholics. St Cyprian held that they would need to be 're-' baptized because there can be no grace outside the Church. Pope Stephen held that their Baptism was valid, and could not be repeated, and his position became the Church's official teaching. St Augustine later explained that human sin could not impede Christ's power, hence baptisms done as he taught do work; nevertheless, people who joined schismatic groups were not in charity until they were reconciled with the Church, because schism is contrary to charity. The resolution of this controversy left a double legacy:

'Sacramental Character'

The Catholic Church teaches that Baptism – and Confirmation and Ordination – impart an objective and indelible 'character' to their recipients. The word 'character' in its modern English meaning does not translate the original Greek word, which refers to the impress made by a stamp or seal to mark something as personal property, or to guarantee a letter. 'Sacramental character' is a spiritual stamp of authentication. In these sacraments men and women are sealed by the Holy Spirit, claimed as their own by God the Father in a distinctive way, irrevocably grafted into Christ. God's call is without change of mind on his part, even if individual Christians fail to live up to, or to live out, the status God has given them.

The 'three levels' in the sacraments

Medieval theologians diagnosed 'three levels' in each sacrament, so as to hold together the truths that (a) Christ's covenanted power, present in the sacraments, cannot be thwarted by human wickedness, yet (b) it is possible to receive sacraments unworthily, resisting their grace and their message, and so to fail to benefit from them.

Sacramentum tantum *(something that is 'just a sign')*

Sacramentum tantum is the 'outward sign', which determines whether or not a sacrament has been celebrated validly. Validity requires that all the following need to be in place:

- A due minister. For Baptism, anyone. For Marriage, a man and a woman able freely to marry each other. For Ordination, a bishop. For the other sacraments, a priest – and in the case of Reconciliation, one who has due jurisdiction.
- A right intention on the part of the minister; basically, the intention 'to do what the Church does'. This is typically manifest by what the minister does, and by the context; sometimes a context can render a valid intention impossible. The *recipient*'s intention is also crucial in some sacraments. Someone forced into a baptismal ceremony, who answered, 'I do not believe', would not be baptized. A 'marriage' can be invalid owing to defect of intention.

- The proper 'matter' – for example, water, duly consecrated Chrism, wheat bread and grape wine; the laying on of hands in Ordination. In the Sacrament of Reconciliation, the 'matter' is the acts of the penitent: confession, contrition, 'satisfaction' (better called 'a gesture of repentance').
- Due 'form' – that is, words that properly convey the sacrament's meaning. Often, much of this meaning is supplied by the sacrament's full, extended rite, some of which can be taken as read in an emergency.

A valid 'outward sign' infallibly causes the:

Res et sacramentum *(something that is both a reality, and a sign of something deeper)*

This is something valuable, but chiefly relevant to the life of the Church now, hence it points beyond itself to something yet more precious. Herbert McCabe calls it 'a mystery of the Church herself, a realization in history of the priestly work of Christ'.[3]

- In Baptism, Confirmation and Orders, the *res et sacramentum* is 'character'. It locates us within Christ's Body, which is something to cherish. But we are in the Body for an ulterior purpose, for eternal loving communion with God and one another. We can fail to attain this, if by refusing to love we give the lie to what our presence in the Church says we strive for.
- In Marriage, the *res et sacramentum* is the marriage bond. This differs from character in that it lasts 'till death do us part'. But it speaks of a love and loyalty that should be there throughout life, and that will last for ever.
- In the Eucharist, the *res et sacramentum* is the presence of Christ beneath the appearances of bread and wine. This reality is precious; but, just as Jesus became incarnate for a purpose, so he remains among us for a purpose – to establish a communion that lasts for ever.
- Regarding Penance, Aquinas sees the more outward feelings and expressions of sorrow (which are part of the *sacramentum tantum*) as working an 'interior repentance', a real change of mind. This is the *res et sacramentum*; it is something good, but it points deeper, to the restoration of our communion with God in love.

- Herbert McCabe sees the *res et sacramentum* of the Anointing of the Sick as either the healing and strength needed to resume one's duties, or the strength to die in union with Christ's Sacrifice. Both point, in distinctive ways, to the coming resurrection world.

A valid 'outward sign', together with the *res et sacramentum*, point to and, ideally, cause the:

Res tantum *(this is 'just a reality', a precious goal that does not point beyond itself)*

Herbert McCabe calls it 'a mystery of the Kingdom, a mystery of the Spirit in each of us, a mystery of grace'.[4] It is our share in the life and love of the Triune God, abiding in us; the life of grace that we hope will grow and flourish to eternal life. In each sacrament, the life of grace comes, or comes back, or is nourished, under some aspect or other. Some of the suggestions that follow are tentative, since (as with the *res et sacramentum*) theologians have not been unanimous in this regard:

- In Baptism, the *res tantum* is justification: the Holy Spirit comes to undo original and any actual sins, making us God's friends and children.
- In Confirmation, the *res tantum* is the Holy Spirit's Seven Gifts invoked in the rite. Aquinas sees them as seven *instincts*: ways in which we grow in empathy with the Spirit who comes to be our Paraclete, our friend for the journey.
- In the Holy Eucharist, the *res tantum* is the Mystical Body of Christ. Jesus comes to us to build us up as his living members; he gives us the Spirit to make us one in Faith and Love.
- In Penance the *res tantum* is, again, justification: the Holy Spirit comes to us to undo actual sins, to restore us to God's friendship if we have lost it, or to make us better friends of God, so that we live again, or live more committedly, the life of grace.
- In the Anointing of the Sick, the *res tantum* is closer union with Jesus who healed the sick, who rose from the dead and will raise us; and with the life-giving Spirit who conforms us to Christ in his priesthood, making us able to bear witness to our hope by using sickness prayerfully and patiently, or by our return to vigour.

- In Holy Orders, the *res tantum* is conformity to the Good Shepherd who made God's truth and mercy incarnate. It includes the graces that flow to others from the clergy's ministry.
- In Marriage, the *res tantum* is the Holy Spirit coming to craft the bond of real love between husband and wife, love that reflects the self-giving of the Divine Bridegroom. It includes the graces that flow to the spouses themselves, and to their children, families and neighbours, from the ministry of the married couple.

Ways in which 'sacramental wholeness' can break down

Whenever a sacrament is properly celebrated, the first two levels cause the third. This is how it should be, rather as human words and gestures should be edifying, and sincere expressions of love stand to call forth a response of love.

But it is possible to thwart the *res tantum* by coming to a sacrament while being unreceptive to its grace. For example, if I receive Holy Communion after murdering my grandfather and while plotting to murder my grandmother, I receive Jesus' Body and Blood, but do not receive grace, since I am unwilling to grow in love. If someone comes to faith and is baptized, but plans all the time to persist in some serious sin that he only pretended he was going to give up, he receives the baptismal character, but is not yet justified. When he does repent of his sin, the character that has been imparted begins to have its effect, and grace flows in.

Conversely, it is possible to lay hold on the *res tantum* without the sacrament. A convert planning to be baptized has begun to live the life of grace, by 'Baptism of Desire' (that is, because of desire for Baptism), and goes to heaven if she dies before Baptism. Someone who attends a 'Mass' celebrated by an impostor, without knowing the celebration is a sham, desires to receive Holy Communion and thereby grows in grace, even though she receives only bread and wine in her mouth.

This possibility of receiving something of the *res tantum* by desiring it does not mean we can do without the sacraments themselves. Someone in prison might not be able to send his wife a birthday present, and at her next visit could sincerely say 'I was thinking about you'. But if a free man failed to give his wife a present when he could, it would not be sufficient for him to say 'It's the thought that counts'. Likewise, if you pretend to yourself that you want to go to Confession when you get a chance, but do not take the chances that come your way, the desire is not really there, nor genuine repentance. The desire for the grace of a sacrament relies on the richer, more 'holistic' normal procedure – you cannot desire Holy Communion if there is no Holy Communion to desire!

The sacramentality of the Christian and of the Church

A consequence of the teaching that character and the marriage bond are *res et sacramentum* is that a reality with sacramental power abides in those who have received these sacraments. In a sense, they become sacramental. An exploration of this theme, which does not seem often to be noticed, will lead us on to an important theme in modern sacramental theology – namely, the Church herself is a sacrament.

A powerful sign abides in the baptized, confirmed, ordained and married

The *character* of being baptized, confirmed and ordained, and the marriage bond, are *res et sacramentum*, reality and sacrament – sign and channel of grace. For Aquinas, character is a sharing in Christ's priesthood; the twentieth-century theologian Yves Congar developed the idea of the priesthood of married people and parents. This implies that dignity and vocation belong to those who are baptized, confirmed, ordained, or married. A God-given reality in them is a potential sign and channel of grace to them and to others. In a sense, this means that they become sacramental. They may at times fail to draw on this *res et sacramentum* and so render it unfruitful. But the resource remains, and is a ground of hope that God who began the good work in them will bring it to fulfilment (Phil. 1.6).

Sacraments of Mission

The sacraments just mentioned *consecrate* Christians for ministry in Christ. In fact, in each sacrament the Risen Christ is among us, saying: 'As the Father has sent me, even so I am sending you . . . Receive the Holy Spirit' (John 20.21–22). By imparting the Spirit, Jesus shares with his followers his mission to make his Father's mercy visible and tangible; he empowers them to share his role as sacrament of encounter with God.

The Spirit who overshadowed Mary so as to craft Christ's Body, overshadows the baptismal font, the womb of Mother Church, to craft those baptized there as members of Christ's Mystical Body. In Confirmation, the Spirit who anointed Jesus for his mission, and comes to anoint the baptized for their share in that mission, is called down after an invitation to ask 'that the Spirit may strengthen [these candidates] by the abundance of his gifts, and by his anointing may bring them to perfection as conformed to Christ'.

In the Eucharist, Christians become what they receive, and so the Mass ends: *Ite, missa est*, 'Go: the assembly is sent.' They are sent out to be Christ's Body in the world, and to imitate the sacrifice they have celebrated.

The old prayer for blessing the oil of the sick implied that the sick who are anointed share Christ's dignity as Priest, Prophet, King and Martyr, and in line with this the Catechism of the Catholic Church (1521–3) says that they are in some way consecrated and given a distinctive role in the Church.

The Church's Sacramentality

Not just each Christian, but the whole Body, is called to be a sacrament, to be the extension into space and time of Christ who is himself *the* sacrament of God. In its Dogmatic Constitution on the Church, *Lumen Gentium*, the Second Vatican Council set out to convince the Church's members, and the world, of the Church's inner nature and mission to the whole world, and at the outset this document declared that 'in Christ the Church is like a sacrament, that is, a sign and instrument, of intimate union with God and of the unity of the whole human race'. That is, in the Church we should see people being drawn into communion with God and with one another, and the Church is called to bring this communion about by gathering and nurturing the faithful. She does this as commissioned by Christ who died so as to gather into unity the children of God who had been scattered abroad by sin.

One sign of this vocation of the Church is the role of the minister in the seven sacraments. Human relationships have been damaged by sin; but in the sacraments encounters between human beings become channels of healing grace, and thereby the healing of relationships is proclaimed. Further, the sacraments are analogous to a society's public rituals into which citizens need to be inculturated, and which themselves inculturate citizens and cement social identity. The sacraments are a core part of *the common Christian heritage*, to whose 'language' we learn to be attuned, and which form us – form us into Christ.

The Church is a sacrament in a different way from Christ, and in a different way from the seven sacraments (hence the Second Vatican Council said she is *like* a sacrament). Each reveals and veils God's saving work; and in the case of the Church she veils God's work because Christ's faithful Bride suffers scandals and the imperfection of her members.

The Eucharist makes the Church, and vice versa

Following Augustine and Aquinas, we said above that the *res tantum* of the Holy Eucharist is the Mystical Body of Christ, the Church. The ultimate purpose and effect of that, and in a way of all the sacraments, is to make the Church, to build up God's eternal dwelling-place. Applying the concept of instrumental causality, we can say God reaches out through the following causal chain:

> *God → Jesus' humanity and sacrifice → Sacraments (involving ministers) → Recipients → Church*

The focus is on God's work in Christ. A complementary 'model' operates in the modern theology that sees the Church as 'the fundamental sacrament'. In this picture, Jesus, who is the primordial sacrament, established his Body to be an ongoing sign and instrument of God's healing presence; the Church, this Body, then celebrates the individual sacraments for her members. This suggests the following causal chain:

God → Jesus' humanity and sacrifice → the Church as structured Body → Sacraments → Recipients

The Catechism of the Catholic Church gives space to both 'models'; for example, 1088, 1114–21. This is valuable, since if taken in isolation the second model can be misread in a way that separates 'the hierarchy' from 'the ordinary faithful' (the 'active' from the 'passive'), and could even tempt those who are called to be *ministers* to have a false sense of *ownership* of the sacraments.

I would prefer to see the Holy Eucharist as the fundamental sacrament, on which both the Church, and the other sacraments, depend. It makes the Church; it teaches her what to be, how to live sacrificially, and what values to preach and promote, including unity, care for the poor, and peace. This approach, which owes much to the twentieth-century theologian Henri de Lubac, will be explored in closer detail in the chapter on the Celebration of the Eucharist (see Chapter 7).

Why *Seven* Sacraments?

Having glimpsed something of how the sacraments form us into Christ, and before moving on to examine the individual rites, we can ask why there are precisely seven. The list of seven later defined by the Church had not been long agreed when Aquinas wrote. He saw a parallel between our natural life and the life of grace:

- In human life we are brought to birth. As children of God we are born in Baptism.
- In human social life we 'come of age'. Confirmation brings us to maturity in Christ. (This does not mean it can only be given to adults. It is a resource to draw on, an identity to grow into, rather as human maturity may be celebrated at 18 or 21, but we have to grow into it.)
- Human life needs to be nourished by food and drink. Our life in Christ needs the Eucharist.
- Human relationships can be inhibited by moral difficulties, and reconciliation may be needed. When our supernatural life is wounded morally, we need Reconciliation and Repentance.

- Social life can be impeded by sickness, so that healing is needed. Our participation in the Church's life is facilitated by the Anointing of the Sick. (This is
not the account *Aquinas* gave.)
- Human life is organized at the domestic level by marriage. Our Christian
domestic life is energized by the same thing, enriched with the dignity of a
sacrament.
- Human life requires leadership at the more political level. The Church needs
the leadership the sacrament of Orders provides.

This is obviously not intended as a complete account of the sacraments and what
they achieve. In particular, the twentieth century witnessed a re-evaluation of
Confirmation that understood it less as a sacrament of maturity and more as a
further stage in the process of initiation into the Christian life. The manner in
which these two ways of understanding Confirmation work out in practice –
and the tensions on the ground – will be considered in Chapters 5 and 6. But
Aquinas' analysis of the seven exemplifies how grace elevates nature, lifting up
things human into realms divine. It points to the ways in which the sacraments
place Christ's pattern, and the pattern of his passing over, upon our lives, shap-
ing them into a journey in Christ, energized by the Spirit, to the Father.

Besides the seven 'moments' in human life on which this list relies, there is
an eighth, namely death. But no sacrament matches that last moment, since the
life of grace restored and nourished by the sacraments does not come to an end
at death; it grows into eternal glory.

Questions for Reflection

- Did Jesus institute all seven sacraments? Is Scripture clear about
this? Does it matter if it isn't clear?
- How useful is it to discuss 'sacraments in general' before examining
each of the seven in detail, and in isolation from the whole liturgy?
- The kind of dispute described above was a live one between the
Dominican and Jesuit missionaries in China; how might it affect
missionary work and evangelization in the West today?
- Do we need to work harder to recover the Jewish roots of the
Christian sacraments?

- Should we try to make our sacramental celebrations 'transparent' or 'mysterious', simple or dramatic?
- Do we need to work harder to bring out the Trinitarian dimension of the sacraments?
- Do we need to work harder to help Christians celebrate the sacraments as eschatological signs and as 'sacraments of mission'?
- Do we need to work harder to convince Christians that *they* are sacramental, both as individual disciples and as a Church?
- Are the sacraments our celebration of our faith, or of existing (but God-given) realities; or are they more a matter of God breaking in to do things for us?
- If the sacraments are 'channels of God's grace', why are we not changed by them more powerfully?
- Is it better to see the Church, or to see the Holy Eucharist, as the 'fundamental sacrament'?
- Is it better to see 'the Church' as dispensing the sacraments to her members, or Christ dispensing them to his members so as to make them into a Church? Or should we hold both 'models' in balance? And what does this imply for who 'owns' the sacraments?

Notes

1 Catechism of the Catholic Church (CCC) (London: Catholic Truth Society 1994, 2016).

2 McCabe, Herbert, OP, *The Teaching of the Catholic Church: A New Catechism of Christian Doctrine* (London: CTS, 1985; London: DLT, 2000). Section 68 (p. 15 of the CTS edition, p. 23 of the DLT edition).

3 McCabe, section 72.

4 McCabe, section 72.

5

Christian Initiation of Adults

CAROLINE DOLLARD AND PETER MCGRAIL

Introduction

Life is filled with beginnings and endings. We start new jobs, move home, form new relationships – and through it all we transition through life, from childhood to adulthood, from maturity to old age. Some of these changes happen unnoticed, others happen suddenly or even traumatically, as at the unexpected death of a loved one. But a number of the transitions we make through life are underpinned by major decisions – such as when we enter into marriage. These more conscious changes can demand so comprehensive a re-orientation of our attitudes or our patterns of life that they take time, and therefore are best understood as processes rather than as single events. Moving from the single life into the married state, for example, demands considerably more of both parties than their attendance at a wedding ceremony.

When those processes involve an individual moving into a new relationship with a community, we frequently speak of them as processes of initiation. Both the individual and the community have active parts to play in initiation: indeed, ultimately, it is the community that initiates. Thus, many societies have marked the transition of their young people into adulthood by complex initiation ceremonies that involve not just ritual actions, but also lengthy periods of instruction of the young people by their elders. In the West such adolescent initiation rites have largely disappeared – but we can still recognize the overall pattern in the manner in which, say, a graduation ceremony marks the end of a period of study and the particular institution initiates its former students into their new status as degree-holders, or in the complex of instruction and rituals that can sometimes mark a period of apprenticeship.

All of the above is true of initiation into the Catholic Church. The Church expects that an individual who seeks membership of it should be radically orientated towards Christ and his members, towards becoming part of a community of believers, and towards a way of life that is marked by faith, hope and charity. Like traditional processes of initiation, admission into the Catholic Church involves both educational and ritual processes. However, when speaking of the Christian initiating community a theological dimension is added; it is the whole Body of the Church – Christ and his members[1] – that initiates. Initiation is thus a divine, as well as a human, activity. Therefore, it takes place within a sacramental framework, and involves the reception of not one but three different sacraments: Baptism, Confirmation, and admission to the Eucharist for the first time. Only when a person has received all three can we speak about initiation being completed.

The ritual complexity is further accentuated by the fact that while the three-sacrament principle holds for both adults and children, very different disciplines of initiation for the two have arisen, and discrete versions of the rituals are provided for use with adults and with children. Furthermore, especially in the case of the initiation of children, local practice on the ground can vary considerably, frequently between different dioceses and sometimes even between neighbouring parishes. For these reasons, this book treats the two sets of rites separately, devoting this present chapter to the rituals for adults and discussing the children's rituals in the next, briefer chapter. It may appear strange to begin with the adult form of the rite, especially as across the world the most commonly performed Catholic initiation rituals have children as their subjects. However, it is with the adult rite that the theological contours of this ritual complex become clear and the inter-relationship of the three sacraments is more sharply brought to the fore than is the case with the initiation of children – at least in the manner in which it is most usually celebrated.

Initiation as Human Process

The processes for the initiation of both adults and children are deeply grounded in the realities of human existence, and both sets of rituals reflect and respect human processes of growth and change. As we shall see in the next chapter, the link between the initiation sacraments and the natural phases of a child's life and human development can be particularly strong – so strong, that the link between sacrament and early life-course risks over-layering a different set of meanings on to the way that the Church formally understands these sacraments. With adults, the question is not one of age, or stage of human development, but a recognition of the intricacy of making the kind of free, informed choices that both inform and follow from a decision to join the Church. Of course, that passage is as varied as there are people making it. Some will have lived their lives very close to the Christian community; for others, a more radical journey will have been undertaken. However, for all adults who seek to join the Church, that request involves a dimension of decision, the engagement with challenges, and the passage from not being a member to becoming one.

Experientially, the passage of adults into the Church has a great deal in common with other human processes of change. At the turn of the twentieth century the anthropologist Arnold van Gennep (1873–1957) noted that such life-course-changing processes as pregnancy and childbirth, betrothal and marriage, death and funerals, and initiation in general, share a common structure across cultures and contexts. In his classic book *The Rites of Passage* van Gennep outlined the processes that articulate a person's progress from one state of life to another.[2] This progress, he argued, involved the negotiation of three discrete phases:

- Separation from the old state of life.
- Period of transition.
- Incorporation into the new state.

This structure is deceptively simple, but it reflects human realities. As a person moves from one state of life to another there is inevitably some kind of letting go, of leaving behind – which can be painful, and at times radical. That necessarily leads into a process of becoming or moving forward – something that psychologically cannot happen overnight, and that might be marked by a degree of inner turmoil and confusion as old ways of thinking or of doing are challenged or no longer prove helpful. Finally, the person achieves a new, settled state of being – different to where they started from, and in many ways the fruit of the time spent in-between.

Van Gennep's insight was two-fold. First, he brought to the fore the significance of the in-between phase of transition, which he described as one of 'liminality' – a term that is derived from the Latin word for a 'threshold', the physical space that marks the boundary between a building and the world outside it. When applied to a human process of transition, it describes a time when the individual is neither in their old state nor their new – as it were, between worlds, 'on the boundary'. Second, he identified the role that rituals play within the whole complex, and especially as they mark the beginning and the end of the liminal period. Thus, the move out from the old life on to the threshold is marked by a 'Rite of Separation'. Then, after time spent on the threshold, the person moves from the liminal state to assume their new identity via another, different, ritual process. In the human processes of initiation, that final ritual step marks the transition of the individual to full group membership. Van Gennep's theory gained wide acceptance across the twentieth century, and his term 'Rites of Passage' is now comfortably adopted in many languages, literature and popular cultures across the world to describe transitions in status. The term is applied, for example, to coming-of-age processes, to belief systems, to military or academic life, to vocational or professional development, and even to sporting achievement.

All too frequently, however, insufficient attention is paid to the dynamics of the essential middle period. The importance of the threshold experience was underscored by British anthropologist Victor Turner (1920–83).[3] Turner developed van Gennep's three-fold structure of Rites of Passage, placing particular emphasis on the liminal phase. Turner described liminality as a 'limbo', as unstructured, possibly uncomfortable, intense and temporary, and yet shared with others, marked by the development of peer relationships and a sense of 'being in this together'. All of this, he insisted, served the basic purpose of the 'betwixt and between' of the threshold: it was a space in which old patterns of identity and behaviour could be broken down and new ones formed. It is characterized by creativity and openness – and key to the process is the formation of a strong group-identity which Turner characterizes as '*communitas*'.

Background to Today's Catholic Rituals for Adult Initiation

The Catholic processes for adult initiation were radically revised after the Second Vatican Council, and they now very closely reflect van Gennep's three-stage Rites of Passage. This similarity did not come about by accident, nor overnight. The basic tripartite structure of the Rites of Passage is itself reflective of the ancient heritage of the Christian Church; both the writings of the Fathers of the Church and early liturgical texts attest to a lengthy (typically three-year) and complex process that involved separation, liminality and, finally, sacramental initiation. The early Church even developed a specialist vocabulary to describe the various stages and rituals of the process – most significantly designating the liminal period as 'the Catechumenate', which means 'the time of hearing'. This gives the related terms of 'catechumen' which describes those who have entered into its liminal space, and 'catechesis' – the educational process that takes place there.

The Catechumenate flourished during the first five or six centuries of the Church's existence, but fell into disuse as Christianity entered society's mainstream and people were baptized more usually as infants rather than as adults. Nonetheless, in the decades before the Second Vatican Council, Catholics in two places began to ask whether the catechumenal model of the early Church might not have something to offer to their modern contexts.

The first was Africa, a site of intense missionary activity since the nineteenth century. Missionaries began to recognize that the transition from African Traditional Religions to Christianity required radical changes of worldview and community practice (for example, with regard to polygamy) – changes that called out for a progressive and staged process of initiation. Therefore, from the late nineteenth century, Catholic missionaries began to develop extended processes of baptismal preparation that drew upon the ancient examples and that gave space for conversion to take root within an individual's life. These initiatives spread and intensified during the early twentieth century, and in the lead-up to the Second Vatican Council many African bishops specifically requested that these experiments should be formalized and that the Church should restore both the Catechumenate and sequenced initiation rites.

Meanwhile, pastors in continental Europe – particularly in France – awakened to the recognition that Europe was no longer uniformly Christian, and that significant numbers of adults were once again seeking Baptism. In post-war Paris, catechists began experimenting with the catechumenate model with such adults, and the model was taken up in a number of French dioceses. This process was community based, initiating more formal education through shared reflection on life and worship. As the Second Vatican Council approached, bishops in mainland Western Europe added their voices to the African bishops in calling for a formal response by the Church in the restoration of the Catechumenate. That response came in article 64 of *Sacrosanctum Concilium*, which stated:

> The catechumenate for adults, comprising several distinct steps, is to be restored and brought into use at the discretion of the local ordinary [bishop]. By this means the time of the catechumenate, which is intended as a period for suitable instruction, may be sanctified by sacred rites to be celebrated at successive intervals of time.[4]

This Conciliar decree set in course a process of ritual revision. Following the pattern discussed in Chapter 2, a 12-member study group of the *Consilium* worked on the new adult rites between 1965 and 1969. A provisional text was approved by Rome in 1966 and was trialled in 50 catechetical centres across the world. In the light of these practical experiments, the study group redrafted the rite, and Pope Paul VI approved it for use in 1972. The revised text carried the name, the *Rite of Christian Initiation of Adults* (henceforth, *RCIA*). It owed much to liturgical studies carried out by scholars active in the Liturgical Movement, but it was far from a slavish recreation of a rite from the early Church. A large number of ancient prayer texts were, indeed, incorporated, but in a surprisingly free and often radically adapted manner – as was the case for the post-Vatican II revision of all the Roman rites. The revised initiation ritual reflected twentieth-century developments in the fields of education, psychology and anthropology as much as it did historical studies. The freedom with which the text was drawn up is reflected in a similar freedom offered to those who use it today: the rite is intended to be adapted to the particular circumstances of individuals, communities and cultures.

Rite of Christian Initiation of Adults

History
- Editio typica, 1972: *Ordo Initiationis Christianæ Adultorum*
- English Translation, First edition, 1988: *Rite of Christian Initiation of Adults* (London: Burns & Oates, 1987)
- English Translation, Second edition, forthcoming: *Order of Christian Initiation of Adults*

Contents
Christian Initiation, General Introduction
Rite of Christian Initiation of Adults, Introduction

Part I: Christian Initiation of Adults
   Period of Evangelization and Pre-Catechumenate
   First Step: Acceptance into the Order of Catechumens
   Period of the Catechumenate
   Second Step: Election or Enrolment of Names
   Period of Purification and Enlightenment
   Third Step: Celebration of the Sacraments of Initiation
   Period of Post-baptismal Catechesis or Mystagogy

Part II: Rites for Particular Circumstances
   Christian Initiation of Children who have reached Catechetical Age
   Christian Initiation of Adults in Exceptional Circumstances
   Christian Initiation of a Person in Danger of Death
   Preparation of Uncatechized Adults for Confirmation and Eucharist
   Reception of Baptized Christians into the Full Communion of the Catholic Church

Structure of the *RCIA*

The relationship between the revised adult rituals and the Rites of Passage model is not immediately apparent, because the rite appears to consist of four – rather than the classic three – phases:

1. Period of Evangelization (or Pre-Catechumenate)
   Rite of Entry into the Catechumenate

2. Catechumenate
   Rite of Election

3. Period of Purification and Enlightenment
   Celebration of Sacraments of Christian Initiation

4. Period of Mystagogy

However, the dimension of liminality, which begins at the start of the second period, is not brought to a definitive conclusion until the end of the third period, at the celebration of the Sacraments of Christian Initiation; the classic three-part process, therefore, underpins the whole.

The Period of Evangelization/ Pre-Catechumenate

The explicit introduction of a first Period of Evangelization/Pre-Catechumenate into the model is not entirely helpful, as it can suggest that this initial phase of initiation involves a structured approach, which it does not. It is better conceived of as an aspect of the 'before' of the Rites of Passage model. Thus, this first period of the *RCIA* ought not to be conceived of as a closely defined activity on the part of either parish or individual. Rather, it stands for an accumulation of encounters between a person and the message of the gospel as lived and spoken by members of the Christian community that may well have taken place over several years. From a parish perspective, therefore, it is best not to think of the

'Pre-Catechumenate' as a discrete process, as something that it does alongside its other activities. Rather, it happens through those activities – it is fundamentally constituted by a parish's everyday encounters with the broader human community that in a real sense form the bedrock of the parish's mission. Focused evangelization projects may well form part of this ongoing reaching out, but they do not sum it up.

The rite gives the formal name of 'Enquirer' to people at this 'Pre-Catechumenal' stage. The term is apt: an extended and multifaceted encounter between the gospel and ongoing life experience has the potential to give rise to significant questions on the part of the individual. These questions may well involve an intellectual dimension, but they can also relate to fundamentally existential issues about personal identity, ethical choices, and so on. At some point an 'Enquirer' may decide that there is a need to address them – to explore in greater detail whether the Catholic Church is offering an answer and a way of life. That is the point at which the Catechumenate comes into play.

The Catechumenate

The heart of the *RCIA* is this second period, which substantially corresponds to van Gennep's liminal phase. The Catechumenate is intended as an extended period of pastoral formation and guidance and has no fixed duration; indeed, depending on the individual and their own inner processes it may last for up to three years. Typically, the Catechumenate includes an ongoing catechesis based on the experience of community life, the experience of the liturgical year through celebrations of the Word and the gradual unfolding of the Paschal Mystery in the Scriptures as they are proclaimed Sunday by Sunday at the Eucharist – with an exploration of core aspects of Catholic doctrine/Tradition that relate to those Scriptures. The rite also provides a range of prayers, blessings and anointings to purify, strengthen and nourish the catechumens along their journey, and to undergird their engagement with the demands made by the gospel to love and serve others. Across this process, they engage in different ways with the Christian community: with the catechists who are responsible for facilitating their exploration of the gospel and unpacking its practical implications, with sponsors who offer a more personal, one-to-one support and example, and with the Sunday Mass congregation.

The rite of entry into the Catechumenate

The beginning and end of the Catechumenate are clearly delineated by two major rituals that mirror each other. The first is the 'Rite of Acceptance in the Catechumenate', which corresponds to van Gennep's 'Rite of Separation'. The rite takes place during Sunday Mass in the Catholic parish and may be celebrated at any time of the year. It begins as the priest and the would-be Christian meet at the door of the church. Thus, visually, it represents the point at which the individual steps on to the threshold of the Church. That first ritual encounter takes the form of a conversation for which a script is provided, but which may be adapted. On the face of it, the questions posed appear quite straightforward: 'What do you ask of God's Church?', and 'What does faith offer you?' And the candidates make a deceptively simple response: 'Eternal life' or 'the grace of Christ' or 'Entrance to the Church'. Yet both question and answer are full of hope and fragility, founded on a gradual impulse towards Christ that has been influenced by the experiences of a lifetime. To be authentic, these questions need to be rather more than routine, and they presume that the person who approaches the Church senses that they are looking for something – and that the Church might possess a response.

The rite continues as the priest leads the enquirers into the building and asks them to make a 'First Acceptance of the Gospel' before the gathered parish community. This 'First Acceptance' is a public statement of the desire of the catechumen to orientate his or her life to that of Christ – but it does not yet constitute a point of arrival: rather, it propels the catechumen on to the threshold of no longer being completely outside the ambit of the Church, though not yet admitted into its membership. That ambiguity is reflected in the language that the Church uses to speak of people at this stage. The Church 'embraces the catechumens as her own with a mother's love and concern', and from now on they become part of the household of Christ,[5] nourished by celebrations of the Word, blessings, and the teaching and life of the community. The rite makes provision for them to be formally 'dismissed' from the Sunday assembly at the end of the Liturgy of the Word. Participation in the Liturgy of the Eucharist pertains to the baptized faithful. The catechumens are making their way towards full initiation – but the fact that they have not yet reached that point is expressed by their exclusion from the Eucharistic rites themselves.[6]

The Rite of Election

The corresponding rite that brings the Catechumenate to its close is the Rite of Election. This differs from the Rite of Acceptance into the Catechumenate in three ways: its place, its minister, and the timing of its celebration. This rite is celebrated in the cathedral of the diocese, and its minister is the local bishop. It is, therefore, a formal act of the local church, and is a powerful reminder that the individual is not preparing for admission into a single congregation (no matter how much 'at home' they may feel there), nor simply into a local 'family' of churches linked by a common culture, history and language, but into a communion of churches that extends across cultures, races and languages. Finally, the rite is celebrated once per year, at the start of the season of Lent. As we shall see, that timing is significant.

At the Rite of Election, the Church determines whether or not the catechumens have reached the point at which they are ready to enter into membership of the Church. The event itself is highly formalized, but it is predicated upon a process of discernment and discussion at parish level between the catechumens and those responsible for their formation. During the rite, the bishop publicly chooses (or 'elects') the catechumens as candidates for reception of the Sacraments of Initiation, and their names are entered into an official Book of the 'Elect' – their new official designation. Core to the whole process is an engagement between the bishop and the godparents of the catechumens. These are members of the parish community who have been serving as companions and guides to the catechumens and who both will represent the community during the initiation ceremonies and will continue to offer spiritual and moral support to the new Christians thereafter. Once again, a series of questions is asked, and these summarize succinctly the whole thrust of the Catechumenate:

> *The Bishop:*
> God's holy Church wishes to know whether these candidates are sufficiently prepared to be enrolled among the Elect for the coming celebration of Easter. And so I speak first of all to you, their godparents.
> *He addresses the godparents:*
> Have they faithfully listened to God's word proclaimed by the Church?
> *Godparents:*
> They have.

The Bishop:
Have they responded to that word and begun to walk in God's presence?
Godparents:
They have.
The Bishop:
Have they shared the company of their Christian brothers and sisters and joined with them in prayer?
Godparents:
They have.

Questions for Reflection

- What does the text tell us about what must happen *before* this rite can be celebrated? What does it say about the nature of the Catechumenate or period of formation?
- What would be key elements in a 'framework' to support the discernment process – for the catechumen? For the community (clergy, catechist, sponsor, godparents, etc.)?

Despite its solemn formality, the Rite of Election does not mark the point of entry into the Church. What lies ahead is not immediately the celebration of the rites of initiation, but a period of intense preparation. An end-date has been set for their liminality, but they have not quite yet arrived at the point of definitive arrival within the Church.

The Period of Purification and Enlightenment

At their election, the candidates for initiation transition from the second to the third period of the *RCIA*, the Period of Purification and Enlightenment. This third period is best understood as the final dimension of van Gennep's threshold phase, and during it the Elect undergo an intense period of preparation for their final arrival at membership of the Church. The period usually corresponds to the six weeks of Lent – and, indeed, the ancient ancestor of this period lies at the origin of the Lenten season itself.

During the Period of Purification and Enlightenment the Elect reflect with the whole community on their forthcoming Baptism, and the Paschal Mystery. The Lenten themes of repentance and enlightenment offer the framework for this reflection, and the process intensifies from the third week of Lent onwards. On the third, fourth and fifth Sundays in Lent, three liturgical ceremonies are celebrated which are intended to purify the Elect of any remaining attachment to sinful patterns of life and to open their minds and hearts to Christ – hence, the 'Purification and Enlightment' of this period's official designation. The three ceremonies bear the ancient name of 'Scrutinies' – and in the early Church they took the form of elaborate exorcism rites. The Scrutinies were one of the most changed aspects of the post-Vatican II reform, and while a prayer of exorcism still remains in each, those are new prayers, seeking God's protection of the Elect rather than driving out demonic forces. It is the Holy Spirit who scrutinizes the Elect and who awakens in them self-recognition and repentance. The Scrutinies follow ancient tradition by relating the experience of the Elect as they progress towards Easter to three sections of John's Gospel:

- Third Sunday of Lent: Christ who offers Living Water (The woman at the well of Samaria, John 4.1–41).
- Fourth Sunday of Lent: Christ, the Light of the World (healing of the man born blind, John 9).
- Fifth Sunday of Lent: Christ, the Resurrection and the Life (raising of Lazarus, John 11.1–44).

Alongside the Scrutinies, the final weeks of Lent contain the formal presentation to the Elect of two representative 'treasures' of the Christian family. During the third week of Lent – that is, after the celebration of the First Scrutiny – the Creed of the Church is formally given to them. Then, during the fifth week they receive the Lord's Prayer. To modern eyes it may appear strange that the Church should hold back until this last minute the formal engagement with texts that are ubiquitous. However, the historical origins of the Creed lie in the profession of faith demanded of new Christians immediately before they were baptized. Ritually, it makes sense to 'hand it over' at this point as Baptism approaches. Similarly, the Lord's Prayer is a succinct expression of the relationship of the children of God to God: following their Baptism, the Elect will join the rest of the faithful as children of God, able to call God 'Our Father'. Using the language of relationship, the rite says the Church *lovingly entrusts* these ancient texts expressing the heart of the Church's faith and prayer in a proclamation of the community to the Elect, in order to fill their hearts and minds with the vision of what it means to be baptized as members of the Body of Christ.

Celebration of the Sacraments of Initiation

The time spent on the threshold of the Church that stretches back to the Rite of Acceptance into the Catechumenate reaches its conclusion at the celebration of all three of the Sacraments of Initiation during the night before Easter. That celebration takes part within a lengthy and multipart liturgy known as the Easter Vigil, which falls into four sections:

- A service of Light, beginning with the lighting of a new fire, the preparation and illumination of the Paschal Candle, and the singing of the *Exultet* – an ancient song of praise to God for the gift of salvation in Christ. The light symbolizes the dawn and the promise of new life in Christ.
- An extended Vigil of Readings, Psalms and Prayers: these offer an overview of salvation history from the story of the Creation to the account of the resurrection of Christ.
- The celebration of the sacraments of Baptism and Confirmation. If the rite is celebrated in the Cathedral Church the bishop is the minister; if it is held in parish churches, priests are delegated the authority to confirm in the bishop's place.
- The celebration of the Eucharist, at which the new members of the Church receive Holy Communion for the first time.

Period of post-baptismal catechesis or mystagogy

The final period of the *Rite of Christian Initiation of Adults* typically corresponds to the period between Easter Sunday and Pentecost. This season is marked by opportunities for post-baptismal reflection or 'mystagogy', as the new members of the Church are given opportunities to reflect back on the journey of initiation, particularly its climax in the experience of the Paschal Mystery at the Vigil. From now on they are known as 'neophytes' – that is, newborn children of God.

Initiation as 'journey'

The language of 'journey', when applied to Christian initiation, retains a reson-ance that it frequently has lost thanks to its over-use in contemporary popular parlance. This is largely because an analysis of physical journeys formed part of van Gennep's original formulation of his Rites of Passage model; the very notion of the threshold implies a physical passage from one space to another. The Rites of Passage model implies the transition through discrete and deline-ated stages – which is particularly clear in the case of the Christian initiation rituals. Therefore, the application of the notion of a 'spiritual journey' to adult initiation is appropriate and, indeed, popular. This is reflected in the common use by many parishes of such expressions as 'Journey in Faith' to designate the entire *RCIA* process.

Theology of Initiation

The theology of the Paschal Mystery, discussed in detail in Chapter 2 of this book, runs through the rites of Christian initiation. Entry into the Christian community – be it by adults or by children – is understood as a profound identification with Christ, especially in his self-giving and obedience to the Father, and emphasizes a corresponding incorporation of the individual into Christ's Mystical Body. Each ritual step on the journey from the First Accept-ance of the gospel, to presentation for election, to reception of the sacraments themselves, requires the candidates to reflect with the community on their en-gagement with the gospel. Each step, therefore, should be a concrete expression of their progressive conversion to Christ. All this culminates in the Sacraments of Initiation themselves:

> In the sacraments of Christian initiation we are freed from the power of dark-ness, and joined in Christ's death, burial and resurrection. We receive the Spirit of adoption and are part of the entire people of God in the celebration of the memorial of the Lord's death and resurrection.[7]

As we saw in the previous chapter, symbols are intrinsic to the sacraments. To understand the Sacraments of Initiation, therefore, it is useful to examine their symbols in a little depth – and to look at the way in which some of the prayers used at initiation forge a link between symbol and theology.

Water

The primary symbol of Baptism is water, heavy with symbolic ambiguity. Water is essential for every form of life and it nourishes all growing things; it both cleanses and refreshes after a busy day and it quenches thirst. Yet, water also possesses destructive power in the storm and the flood. The same natural element that can nurture and protect life – for example, around a baby in the womb – can also take life, as in a drowning accident. The same ambiguity can be seen in the Scriptures: water is a sign of the initial creation and was the medium by which the Israelites passed from slavery to freedom. Yet for the Hebrews the forces of water also had the capacity to evoke a fear of untamed and unpredictable destructiveness – which is why Jesus' capacity to control the element and even to walk on water produced a response of awe on the part of his disciples. Jesus himself alluded to the death-dealing capacity of water when he speaks to his own disciples of his own forthcoming passion and death as a 'baptism'.[8] Both of these symbolic dimensions – positive and negative – are at play in the use of water in the sacrament of Baptism: through it the individual dramatically enters into the Paschal Mystery of Christ: they ritually 'die' to their old life, and 'rise' to a new life in Christ. All this is encapsulated in the Blessing and Invocation of God over Baptismal Water.[9] The prayer falls into several broad sections:

1   *Invocation of God*
     O God, who by invisible power
     accomplish a wondrous effect
     through sacramental signs
     and who in many ways have prepared water, your creation,
     to show forth the grace of Baptism;

2a   *Recalling God's Action, Part 1 – Old Testament*[10]
     O God, whose Spirit
     in the first moments of the world's creation
     hovered over the waters,

so that the very substance of water
would even then take to itself the power to sanctify;

O God, who by the outpouring of the flood
foreshadowed regeneration,
so that from the mystery of one and the same element of water
would come an end to vice and a beginning of virtue;

O God, who caused the children of Abraham
to pass dry-shod through the Red Sea,
so that the chosen people,
set free from slavery to Pharaoh,
would prefigure the people of the baptized;

2b   *Recalling God's Action, Part 2 – New Testament*
O God, whose Son,
baptized by John in the waters of the Jordan,
was anointed with the Holy Spirit,
and, as he hung upon the Cross,
gave forth water from his side along with blood,
and after his Resurrection, commanded his disciples:
'Go forth, teach all nations, baptizing them
in the name of the Father and of the Son and of the Holy Spirit',
look now, we pray, upon the face of your Church
and graciously unseal for her the fountain of Baptism.

3   *Intercession*
May this water receive by the Holy Spirit
the grace of your Only Begotten Son,
so that human nature, created in your image
and washed clean through the Sacrament of Baptism
from all the squalor of the life of old,
may be found worthy to rise to the life of newborn children
through water and the Holy Spirit.
The celebrant touches the water with his right hand and continues:

4   Request for the Outpouring of the Holy Spirit[11]
May the power of the Holy Spirit,
O Lord, we pray,
come down through your Son
into the fullness of this font,
so that all who have been buried with Christ
by Baptism into death
may rise again to life with him.
Who lives and reigns with you in the unity of the Holy Spirit,
one God, for ever and ever.
Amen.

Questions for Reflection

- What stories from the Old Testament are contained in this prayer? What do these images tell us about the way that this prayer understands Baptism?
- What stories from the New Testament are contained in this prayer? What do these images tell us about the way that this prayer understands Baptism?
- What does this prayer ask God to do for those who will be baptized?

Oil

The second Sacrament of Initiation is Confirmation, in which the minister anoints the forehead of the newly baptized with the oil of Chrism. This is a mixture of olive oil and an ancient perfume called 'balsam', and is only used in the sacraments of Confirmation and Ordination. In the adult rituals it is conferred immediately after Baptism. If Baptism represents a radical incorporation into Christ, and especially into those aspects of the Paschal Mystery that focus on his death and resurrection, the focus here shifts to the related themes of the Holy Spirit and of mission.[12] The link between the two sacraments is brought out by the minister as he introduces this phase of the rite:

My dear newly baptized, born again in Christ by baptism, you have become members of Christ and of his priestly people. Now you are to share in the outpouring of the Holy Spirit among us, the Spirit sent by the Lord upon his apostles at Pentecost and given by them and their successors to the baptized.

The promised strength of the Holy Spirit, which you are to receive, will make you more like Christ and help you to be witnesses to his suffering, death and resurrection. It will strengthen you to be active members of the Church and to build up the body of Christ in faith and love.[13]

Questions for Reflection

- What does this passage tell us about the relationship between Baptism and Confirmation?
- What does the gift of the Holy Spirit in Baptism specifically empower the new Christians to do?

The use of oil in this ritual closely relates to its natural properties and to the use made of it in the Scriptures. The natural properties of oil and its cultural uses down the ages resonate with a theology of anointing: protection for new life, healing, strengthening as life progresses, nourishing and sealing in goodness. In the Scriptures oil is a potent symbol with a theological purpose. In the Old Testament, for example, oil is used to signify the holiness of God's calling in the anointing of prophets, priests and kings, and in the sprinkling of the tabernacle as the focus for worship of God (e.g. Exod. 25.6; Lev. 8.30; Num. 4.16). In the New Testament, oil is used as a sign of God's power at work in healing the sick (e.g. Mark 6.13; James 5.14), and as a sign of honour and worship in the presence of holiness (e.g. Mark 14.3–9). In the sacrament of Confirmation those properties of strengthening and the biblical resonances of calling and setting aside for a sacred purpose combine in expressing the reality that new Christians are called to mission. In other words, while the reception of the sacraments marks the end of a process of initiation, it also sets the new Christian on a future trajectory – to take part in the mission of the Body of Christ in the world.

Food

The Eucharist, as 'source and summit' of the Christian life, towards which all other sacraments are orientated, completes Christian initiation. Having entered into Christ's death and resurrection through Baptism, configured by Confirmation to the mission of Christ and his Body, the neophyte now participates in the climax of the Easter celebration of the Paschal Mystery, by participating for the first time in the Eucharist.

Bread

Over millennia, bread has been and remains a staple in the diet of many cultures, and supplies many of the nutrients needed in a balanced diet to grow and remain healthy. It is a symbol of the essentials of sustenance. In the Old Testament, 'breaking bread' with another was a sign of hospitality. In the Jewish celebration of Passover (Pesach) the unleavened bread symbolizes the hasty departure from Egypt, and liberation from slavery and oppression. Bread symbolized and expressed the Israelites' covenant relationship with God, made at Sinai. During the Exodus, God had provided 'bread' in the form of 'manna' enabling their survival in the desert. This was a reminder to Israel that they lived by the bread of the word of God, and God's pledge of faithfulness. The prophet Isaiah uses the image of a banquet to refer to the coming of the Lord at the end of time (Isa. 25.6–9).

The New Testament depicts Jesus as a guest at many meals, but he also appears there as a generous host. For instance, John's Gospel describes the miracle of the multiplication of the loaves; Jesus blessed a small number of loaves of bread, which were then broken and given to a large crowd. Explaining later the significance of this event, he spoke of himself as 'the bread of life':

> 'Very truly, I tell you, it was not Moses who gave you the bread from heaven, but it is my Father who gives you the true bread from heaven. For the bread of God is that which comes down from heaven and gives life to the world.' They said to him, 'Sir, give us this bread always.' Jesus said to them, 'I am the bread of life. Whoever comes to me will never be hungry, and whoever believes in me will never be thirsty.' (John 6.32–35)

The generosity of Jesus' miraculous feeding of the crowd prefigured the super-abundant giving of himself as food in the Eucharist. On the night before he died, as host to his disciples at supper, Jesus instituted the Eucharist. This sacrament of unconditional love, and the sign of the unity of the Church, is a banquet in which Christ is consumed under the form of bread and wine. By the words of Christ and the power of the Holy Spirit, these gifts (which are a combination of divine gift in creation, 'fruit of the earth', wheat and grapes, and human labour in making bread and wine) become in the liturgical action the 'bread of life', and the spiritual drink.[14] Jesus commands the Church to continue to celebrate these mysteries until he comes again in glory at the end of time.

Wine

The fermented fruit of the vine has properties that can soothe or sting. It can richly enhance life – sharing wine together is a potent sign of human fellowship and of pleasure in the company of others. Over wine we celebrate joys or soothe sorrows, set the world to rights, and gratefully celebrate the present moment. Yet, the drinking of wine can also bear a sting in its tail, as we turn to it at times of rejection or betrayal, opposition, or regret. In the Old Testament, the vine-yard and the vine are symbols of fruitfulness, and Israel is likened to a vineyard planted by the Lord. Wine was an essential part of Jewish ritual meals, symbol-izing both life and death – joy and celebration, and the shedding of blood in the struggles for freedom from oppression. So, it expressed the recognition that new life comes *through* suffering and death; 'the blessing cup' of wine is an expression of joyful hope. For example, at the Passover meal, the fourth cup at the end of the meal is raised, and songs of praise are sung, full of confident hope in God's power to save and triumph over any trial.

Jesus' parables contain many references to vineyards. Jesus refers to himself as the vine, and to his father as the vinedresser (John 15.1). The water at the marriage feast of Cana is transformed into the fruit of the vine, as a foretaste or sign of the Kingdom to come, where everyone will drink the new wine that is Christ (cf. John 2.11; Mark 14.25). This new wine requires new wineskins (Mark 2.22) – its fermentation is powerful, and will burst old skins. To contain it, we must be baptized, and configured to Christ. And it is this richly potent symbol of wine that in the Eucharist becomes a sign of Christ's outpouring of himself: the cup of blessing is at the same time the chalice through which Christ's members are drawn into communion with him in his sacrifice.

The sacrament of the Eucharist: the culmination of Christian initiation

As the neophyte receives Holy Communion for the first time their Christian initiation is completed. This is because the Eucharist draws them into two closely inter-linked relationships. The first is with Christ: the Paschal Mystery is no longer something that the newly baptized have heard about; now it is something into which they have themselves been plunged. In the waters of Baptism they ritually entered into the death and resurrection of Christ as their former life drew to a close and a new life began. By the gift of the Spirit at Confirmation, they became sharers in Christ's mission in the world. Now, they receive the sacrament of his body and blood so that their lives will become progressively modelled on the pattern of his self-sacrificial generosity. The second relationship is with Christ's mystical body, the Church – of which the neophytes are now members. Holy Communion also draws those who receive it into that body, and strengthens the bonds between them. The Eucharist makes the Church.

The Reception of Baptized Christians into the Full Communion of the Catholic Church

The *RCIA* includes texts for the ritual reception into the full communion of the Catholic Church of persons who have been previously baptized in a different Church community.[15] This rite gives guidance as to the manner of celebration. It should take place during Mass and there should be not the slightest whiff of triumphalism, respecting the Baptism that the person has already received. By way of preparation, the candidate should receive doctrinal and spiritual preparation that is adapted to their pastoral requirements and, most importantly, 'anything that would equate candidates for reception with those who are catechumens is to be absolutely avoided'.[16]

When *RCIA* was first introduced into the English-speaking world, many of those who came forward had in fact already been baptized in another Christian denomination, and were now seeking to become Catholic Christians. For example, some were married to Catholics, and had been attending Mass with their spouses for years; others had been influenced by Catholic relations or friends. For some, knocking on the door of the Church came at the end of a long and intellectual or spiritual search. Many had received rich biblical and spiritual formation in their original church, and had spent their entire lives as Christians. Others, although baptized as infants in another church, had never received any Christian formation, and had never practised their faith. Alongside them another category of people began to appear in the parish groups that formed around the *RCIA*; these were people who had been baptized as infants in the Catholic Church, but never received any formation, nor received First Holy Communion or Confirmation.

In many parishes, indeed, the majority of those who took part in the *RCIA* were from these two groups of the already baptized. The catechumenal model was adapted to accommodate their own progress into the Church, and was effectively an extended post-baptismal catechesis. The result was that rather than the extended period of liminality envisaged by the rite, the *RCIA* in many places became a roughly six-month-long course, which was punctuated either by rituals that had been adapted to reflect the post-baptismal status of those for whom they were celebrated, or that were omitted altogether. More recently, the demographic has shifted, and it is becoming more usual for adults to request Baptism. Two principal reasons are driving this shift – a reduction in the numbers of people who are being baptized into any Christian church as infants, and immigration. As the ratio shifts towards the unbaptized, many parishes that have long used a cut-down version of the *RCIA* to welcome previously baptized Christians into the Catholic Church are being challenged to recalibrate their practice.

Questions for Reflection

- What are the particular challenges posed by bringing unbaptized and baptized candidates together into a single group for catechesis and for ritual?
- What might be appropriate times during the course of the year to receive (rather than baptize) people?

Conclusion

The fact that the *RCIA* was quickly adapted for use with Christians who had already been baptized indicates the flexibility of the catechumenal model that it proposed. With sensitivity both to the particular 'journey' of each individual and also to the theological integrity of the rite, there is real scope here for adaptation. The catechumenal model also has proved attractive beyond the *RCIA* – not least within the rites for the initiation into the Catholic Church of children. It is to these rites that the next chapter turns.

Notes

1 See Chapter 2 for an explanation of this idea.

2 Van Gennep, Arnold, *Rites of Passage*, 1909 (London: Psychology Press; hardback in English, 1960, paperback, 1977).

3 Turner, Victor, *The Ritual Process: Structure and Anti-Structure* (Chicago, IL: Aldine Transaction, 1969; London: Routledge, 2017).

4 See also *SC* 65 and 66; Second Vatican Council, 1965, Decree concerning the Pastoral Office of Bishops in the Church, *Christus Dominus,* 14; Second Vatican Council, 1965, Decree on the Mission Activity of the Church, *Ad Gentes* (*AG*), 14.

5 *RCIA*, 437.

6 See *RCIA*, 75.3.

7 *AG*, 14; *Christian Initiation, General Introduction*, 1.

8 Luke 12.50 and many related texts.

9 *RCIA*, 215.

10 The technical term for this kind of liturgical 'memory' is 'anamnesis'.

11 The technical term for a request that the Holy Spirit should act in the liturgy is 'epiclesis'.

12 See Chapter 2.

13 *RCIA*, 235 and 236.

14 Cf. *RM*, Order of Mass (*OM*), 23.

15 *RCIA*, Part II: Rites for Particular Circumstances.

16 *RCIA*, 387–99.

6

Christian Initiation of Children

CAROLINE DOLLARD

With this chapter we turn from the exploration of the ritual processes provided for the initiation of adults into the Catholic Church to those rituals explicitly designed for use with children. It is immediately important to note that the Catholic rituals distinguish between two different groups of children, differentiated by age:

- For those children who have reached 'catechetical age', generally taken to be 7 years and older, a specially adapted and simplified version of the Catechumenate is provided.[1] This provides discrete stages and ritual steps that lead to a unified celebration of the three Sacraments of Initiation: Baptism, Confirmation and admission to the Eucharist.
- Children aged under 7 years are treated as 'infants' and are baptized according to the rite of Infant Baptism. The Church invites the Christian community thereafter to take responsibility for nurturing and accompanying the parents and godparents of the child in the years following Baptism. This especially involves offering support to parents in their role as first teachers in the faith, helping them 'persevere in the faith and in their lives as Christians'.[2] Effectively, the years after Baptism are understood as a gradual post-baptismal catechesis that builds on the child's innate spiritual awareness and which respects their human development.

This chapter explores the rites that have been developed to serve the needs of the second of these two groups. This will involve a consideration not only of the Rite of Baptism of infants, but also the separate rite of Confirmation and the admission of children to the Eucharist at their First Holy Communion. The chapter opens with a historical summary that sets out the background for the celebration of the three rites today and that focuses especially on the changes desired by the Second Vatican Council. It then explores the application to the celebration of these rites of a 'catechumenal model' derived from the adult rituals.

Historical Background

As noted in the previous chapter, the practice of the early Church was to baptize adults – although it seems that when the head of a family became a Christian, all the members of their household, including children, would have been baptized with them.[3] In that sense, the initiation of children has always taken place. From the fourth century onwards, as Christianity moved from minority status to become the official state religion, the initiation of infants became the norm. At first, the unified ritual originally designed for adults was used for children, who were baptized, confirmed and admitted to the Eucharist at the Easter Vigil. There is evidence that the Catechumenate too was retained in a stripped-down form – reduced to the season of Lent, it was used to instruct the parents rather than the infants.

Gradually, however, the three ritual elements of Baptism, Confirmation and admission to the Eucharist became separated from one another. The process was lengthy and complex, and frequently came about as a result of the need to respond to practical challenges. High rates of infant mortality led to the celebration of Baptism immediately after birth, and brought an end to the last vestiges of the Catechumenate. The impossibility of the bishop being present at each celebration of baptism in his diocese led to the delay of Confirmation, potentially by years. A decline in the practice of lay people receiving Holy Communion from the chalice impacted negatively on the earlier tradition of admitting infants to the Eucharist from their Baptism – children who could not digest solid food had nonetheless been able to suck on a finger that had been dipped into the chalice. Concerns that children could only be admitted to the Eucharist once they had acquired an intellectual capacity to grasp its meaning also fuelled the separation of Baptism from admission to the Eucharist.

Three discrete sacraments

Thus arose the practice of children receiving across a number of years the sacraments that had originally formed a unified initiatory complex. This gave rise to the question as to how in this very different set-up the sacraments should be understood. The natural response was to link them to the child's life-course – effectively, to stages of human development. This particularly made sense when a child's developing intellectual capacity was regarded as a key determinant for their readiness to receive at least one of them. St Thomas Aquinas' neat summation of this has been given in Chapter 4. The process was further developed by the emergence in the late sixteenth and early seventeenth centuries of carefully structured catechetical processes leading to the admission of children to the Eucharist, and the development of elaborate ceremonies of First Holy Communion. Continuing concerns about the need properly to understand what was happening theologically in the Eucharist simultaneously pushed upwards the age at which First Holy Communion was received. By the turn of the twentieth century the following pattern was normal:

- Immediately after birth – Baptism. Theological emphasis lay on the cleansing from Original Sin.
- Between ages 7 and 11 – Confirmation: the timing usually coincided with one of the bishop's formal periodic visitations to the parish.
- Age 11 – Reception of First Holy Communion: the event by 1900 carried strong resonances of a transition from childhood to puberty. In some parts of Europe there was pressure for an even older age to be adopted.

Early twentieth-century developments

This 1900 sequence respects the original order of Baptism, Confirmation, Eucharist. However, in 1910 the sequence was unintentionally disrupted by the Decree *Quam Singulari* of Pope St Pius X.[4] This Decree reduced the age of reception of First Holy Communion to 7 years. Rather than being expected to possess a detailed theological understanding of the Eucharist, the child was required only to show the initial indications of a capacity for rational thought – in practice, to be able to distinguish the Eucharistic species from ordinary bread. Pope St Pius did not legislate for any change in the age or practice of Confirmation, so in some places it continued to be celebrated prior to First Holy Communion. However, in practice the periodic nature of episcopal visitations to parishes meant that most children were confirmed at a later date – perhaps years later. The sequence in which most received the sacraments was: Baptism, Eucharist (as First Holy Communion), Confirmation. This was the prevailing situation on the eve of the Second Vatican Council.

Questions for Reflection

- What is gained by linking these sacraments to the life-course of the child? What is lost?
- What might have been the motivations behind the 1910 reduction in the age of admission to First Holy Communion?

The Revision of these Sacraments after the Second Vatican Council

The Constitution on the Sacred Liturgy of the Second Vatican Council, *Sacrosanctum Concilium*, made two statements that profoundly impacted on the Church's understanding and practice of these sacraments:

> The rite for the baptism of infants is to be revised, and it should be adapted to the circumstances that those to be baptized are, in fact, infants. The roles of parents and godparents, and their duties, should be brought out more clearly in the rite itself.[5]

> The rite of Confirmation is to be revised also so that the intimate connection of this sacrament with the whole of the Christian initiation may more clearly

appear. For this reason the renewal of baptismal promises should fittingly precede the reception of this sacrament. Confirmation may be conferred within Mass when convenient. For conferring outside Mass, a formula introducing the rite should be drawn up.[6]

Question for Reflection

- These two passages ask for a number of changes in previous practice: identify them, and consider what might their impact have been on the way the sacraments were prepared for and celebrated?

Perhaps the most significant development here is a return to the language of initiation: SC 71 draws Confirmation and admission to the Eucharist (back) into the ambit of Christian initiation. The Council Fathers wished to ensure that the essential connectedness of the three sacraments could be clearly seen, and felt that their unity could be witnessed most eloquently through the celebration of the sacraments within the Eucharist itself, the reception of which marks the climax of Christian initiation. This set the tone for the subsequent renewal of the Rites of Baptism and Confirmation: they were understood as forming part of an initiatory process that culminated in the Eucharist, rather than as free-floating rituals.

Changes to the rites of Baptism of children

Two significant changes were called for by the Council in the revision of the rites for the Baptism of children. The first is that an end should be brought to the centuries-long practice of using a compressed form of the adult rite of Baptism when baptizing children. What the Council requested was a ritual that acknowledged the subjects of Baptism to be (usually) very young children. The second change related to the first: the respective roles of parents and godparents were to be clearly articulated. It might appear odd to today's sensibilities, but up to this point the parents of a child had played no active role at its Baptism. The child was presented by its godparents, and it was they who spoke in its name. This was an echo of the adult initiation ritual that had passed almost unchanged into the pre-Vatican II rite for the Baptism of children. However, it did not reflect the reality that a child's early faith is most informed and formed by daily contact with its parents.

By giving the parents a prominent role within the revised rite and by emphasizing the ongoing responsibilities that presenting their child for Baptism laid upon them, today's ritual explicitly sets the child and its family upon a natural experiential catechesis that will take place gradually and progressively over the infant and childhood years. The ritual also adds a further, community dimension that offers a broader context for this catechesis. Whereas the previous ritual had usually been attended only by the child's immediate family, the revised rite presumes that the broader parish will be involved not only in helping the parents and godparents to prepare for this day, but also through the presence and ministration of members of the community at the Baptism itself.[7] Indeed, the rite makes provision for the sacrament of Baptism to be conferred during a celebration of the parish Sunday Eucharist, thereby reinforcing the communal dimension.

Changes to the rite of Confirmation

The changes the Council desired for the celebration of Confirmation underscore the unity of the three Sacraments of Initiation. First, the Council required an explicit link to be made with the sacrament of Baptism by requiring the candidates publicly to renew the promises that had been made in their name by their parents and godparents at Baptism. These promises involve a basic version of the Creed, preceded by the renunciation of Satan and of evil. Second, the reversal of centuries of practice by permitting the celebration of Confirmation within Mass reinforced the link between membership of the Body of Christ and active sharing in its mission.

A Catechumenal Model

The post-Vatican II reform required the Catholic community to appreciate that initiation into its membership is a protracted and multi-staged approach. The renewed emphasis on the role of the family in this process raises a number of challenges. How are they to understand that these very different rituals, spread out across several years, constitute a unified expression of initiation into the Christian community? How best does the Church support the child and its family across this process? What role might the Catholic school play in all this? What educational and catechetical processes are best suited to this task? The most fruitful response appears to be to draw on the insights of a similar extended catechetical process – the Catechumenate of adult initiation – and creatively to apply those insights to the situation of children. Thus, in June 1986, the Bishops' Conferences of England and Wales, and Scotland wrote in their Decree introducing the *RCIA* into their dioceses, that this rite 'is the exemplar and rule for all Christian Initiation'.[8]

The notion of the catechetical 'journey', frequently applied to the process of adult initiation as outlined in the previous chapter, provides a useful way of holding these three sacraments together across an extended period of time. The essential dimension of continuity is provided above all by the community: any 'journey in faith' process is rooted within the life and worship of the community and the ongoing participation of its members in the Paschal Mystery through its mission and in its celebration of the sacraments. As the different stages of initiation unfold, a child and its family engage in different ways with the community. That engagement will take place across different settings which may well include the Sunday Eucharistic Assembly, parish catechetical contexts, and Catholic schools. The intensity of the engagement will vary from the build-up to reception of one of the sacraments, to a background hum. But in all of that, the parish community seeks to act as servant – not only to the children and their families, but also to God: in a sacramental economy it is fundamentally the Holy Spirit who is at work, preparing the Church to encounter the Lord, and making present the Mystery of Christ in all the different ritual experiences of Christian initiation.

Catechumenal approaches and the family

If a catechumenal approach is to be effective, it must be strongly family focused, affirming, respecting and resourcing family and home as the places of God's activity. The challenge to the parish community is to welcome families into its life and worship, and, in the words of Pope Francis, to be a sign of mercy and closeness to them, connecting the 'dying and rising' in their experience with the dying and rising of Christ in the Paschal Mystery,[9] exploring the ways in which the frequently vulnerable, tenacious, self-giving love that goes on in families can reflect the experience of Christ, and the life of the Trinity. Yet, the complexities of early twenty-first-century life can make the encounter between parish and family far from straightforward. Parents present their children for Baptism for a wide range of reasons – the following would be typical in most parishes:

- Some are practising members of the community and act out of a profound sense of personal belief.
- Some do not practise their faith, but nonetheless present their children for Baptism from a strong sense of family tradition or identity, or because they may be sensitive to the expectations of parents or grandparents.
- Some come because Baptism is required for entry into the Catholic school.
- Some have parted company with the Church earlier in their lives over a particular pain or difficulty, and have felt judged for less than perfect lives, but now, with the baby, they want to try again.
- Some may be in relationships where one partner has no faith at all, and the other's faith is somewhat tenuous. Others are not married, and wonder if this is a barrier to having their child baptized.

All these parents are living through the life-changing event that is the birth of their child, and they are developing and growing into their identity as parents – with all the physical, mental, emotional and spiritual impact that can bring. Whatever their motives for requesting the Baptism of their child, the encounter with the parish community offers an opportunity for them to encounter there something of significance. The response of that community is to draw on the life experience and expertise of its members to provide a welcoming, supportive environment in which it can encounter the parents and to encourage an exploration of their own faith.

The creation of that environment lies at the heart of the catechumenal approach. In practice, it calls upon parishes to engage with parents openly and without cynicism, to discern what they are looking for; then, to accompany them (and wherever possible the godparents) along a pathway of preparation. If that experience is to be authentic, the involvement of parishioners who are themselves parents, who have walked that path before and can share their own experiences, is essential. At the same time, an effective catechumenal approach would facilitate parental reflection on what they are asking in bringing their children, what they will be asked by the Church, what their responsibility in bringing up their children in faith is, and what support they might expect from the parish community now and in the years ahead.

Questions for Reflection

- What practical steps might a parish community take to help parents fulfil their duties as parents?
- How can we celebrate good liturgy that gathers in families, nurturing their gradual accomplishing and expressing of their conversion to love and continuing renewal in commitment to love, and to celebrate this in the sacraments of God's love?
- How do we support and resource parents as leaders of the home and first teachers in faith?

The age at which these sacraments are administered, and their order

As the historical overview offered at the start of this chapter makes clear, the age at which these sacraments have been administered, and the order, have been remarkably fluid. While for many centuries Baptism was celebrated immediately after birth, more recent trends suggest that many families are delaying requesting it for their children; not infrequently until shortly before a child starts Primary School. The discipline for First Holy Communion established in 1910 has proved remarkably stable, although it is not uncommon to find that it has been delayed in England and Wales for a year for school curricular reasons. Confirmation, however, has wandered the most of the three sacraments. An unintended consequence of the revision of Pope Pius X was that the age at which this sacrament was celebrated crept upwards until by the second half of the twentieth century it came to be celebrated at more or less the same point that had previously been occupied by First Holy Communion – that is, around 12–14 years. Increased numbers of auxiliary bishops and the common practice of celebrating the Confirmation of young people from a number of adjacent parishes in a single celebration rather than in their individual parishes allowed for more frequent celebrations. This, in turn, narrowed and stabilized the age range of participants.

The traditional catechesis for Confirmation had elaborated the notion that the sacrament strengthened the young Christian for warfare – primarily internal – against the forces of evil. It constituted them, therefore, a 'Soldier of Christ'. As the twentieth century progressed this catechetical perspective was increasingly replaced by one that emphasized Confirmation as a sacrament of maturity and as a rite of passage into adult Christianity – establishing the point from which the young person could assume a public role/responsibility in the Church. The positive dimension of this is that it can give the opportunity to explore the theme of the mission of the Church, which is a core theological thrust of Confirmation. The risk, however, is that the rite becomes a teenage rite of passage. The challenge is how that might be accommodated into an overarching theological perspective that understands it as part of the initiation into the communion and mission of the Church.

'Restoring the original order'

In response to such questions, bishops in some dioceses across the English-speaking world have engaged in a process of re-ordering the sacraments. They have reverted to the original initiatory order. Infant Baptism is followed at age 7 by Confirmation, shortly after which First Holy Communion is administered. Participation in the Eucharist thus completes the process. Theologically, the move makes sense – and in many places the catechumenal model has been used to create and resource programmes of family catechesis to enable parents to engage with the process.

It is, however, telling that the instinct down the centuries has been to link one of the sacraments with early adolescence – First Holy Communion until 1910 and Confirmation more recently. The restoration of the traditional order of the sacraments and the completion of initiation around the age of 7 is experienced by many as leaving a gap further down the line. Arguably, the celebration of either First Holy Communion or Confirmation at early adolescence imposes an alien theological meaning on those sacraments. There is a real need, therefore, to offer young people opportunities to live out their initiation in a meaningful and challenging way, and to give them real possibilities to share in the active mission of the Church.

Pope Benedict has suggested:

> It needs to be seen which practice better enables the faithful to put the sacrament of the Eucharist at the centre, as the goal of the whole process of initiation. So that the faithful can be helped both to mature through the formation received in our communities and to give their lives an authentically Eucharistic direction, so that they can offer a reason for the hope within them in a way suited to our times. (*SacCar* 18)

Questions for Reflection

- What might a parish do to enable teenagers and young adults to live out their Christian mission?
- The passage into young adulthood can be difficult for both young people and their families: is there a role for the parish in helping people to mark – and to find their way through – this transition?

The Celebration of Infant Baptism

Having considered the pastoral issues that surround these sacraments, we can now turn to the liturgies themselves. As they share so much with the adult rites, we will focus just on a number of salient points, offering suggestions for reflection. We begin with the *Rite of Baptism for Children* (henceforth, *RBC*).

Rite of Baptism for Children

History

Ordo Baptismi parvulorum
- Editio typica, 1969
- Editio typica altera, 1973

Rite of Baptism of Children
- First edition, 1969 (London: Geoffrey Chapman, 1992)
- Second edition, New translation, forthcoming – *Order of Baptism of Children*

Contents

Christian Initiation: General Introduction
Baptism for Children, Introduction
Baptism for Several Children
   Baptism for Several Children at Mass
Baptism for One Child
   Baptism for One Child at Mass
Baptism for a Large Number of Children
Baptism for Children in Danger of Death
Bringing a Baptized Child to the Church
   Bringing a Baptized Child to the Church at Mass

The ritual of Infant Baptism is complex and lengthy. At its core, however, is the simple pattern of Liturgy of the Word/Liturgy of the Sacrament that is found at the heart of each liturgy. This Word/Sacrament unit is preceded by an Introductory Rite that takes the form of the reception of the child and its family; it is followed by a sequence of 'explanatory rites' that use the language of symbols to draw out the meaning of Baptism for the child and its family. The rite concludes with the Lord's Prayer and Blessings.

Rite of Baptism of One Child

Rite of Receiving the Child
  Welcome
  Questioning of the Parents and Godparents
  Signing of the Forehead
  Procession to the Place of Celebration of the Word of God
Celebration of the Word of God
  Biblical Readings and Homily
  Prayer of the Faithful
  Litany
  Prayer of Exorcism
  Anointing before Baptism
  Procession to the Baptistery
Celebration of Baptism
  Blessing of Water
  Renunciation of Sin and Profession of Faith
  Rite of Baptism
  Explanatory Rites
    Anointing after Baptism
    Clothing with a White Garment
    Handing on of a Lighted Candle
    Ephphatha Rite
Concluding Rite
  Procession to the Altar
  Lord's Prayer
Blessing and Dismissal

As the theology of the rite is identical with that of the adult rite, it is useful here to explore the relationship between the scriptural readings and the meaning of the sacrament. Listed below are some of the passages from the Gospels that may be read at a celebration of Infant Baptism. Read each one, and then consider the Questions for Reflection:

- Matthew 28.18–20, The Apostles are sent to preach the gospel and to baptize.
- Mark 1.9–11, The baptism of Jesus.

- Mark 10.13–16, Let the little children come to me.
- John 3.1–16, Jesus' meeting with Nicodemus.

Questions for Reflection

- What understanding of Baptism emerges from each of these readings?
- If you were arranging for the Baptism of a child within your own family, which of these readings would you use, and why?
- What other reading(s) from Scripture might be appropriate for use at the Baptism of an infant? Why?

The Explanatory Rites

The act of Baptism itself takes place surprisingly quickly; following ancient tradition it is, however, followed by three 'explanatory' rituals. These do not 'do' anything in their own right – rather, they illustrate three different dimensions of what has happened in Baptism, and set out the challenges that lie ahead for the newly baptized child and (more immediately) for its family.

The anointing with Chrism

One of the particularities of the Roman Rite is that from an early date new Christians were anointed with chrism by a priest immediately as they stepped up from the baptismal font. This is not the sacrament of Confirmation, but is a practical illustration of what has taken place in the water – how closely Baptism has configured the individual to Christ, and the essential nature of their relationship with other members of the Church. Before he anoints the crown of the child's head, the priest (or, today, deacon) says:

The God of power and Father of our Lord Jesus Christ
has freed you from sin

and brought you to new life
through water and the Holy Spirit.
He now anoints you with the chrism of salvation.
So that, united with his people,
You may remain for ever a member of Christ
who is Priest, Prophet and King.[10]

This text takes forward our understanding of Christ's priesthood, which was initially discussed in Chapter 2. That priesthood is here presented as having three dimensions: a ministry of worshipping the Father, of proclaiming the Good News and of ruling through service as the one 'who came not to be served, but to serve and give his life as a ransom for many'.[11] What this ritual of anointing underlines is that each Christian shares in that three-fold priesthood. This theme – and the relationship between the baptismal priesthood of all believers and that of the ordained – will be further explored in Chapter 10.

The clothing with the white garment and the presentation of a lighted candle

The two other explanatory rites involve first the robing of the child in a white garment and then the presentation to its parents and godparents of a candle that was lit from the Paschal Candle.

Questions for Reflection

Please read the ritual texts spoken by the minister at the clothing of the child in white and the handing over of the lighted candle (below).

- What do they tell us about the relationship of the child with Christ that has been established by Baptism?
- What do they say about the future life of the child?
- What responsibilities do they set before parents and godparents?

Clothing with White Garment

N. and N., you have become a new creation
and have clothed yourselves in Christ.
See in this white garment the outward sign of your Christian dignity.
With your family and friends to help you by word and example,
bring that dignity unstained into the everlasting life of heaven.[12]

Presentation of a Lighted Candle

Receive the light of Christ.
Parents and godparents, this light is entrusted to you to be kept burning
   brightly.
These children of yours have been enlightened by Christ.
They are to walk always as children of the light.
May they keep the flame of faith alive in their hearts.
When the Lord comes,
may they go out to meet him
with all the saints in the heavenly kingdom.[13]

The Celebration of Confirmation

Order of Confirmation

History
Ordo Confirmationis
• Editio typica, 1971
Rite of Confirmation
• First edition, 1971
Order of Confirmation
• New translation, 2015 (London: Catholic Truth Society)

Contents
Introduction
The Order for the Conferral of Confirmation within Mass
The Order for the Conferral of Confirmation without Mass
Those things to be observed when Confirmation is Conferred by an Extraordinary Minister (Priest)
Confirmation to be Administered to a Sick Person in Danger of Death
Texts to be used in the Conferral of Confirmation

Structure
The Order for the Conferral of Confirmation within Mass
Introductory Rites
The Liturgy of the Word
The Celebration of Confirmation
    Presentation of the Candidates
    Homily
    Renewal of Baptismal Promises
    Laying On of Hands
    Anointing with Chrism
    Prayer of the Faithful
Liturgy of the Eucharist
Concluding Rites

Whether or not it takes place within a celebration of the Eucharist, the conferral of Confirmation is always preceded by a Liturgy of the Word. At the core of the ritual stand four interlinked actions by the bishop:

- The laying on of hands.
- The prayer for the outpouring of the Holy Spirit.
- The Anointing with Chrism.
- The exchange of the Sign of Peace with each candidate.

The laying on of hands

Bishop: Dearly beloved, let us pray to God the almighty Father, for these, his adopted sons and daughters, already born again to eternal life in Baptism, that he will graciously pour out the Holy Spirit upon them to confirm them with his abundant gifts, and through his anointing conform them more fully to Christ, the Son of God.

All pray in silence for a while.

Then the Bishop lays hands over all those to be confirmed. The Bishop says:

Almighty God, Father of our Lord Jesus Christ,

who brought these your servants to new birth

by water and the Holy Spirit,

freeing them from sin:

send upon them, O Lord, the Holy Spirit, the Paraclete;

give them the spirit of wisdom and understanding,

the spirit of counsel and fortitude,

the spirit of knowledge and piety;

fill them with the spirit of the fear of the Lord.

Through Christ our Lord.

R. Amen.[14]

The Anointing with Chrism

The Bishop dips the tip of the thumb of his right hand in the Chrism and, with the thumb, makes the Sign of the Cross on the forehead of the one to be confirmed, as he says:

N., be sealed with the Gift of the Holy Spirit.

The newly confirmed replies: Amen.

The Bishop adds: Peace be with you.

The newly confirmed: And with your spirit.[15]

Questions for Reflection

- What links are made here between Confirmation and Baptism?
- What does this text tell us about the action of the Holy Spirit in Confirmation? How might this impact on the life of the person being confirmed?
- What might it mean to be 'sealed with the gift of the Holy Spirit'?

Admission to the Eucharist

There is no formal ritual for the admission of children to the Eucharist for the first time. It is perfectly possible that when those responsible for the child's formation, and its parents, agree that the child is ready to begin receiving Holy Communion, then the child could simply attend a regular parish Mass with the parents and go forward for Holy Communion with the rest of the congregation. In practice this rarely happens. From the seventeenth century the process of preparation for First Holy Communion has generally culminated with elaborate celebrations of the Eucharist in which the First Communicants play a visible role. That visibility is reinforced by the common practice of clothing the girls in sometimes extravagant white dresses and veils. The tendency to prepare the children as age-related cohorts has generally resulted in their receiving the sacrament alongside their peers – sometimes in very large numbers. Today, parishes frequently break the cohort into smaller sub-groups, and distribute the First Holy Communion of their 7- or 8-year-olds across a number of Sundays. The ostentatious display that the celebration of First Holy Communion can sometimes trigger has made the ritual a source of contention for centuries. It remains, nonetheless, one of the most popular Catholic rituals, and participation in it is frequently seen as a hallmark of Catholic identity.

Questions for Reflection

- Why might First Holy Communion be regarded as a 'hallmark of Catholic identity'?
- What human processes relating to a child's development or its identity might feed into the First Holy Communion event? How might they be accommodated?
- What might be the role of the broader parish community at First Holy Communion?

Conclusion

The revision of these three sacraments has proved to be one of the most challenging aspects of the post-Vatican II liturgical reform. Not only have the rites themselves been radically changed – especially in the case of the Baptism of Infants – but they have been placed in a renewed theological framework of initiation. Implementing those changes has required the Catholic community to revisit in depth not only its liturgical practices, but also its catechetical and pastoral ones. More than 50 years on from the Council, there is still a sense that Catholics are looking for the best way of bringing all these things together. The pull of these sacraments towards different stages of the human life-course remains strong, and it is probably still too early to evaluate fully the long-term impact of the various attempts to restore the traditional order of the sacraments. What is certain is that the future of these rituals lies very closely linked to the manner in which the parish community perceives itself to have a stake in them, and in the extent to which it marries a sense of mission, a commitment to developing a catechumenal approach in all its catechetical endeavours, and in the care it gives to celebrating the liturgies themselves.

Notes

1 See *RCIA*, Part II, Section 1, *RCIA*, 242–9.
2 See *RCIA*, *Christian Initiation, General Introduction*, 7 and 8.
3 Cf. Acts 16.15, 33; 18.8; 1 Cor. 1.16.
4 Sacred Congregation of the Discipline of the Sacraments, *Quam Singulari: Decree on First Communion*. https://www.ewtn.com/library/curia/cdwfirst.htm.
5 *SC*, 67.
6 *SC*, 71.
7 *General Introduction to Christian Initiation*, 7; *RBC*, 4.
8 Congregation for the Clergy, 1997, General Directory for Catechesis (London: Catholic Truth Society).
9 Pope Francis, 2016, Apostolic Exhortation, on love in the family, *Amoris Laetitiae* (*AL*), 5, 7.
10 *RBC*, 62.
11 Matt. 25.28 and parallels.
12 *RBC*, 63.
13 *RBC*, 64.
14 *OC*, 25.
15 *OC*, 27.

7

The Celebration of the Eucharist

STEPHEN DEAN AND MARTIN FOSTER

The Mass or the Eucharist is the principal liturgical celebration in the regular life of the Church. For the majority of Catholics, attendance at it will be their primary ongoing experience of the Church, and their membership of the Eucharistic Assembly informs their Christian identity. The centrality of the Eucharist in the life of the Church was underscored by the Second Vatican Council, which declared it to be 'the source and summit of the Christian life'.[1] In other words, everything that the Church does flows from its celebration of the Eucharist – and ultimately leads back into it. This flows from the particularly intimate connection between the Eucharist and the Paschal Mystery of Christ.

The theological significance of the Eucharist will be explored in the next chapter of this book. The purpose of this chapter to guide the reader step-by-step through the admittedly complex ritual that is the Roman Mass today. After a brief review of some of the earliest historical evidence for the development of the Mass, there will be a consideration of the underlying structures of the celebration, and the various parts of the Mass will be identified. These parts will then be discussed in sequence and the way in which they contribute to the whole will be drawn out.

Scriptural Sources

For I received from the Lord what I also delivered to you, that the Lord Jesus on the night when he was betrayed took bread, and when he had given thanks, he broke it, and said, 'This is my body, which is for you. Do this in remembrance of me.' In the same way also he took the cup, after supper, saying, 'This cup is the new covenant in my blood. Do this, as often as you drink it, in remembrance of me.' For as often as you eat this bread and drink the cup, you proclaim the Lord's death until he comes.[2]

St Paul's letter to the Corinthians is generally held to be the earliest account of the Eucharist we have, pre-dating the accounts of the Last Supper in the Gospels of Matthew, Mark and Luke (John's account of the Last Supper focuses on Jesus washing the feet of his disciples). Scripture scholars argue about how to date the various texts and where one influences another, but the different accounts suggest that there are signs from the beginning of a multiplicity of practice.

Questions for Reflection

Compare 1 Cor. 11.23–26 with one of the Gospel accounts of the Last Supper: either Matt. (26.20–30), Mark (14.17–26) or Luke (22.14–20).

- What similarities are there?
- What differences do you notice?

Paul's purpose in writing to the Corinthians was to discuss (indeed, criticize) the manner in which they were celebrating the Eucharist there – he was not concerned to set the Last Supper in the context of the life of Jesus. Indeed, Paul already stood at one remove from the Last Supper – after all, he did not attend it. His perspective was already shaped by his understanding of the Paschal Mystery, as he drew connections between the act of eating and drinking, the sacrificial death of Jesus, and his coming again.

Scripture does not provide a simple and full account of the celebration of the Eucharist in the early Church. However, there are many passages across the New Testament that may either reflect how people were celebrating the Eucharist or that may have affected liturgical practice. These passages would include stories from the life of Jesus, such as descriptions of the occasions when he miraculously fed large crowds of people (e.g. Matt. 14.15–21), the accounts of meals that he shared with others (e.g. Luke 14.1–24), and his teaching on the 'bread of life' in John (6.22–59). There are also hints about the Eucharistic celebrations of the early Church in the Book of Acts and in the letters of Paul.

The Structure of the Eucharistic Celebration

Around AD 155 Justin, a Roman citizen and philosopher, wrote to the emperor Antoninus Pius to give an account of the ways of Christians who were a minority in the empire. He described the Eucharist as follows:

> On the day called Sunday, all who live in cities or in the country gather together to one place, and the memoirs of the apostles or the writings of the prophets are read, as long as time permits; then, when the reader has ceased, the president verbally instructs, and exhorts to the imitation of these good things. Then we all rise together and pray, and, as we before said, when our prayer is ended, bread and wine and water are brought, and the president in like manner offers prayers and thanksgivings, according to his ability, and the people assent, saying Amen; and there is a distribution to each, and a participation of that over which thanks have been given, and to those who are absent a portion is sent by the deacons. And they who are well to do, and willing, give what each thinks fit; and what is collected is deposited with the president, who succours the orphans and widows and those who, through sickness or any other cause, are in want, and those who are in bonds and the strangers sojourning among us, and in a word takes care of all who are in need.[3]

This passage tells us several things: that in the mid second century Christians were meeting on Sunday; that this celebration consisted of readings and a homily by the president of the assembly, after which bread and wine were brought, over which prayers and thanksgivings were made; that all present partook of them, not as 'common bread and common drink'[4] but as the flesh and blood of our Saviour; and that the celebration of the Eucharist derives from the command of Jesus, found in the Gospels, to do this in remembrance of him. If we look at the broad outlines of the Eucharist as described by Justin, we can recognize that the liturgy fell into two broad parts – the first focusing on the Scriptures, and the second on the sacrament. This became the typical structure of Christian worship – the community listens to Scripture and responds to it by a communal act of thanksgiving in response to a divine command. The two parts of the Mass are described as the 'Liturgy of the Word' and the 'Liturgy of the Eucharist'. These two parts are so closely interconnected that they form but one single act of worship. The liturgical books, therefore, speak of the community being nourished at two 'tables' during the Mass – the table of God's Word and the table of the Eucharist.

The Word-Sacrament pattern provides the most basic shape, but it raises two questions: how does a group of people become a liturgical assembly in the first place, and what happens to them at the end of the liturgy? A useful way of incorporating a response to these questions is to map the structure of the Mass on to a story of an encounter between Jesus and two of his disciples that took place after the resurrection.

The story begins with the disciples on a journey from Jerusalem to a village called Emmaus. They are concerned about recent events.	**Gather**
They are joined by a stranger who explains the Scriptures to them.	**Word**
They stop for an evening meal and the stranger blesses and breaks the bread.	**Sacramental Action** or **Response**
The disciples return to Jerusalem to tell others that they have seen the Lord.	**Send**

This story invites us to elaborate the structure. Before the community can hear the Scriptures, it must gather in response to the call of God and form an assembly. Similarly, when the worshippers have received the sacrament, they do not simply disperse, but actively are sent out into the world to fulfil the mission of Christ and his Church. This provides a four-fold pattern of Gather–Word–

Response–Send, which is often used as a way of looking at the structure of any liturgy or prayer, from another sacrament to a simple service at a catechetical session.

The Celebration of the Eucharist

The analysis of a liturgical rite such as the Mass can be approached from a number of directions. The first is by examining the texts that are used at its celebration – these would include the text provided by the liturgical books of the Missal and the Lectionary, but we might also consider texts drawn from other sources – for the music, for example.[5] The Eucharist can also be analysed in terms of its performance, focusing on the part played by its 'players' or ministers: the whole assembly sings, the priest and servers process, etc. Another approach would be to analyse how an individual person participates in the Mass: how they listen to the proclamation of the readings, how they make connections with words of Scripture and their own life of faith, etc. Finally, the celebration can be examined from a theological viewpoint. In discussing the celebration of Mass all these approaches need to be included. So, we will ask of the various actions of the Mass what is the text and context, who is performing it, what does it mean, and how does it enable participation?

Introductory rites

Starting points

Liturgy is not a solitary activity, but always draws participants into a shared experience. This is underlined by the very initial rubric that occurs at the beginning of the Order of Mass: 'When the people are gathered'.[6] Although people come to the Eucharist from different backgrounds and with different experiences, they gather because they share a common identity. In gathering they reforge that identity. Furthermore, gatherings in a liturgical context are never merely human initiatives. It is God who invites, it is the Spirit who draws people together, and the Christian assembly offers a visible sign of the presence of the Body of Christ in the world.

Although the Introductory Rites are brief, they are rich in words and gestures that express who the people are, and that draw their diversity into a unified worshipping community. To take a simple example, by making the Sign of the Cross at the start of the Mass, the people establish from the onset that what they do at Mass is done in the name of the Trinity. At the same time, they acknowledge their common Baptism (which makes them members of the Body of Christ) and through the tracing of the cross recall the Paschal Mystery of Christ's death and resurrection which gives the whole liturgy its foundation. The simple gesture is rich in meaning.

Purpose

The Introductory Rites do not only draw together the liturgical assembly: they also prepare the people to hear God's word and to participate in the Eucharist.[7]

Introductory Rites: Structure

Entrance Procession
Sign of the Cross
Greeting
(brief introduction)
Penitential Act
Gloria
Collect

Entrance Procession

The Mass contains a series of processions: at the Entrance, at the Preparation of Gifts, at Communion and at the end. These occur at transitional moments, when the liturgical action flows from one section of the Mass to another, and they help to drive forward the momentum of the celebration. A further, theological, aspect of the processions is that as members of the congregation process forward, they present an image of the Church as a pilgrim people, moving forwards through time until its culmination when Christ will be all in all.

Liturgical actions usually have a functional or practical purpose. That of the Entrance Procession is to bring the ministers to the sanctuary in an orderly fashion. Catholic liturgy, like the Church, is hierarchical, so there is an order to the procession, who comes where. Hierarchy is more about relationship than it is about status, and so the procession passes through the midst of the faithful as a sign that the priest acts on behalf of the gathered church. This passage through the church is one of the ways that the whole community is gathered into one in the Introductory Rites.

The procession will usually be accompanied by singing – many voices become one voice. The *Roman Missal* provides a text for singing the Entrance Antiphon. Though not commonly sung in parishes, the Entrance Antiphon does offer some pointers about what might be chosen at this point. The text of the antiphon is usually scriptural and addressed to God – at the beginning of worship the assembly orientates itself to the divine. Psalm verses, sung by a cantor, come between the repetition of the antiphon. This model of listening and responding is another example of the relational nature of liturgy. That not everything is sung by all also means that there is a chance to look and see the procession – to observe the action the music is accompanying.

Many communities will be more familiar with a hymn or song at the beginning of Mass. In contrast to the antiphon, the hymn text can be directly connected with the readings of the day and the musical form of everyone singing together a strong, regular melody can express the coming together as one voice more easily.

Sign of the Cross, Greeting and Brief Introduction

The first words of the presider are 'In the name of the Father' accompanying the Sign of the Cross. This is followed by the Greeting:

The grace of our Lord Jesus Christ, and the love of God, and the communion of the Holy Spirit be with you all.
Or:
Grace to you and peace from God our Father and the Lord Jesus Christ.
Or:
The Lord be with you.
The people reply:
And with your spirit.

The significance of the Sign of the Cross has already been discussed above. The greeting and the response 'And with your spirit' are once again expressing a relationship. The priest does not greet the people in his own name, but in that of the Trinity; it is ultimately in response to God's invitation (and not that of the priest) that they have gathered. Even the simple form 'The Lord be with you' points to the presence and activity of God.

Question for Reflection

The dialogue 'The Lord be with you'/'And with your spirit' occurs a number of times during the Order of Mass. Identify the different places.

• Why might it be used in each place?

Penitential Act

Each of the three forms of Penitential Act begins with the same invitation, 'Brothers and sisters, let us acknowledge our sins, and so prepare ourselves to celebrate the sacred mysteries.' Like the rest of the Introductory Rites, the Penitential Act is preparatory, and its focus is on human sin and God's mercy. After the invitation, a silent pause is held as an opportunity for personal reflection. Each form of the Penitential Act is different. The first, 'I confess to almighty God', is a personal confession of sin but also invokes the support of the community and the angels and saints in turning away from sin. The second, 'Have mercy on us, O Lord', is brief and in the plural. The first two forms are followed by the Kyrie or 'Lord, have mercy'. *Kyrie eleison* is a Greek text. It is like a layer in an archaeological dig, pointing back to the continuing use of Greek in the early Church in Rome.

The third form, 'You were sent to heal the contrite of heart', incorporates the Kyrie, which is said or sung after an invocation. The Order of Mass incorporates one set of invocations into its main text, and offers additional examples in an Appendix. Unlike the first two forms of the Penitential Rite, these are not confessions of sin, nor are they pleas for mercy. The texts are about the mercy and action of Christ. In this context, *Kyrie* or 'Lord, have mercy' is closer to an acclamation.

Questions for Reflection

The following two texts are from the Appendix of the *Roman Missal*.

A　Lord Jesus, you are mighty God and Prince of Peace:
Lord, have mercy.
Lord, have mercy.
You are Son of God and Son of Mary: Christ, have mercy.
Christ, have mercy.
You are the Word made Flesh, the splendour of the Father: Lord, have mercy.
Lord, have mercy.

B　Lord Jesus, you call your people to turn away from sin: Lord, have mercy.
Lord, have mercy.
You teach us wisdom, and write your truth in our inmost heart: Christ, have mercy.
Christ, have mercy.
You forgive sins through the ministry of reconciliation: Lord, have mercy.
Lord, have mercy.

- To whom are the Invocations addressed?
- What are they saying and how? Are they questions, requests or statements?
- During which season of the liturgical year might each most appropriately be used?

Gloria

The Gloria is a hymn of praise, and its title comes from the first word of the Latin text: 'Gloria in excelsis Deo' – 'Glory to God in the highest'. The Gloria entered the Roman Order of Mass only gradually. It was first sung in Rome just at Christmas and then also at Easter. It was not until the twelfth century that the practice we have today was finally established – with the hymn sung on the Sundays of Christmas, Easter and Ordinary Time, and on Solemnities and Feasts. It is omitted in Advent, Lent and Ordinary weekdays (i.e. not Solemnities or Feasts). The hymn has a three-part structure: the outer sections offer praise, the middle section seeks God's mercy.

Collect

The last element in the Introductory Rites is the Collect, the priest's prayer that concludes this section. This is the first of four Proper or variable texts prayed by the priest: the other three are the Prayer over the Offerings, the Preface and the Prayer after Communion. The Collect begins with the invitation, 'Let us pray', and is followed by a pause for silent prayer. The priest then prays the Collect prayer – which at the same time gathers together the silent prayers of the faithful and is spoken on their behalf. The Collect is frequently unique to a particular day or celebration. Some Collects express something about the celebration; this is generally the case during the seasons of Advent, Christmas, Lent and Easter, on saints' days and at Masses during which other sacraments are celebrated. On the Sundays of Ordinary Time the subject of the Collect is more general. Although Collects can contain scriptural references, the purpose is not to directly prepare for the readings of the Liturgy of the Word.

Structure

The Collects of the Roman liturgy are usually quite short and simple. They share a common structure, which can be characterized as **You-Who-Do-Through**. This pattern is not only the basis for the Collect, but also for other prayers such as the Prayer over the Offerings and the Prayer after Communion. Appreciating this structure is not only helpful when looking at a text or proclaiming it, it also provides a template for writing prayers.

You: Collects generally reflect the Trinitarian nature of the liturgy. They are addressed to God the Father. This address can be as simple as 'O God' or 'Lord God' or it can mention various attributes of God, often drawn from Scripture. These attributes may reflect the context or content of the prayer – for example, God of mercy and compassion in Lent.

Who: The second stage speaks of what God has done. It is usually related to the third stage: because you have done that in the past, so now we ask you to do this.

Do: This states the purpose of the prayer, and clearly expresses what it is asking for. It is often signalled in the current *Missal* by the word 'grant'.

Through: To complete the Trinitarian dynamic the prayer is made through the Son and in the Holy Spirit, which is expressed in a final section of praise. Such concluding sections are generally known as 'Doxologies', a Greek-derived word for the praise of God. The people's 'Amen' is a word of assent and conclusion.

The form of the Collect is very flexible. It can be addressed to Christ (see, for example, the Collect for 24 December). It can begin with Who or Do but the four elements can usually be discerned. Usually the Do is the longest part, but it can also be Who. The elements can all be seen in the Collect for the tenth Sunday in Ordinary Time.

O God,	**You**
from whom all good things come,	**Who**
grant that we, who call on you in our need,	**Do**
may at your prompting discern what is right,	
and by your guidance do it.	
Through our Lord Jesus Christ, your Son,	**Through**
who lives and reigns with you in the unity of the Holy Spirit,	
one God, for ever and ever.	
Amen.	

Questions for Reflection

Look at a couple of examples of Collects and see how the structure can be applied. One way to do this is to ask a series of questions:

- Who is being addressed?
- How is this expanded?
- What is being asked for?

Write a Collect using this structure. It might be helpful to use a Gospel passage as a starting point. Try to write two versions: one pared down and simple; the second drawing on the language and images of the text. Read them aloud. Which do you prefer?

Adaptations

Blessing and Sprinkling of Water

The Penitential Act on Sundays may be replaced by the Blessing and Sprinkling of Water. The primary purpose of this ritual is to serve as a reminder of Baptism – which is why it is particularly appropriate during the Easter Season. After the water has been blessed, the priest sprinkles the ministers and the whole congregation with the blessed water. As he moves through the church a chant or baptismal song is sung. Mass then continues with the Gloria.

Other rites

On a number of occasions, the Introductory Rites are replaced by some other liturgical action. This can take the form of a procession – as at the Feast of the Presentation of the Lord (2 February) and on Palm Sunday, when Mass begins in a place other than the church, and the congregation process from there with candles or palms. In a similar way, the Greeting and Penitential Act are omitted at the beginning of a Wedding Mass or when the coffin is brought into church for the Funeral Mass.

Summary

The Introductory Rites are a prelude to the Liturgy of the Word and the Liturgy of the Eucharist. Their function is preparatory and the different stages suggest a process: the assembly is formed into one Body, reminded of Baptism, reflects on failings and receives mercy, offering glory and praise, turning to God in prayer.

Liturgy of the Word

As noted above, the Liturgy of the Word forms one of the two main parts of the Mass. A number of passages of Scripture are read, culminating in the proclamation of the Gospel. This is followed by a series of responses: the homily, the profession of faith and the intercessions.

Scripture

The public proclamation of the Scriptures played a significant role in the Jewish synagogue worship. This we can recognize in the life of Jesus when, at the beginning of Jesus' ministry, he went to the synagogue at Nazareth, was given the scroll of the Book, and read aloud from the prophet Isaiah. After returning the scroll, Jesus said, 'Today this Scripture has been fulfilled in your hearing.'[8] Similarly, the excerpt from Justin Martyr's *Apology*, given at the beginning of the chapter, includes the expression, 'the memoirs of the apostles or the writings of the prophets are read'. This appears to refer to both the Christian and the Hebrew Scriptures.

Structure

Sundays	Weekdays
Reading 1 – Old Testament or Acts of Apostles in Easter Season	Reading 1 – Old or New Testament
Responsorial Psalm	Responsorial Psalm
Reading 2 – New Testament	Gospel Acclamation
Gospel Acclamation	Gospel
Gospel	(Homily)
Homily	(Prayer of the Faithful)
Profession of Faith	
Prayer of the Faithful	

The Lectionary

History

Ordo Lectionum Missae
- Editio typica, 1969
- Editio typica altera, 1981

Lectionary
- First edition, 1969
  - one volume, 2 editions using Jerusalem Bible and Revised Standard Version, both with Grail Psalter
- Second edition, 1981 (London: Collins and Geoffrey Chapman)
  - three volumes, 1 edition using Jerusalem Bible and Grail Psalter

Contents

Volume 1:

Proper of Seasons

Sundays and Weekdays of:

   Advent

   Christmas

   Lent

   Triduum

   Easter

Sundays of:
　Ordinary Time
Solemnities and Feasts of the Lord
Common Responsorial Psalms

Volume 2:
Proper of Seasons
Weekdays of:
　Ordinary Time
Proper of Saints
Commons

Volume 3:
Ritual Masses
Masses for Various Needs and Occasions
Votive Masses
Masses for the Dead

The Liturgy of the Word on Sundays

Sundays follow a three-year Lectionary Cycle which is based on one of the Gospels: Year A – Matthew; Year B – Mark; Year C – Luke. The Gospel of John is distributed across all three years, particularly in the seasons of Christmas, Lent and Easter. It is also used on a number of Sundays in Ordinary Time in Year B.

Advent, Christmas, Lent and Easter

Four passages of Scripture are provided (Reading 1, Psalm, Reading 2 and Gospel) and they are intended to form a coherent, thematically linked whole. This is also the case for Solemnities, whenever they occur.

　The Scriptures are organized differently according to the season. For example, the Sundays of Advent follow a similar pattern across each of the Lectionary cycles: the Gospel for the fourth Sunday of each cycle is concerned with events relating to the preparation for the birth of Jesus. Thus, in Year A the Gospel is the

Annunciation to Joseph (Matt. 1.18–24), in Year B, the Annunciation to Mary (Luke 1.26–38), and in Year C, the Visitation (Luke 1.39–45). In Lent, on the other hand, each of the three years has a distinct focus: in Year A it is Baptism, and the preparation for initiation at the Easter Vigil; the Lenten Sundays of Year B focus on the Covenant; in Year C the theme is reconciliation and forgiveness.

During the Easter season the first reading is always taken from the Acts of the Apostles rather than the Old Testament.

Ordinary Time

Across the Sundays of Ordinary Time, a semi-continuous approach is taken to the reading of the Gospels. In other words, each year one of the Gospels is read through in sequence, Sunday by Sunday, but with verses or sections omitted. The run through the Gospel is, of course, interrupted each year by Lent and Eastertide. The Lectionary provides a table to show how each Gospel is organized over the year and how a series of Sundays is grouped together – for example, for the Sermon on the Mount in Year A.

The first reading, which is taken from the Old Testament, is chosen because of its relationship to the Gospel: there will be a direct or indirect connection between them. This connection is made in one of three ways:

- Direct quotation – either an Old Testament text quoted in the Gospel is given its original context or a story mentioned in the Gospel is the subject of the first reading (e.g. 18th Sunday, Year B).
- Parallel narrative – the Gospel story is echoed in the first reading: a healing miracle or a story of feeding (e.g. 17th Sunday, Year B).
- Thematic link – the themes of the Gospel are shared by the first reading (e.g. 20th Sunday, Year B).

Although the responsorial psalm is frequently understood as a response to the first reading, it is better to regard it as forming a bridge between the first reading and the Gospel. It is frequently the text of the response that forges the link between the two. On the other hand, the second Sunday reading, which is a semi-continuous reading of the epistles of the New Testament, does not relate directly to the first reading, the psalm or the Gospel.

> ### Questions for Reflection
> - Look at the readings provided for a Sunday.
> - What connections between the different readings do you see?

The proclamation of the Gospel

Because the proclamation of the Gospel is the high point of the Liturgy of the Word, it is distinguished from the other readings by special marks of honour. Its proclamation is reserved to a deacon or, when there is no deacon, a priest:

- The one who proclaims the Gospel reading prepares himself: the deacon by receiving a blessing, the priest by prayer.
- The people stand to hear the Gospel reading and acclaim Christ present and speaking to them.
- Servers with candles may stand on each side of the lectern (the ambo).
- The book may be incensed before the text is proclaimed and it is reverenced by the minister after the proclamation.[9]

Homily

After the Gospel has been proclaimed, the priest or deacon gives the homily. He reflects on the Scripture passages, on the liturgy being celebrated, and on the circumstances of those who hear it. The General Instruction describes a homily as 'necessary for the nurturing of the Christian life'.[10] The homily is followed by a period of silent reflection.

For many adults the homily is the only formal formation in faith they receive. The Appendix to the Homiletic Directory (2014) provides references to paragraphs in the Catechism for every Sunday, making connections between the readings and the teaching of the Church. This reinforces the practice of Lectionary-based catechesis which sees the Sunday readings as the foundation for exploring faith. It also suggests a more considered approach to the homily as part of a larger picture.

Creed

The profession of faith is said or sung on Sundays and Solemnities. Two forms are given in the *Roman Missal*: the Niceno-Constantinopolitan Creed and the Apostles' Creed. The former, as its name indicates, was produced by early Church Councils which had arrived at agreements about the person of Christ and the relationship between the members of the Trinity. The Apostles' Creed (though ancient in origin it was not written by the Apostles) is associated with Baptism. It forms the basis of the profession of faith made by baptismal candidates and renewed by the whole congregation at the Easter Vigil. The *Missal* recommends its use, therefore, in Lent and Easter.

Prayer of the Faithful

Having professed their baptismal faith, the congregation exercise their baptismal priesthood[11] by praying for the Church and the world.[12] The Prayer of the Faithful takes a standard, three-part form:

- Intentions are read by the deacon or a reader.
- Silence is kept.
- The people make a shared response, for example, 'Lord, in your mercy hear our prayer'.

Something rather subtle is happening here: the naming of the intention is not of itself a prayer. Rather, the deacon or reader is inviting the people to pray for some particular need or other. This they do in the silence between the statement of the intention and the response.

Music in the Liturgy of the Word

The proclamation of the Gospel is the high point of the Liturgy of the Word. This is prepared for by the singing of the Gospel Acclamation, which can accompany a procession of the ministers to the ambo. The acclamation usually takes the following form:

- A Cantor sings 'Alleluia', which is repeated by the congregation.

- The cantor sings a verse, which is usually a short phrase of Scripture which can be related to the Gospel.
- The congregation sing 'Alleluia' once again.

During Lent, the Alleluia is replaced by another acclamation such as 'Praise to you, O Christ, King of eternal glory'. If the procession warranted it the acclamation could be extended, but it is the needs of the liturgical action that should dictate the musical form, and not vice versa.

The psalm following the first reading can be set to a number of musical forms. The Introduction to the Lectionary allows for the psalm to be sung 'directly' – that is, without a response. In such a case the verses would be sung by everybody, or, perhaps, with a cantor and congregation singing alternate verses. However, by far the most common mode of singing the psalm is responsorially. It is this form that is given in the Lectionary: the verses are sung by a cantor, and everybody joins in the response. The verses are usually sung to a simple tone or melodic formula. This not only helps to make the words clear to the congregation, but it also facilitates ease of learning.

The Liturgy of the Eucharist

The Liturgy of the Eucharist falls into three parts: the Preparation of the Gifts, the Eucharistic Prayer and the Communion Rite. In the Preparation the gifts of bread and wine are brought to the altar, in the Eucharistic Prayer the bread and wine become the Body and Blood of Christ which are distributed to the faithful in the Communion Rite.

Starting points

If the Mass as a whole follows the structure of Gather, Listen, Respond and Go, then the Liturgy of the Eucharist can be internally structured according to another four-fold action, which is Take, Bless, Break and Share. This, too, can be recognized in the Emmaus story, and is also to be found in the Gospel narratives of the Last Supper. It was the Anglican liturgist Gregory Dix who in his book *The Shape of the Liturgy* traced this pattern through early liturgies.[13]

Question for Reflection

Look at one of the feeding miracles in the Gospels, e.g. Luke 9.10–17.

• Can you identify the stages of Take, Bless, Break and Share?

Liturgy of the Eucharist: Structure

Preparation of Gifts
Eucharistic Prayer
  Sanctus
  Memorial Acclamation
  Doxology and Amen
Communion Rite
  Lord's Prayer
  Sign of Peace
  Fraction and Agnus Dei
  Communion
  Prayer after Communion

The preparation of gifts

Procession and preparation

The beginning of the Liturgy of the Eucharist, like many aspects of liturgy, serves a functional purpose – the gifts of bread and wine have to be brought to the altar. The action, however, carries a deeper symbolic significance. The bread and wine are the fruits of natural gifts from God, the wheat and the grape, which have been worked by human hands and are 'gifted' back to God. These gifts in turn will be transformed and offered back as the Body and Blood of Christ. The preparation is frequently accompanied by a collection of money. Once again, an apparently practical action has symbolic weight: money, a fruit of human work, is given for the needs of the Church and the poor. Once again, it is an exchange of gifts that is taking place.

Prayer over the Offerings

The Preparation of Gifts concludes with a Prayer over the Offerings. This short text is 'proper' (that is, it is taken from the texts of the day) and follows the pattern, in reduced form, of the Collect. For example,

> May the oblation of this day's feast
> be pleasing to you, O Lord, we pray,
> that through this most holy exchange
> we may be found in the likeness of Christ,
> in whom our nature is united to you.
> Who lives and reigns for ever and ever.[14]

The Eucharistic Prayer

The General Instruction describes the Eucharistic Prayer as the 'centre and high point of the entire celebration'.[15] The word 'Eucharist' derives from the Greek word for thanksgiving, which sets the tone for the whole prayer. It is also a prayer of sanctification where the gifts of bread and wine become the Body and Blood of Christ.

Choices

The current *Roman Missal* contains ten Eucharistic Prayers. Embedded in the Order of Mass are Eucharistic Prayers I–IV, which are intended for common use. In addition, the *Missal* provides two Eucharistic Prayers for Reconciliation and four 'Eucharistic Prayers for Use in Masses for Various Needs'. This second set is themed – focusing, for example, on 'The Church on the Path of Unity' and 'Jesus, Who Went About Doing Good'. These may be used when appropriate at particular times or in appropriate contexts: for example, the first one given above would be appropriate for use during the Week of Prayer for Christian Unity. The Catholic Church has also authorized four other prayers that are not contained in the *Missal*: a Eucharistic Prayer for the Deaf (which is signed and spoken) and three Eucharistic Prayers for Masses with Children. The large number of Eucharistic Prayers marks a significant change from the pre-Vatican II *Missal*, which only contained the ancient prayer known as the 'Roman Canon', and which is found in the revised *Missal* as the First Eucharistic Prayer.

Further variation is possible in some of the Eucharistic Prayers because they incorporate a significant element that can be varied from Mass to Mass, depending on the context of celebration and the liturgical season. This element is the Preface. It is a necessary part of all Eucharistic Prayers, but only for some of them does the *Roman Missal* incorporate a Preface text into the text of the Prayer itself. In some of these cases the content of the Preface is so closely integrated into the Prayer as a whole that it may not be varied (Eucharistic Prayer IV, and those for Use in Masses for Various Needs). Other Prayers similarly have their own Preface, but here the link between the Preface and the body text is lighter, and so a different Preface may replace the one provided (Eucharistic Prayer II and the Prayers for Reconciliation). For all the other Eucharistic Prayers the celebrant selects a Preface from the broad range provided by the *Missal*, bearing in mind that some Prefaces are prescribed for particular days or seasons, or for the celebration of a sacrament such as Marriage.

Eucharistic Prayer: Structure

Eucharistic Prayers are built up from a series of common elements of thanksgiving, blessing and prayer. These elements are generally all present and follow the same order – though there are exceptions. The pattern given below is that followed by Eucharistic Prayer II.

Preface
   Preface Dialogue
   Preface
   Sanctus
Prayer
   Epiclesis I
   Institution Narrative and Consecration
   Memorial Acclamation
   Anamnesis and Offering
   Epiclesis II and the Prayer of the Faithful (the Intercessions)
   Doxology and Amen

Preface

Each Eucharistic Prayer begins with the Preface. Its purpose is to draw people into the prayer and introduce the themes of thanksgiving, both general and particular. There are four parts: the Preface Dialogue, the introduction, the 'embolism' – the term used for a piece of interpolated text slotted between two more or less standardized blocks of text – and the ending. The Preface Dialogue is always the same. The beginning and the ending of the Preface itself express common themes that are stated simply or more elaborately. The embolism is the variable part, something inserted between two other unchanging elements.

The Preface Dialogue is a call to order, a clear marking of a new section. The dialogue of 'The Lord be with you' is developed with an invitation to give thanks. The beginning of the Preface affirms this desire to give thanks, in all time and places, and names the object of the thanksgiving, the 'Father most holy'. The embolism offers specific reasons to give thanks. These can be related to the specific feast or occasion being celebrated or be more general. Often this text weaves together a number of scriptural images and allusions. The conclusion of the Preface takes the thanksgiving expressed at the beginning and connects it with the hosts of heaven, introducing the next section of the Eucharistic Prayer.

Sanctus

Heaven and earth join their voices in the singing of the Sanctus or Holy, Holy. Though most of the Eucharistic Prayer is prayed aloud by the priest it is clear that he is expressing the prayer of the faithful who participate by listening and by a number of acclamations. The first of these is the Sanctus, an ancient Christian hymn, which draws on Isaiah's vision of God in the Temple and Christ's triumphal entry into Jerusalem.[16]

Epiclesis I

In a similar way to how Kyrie was a remnant of a Greek-speaking early Church, the terms used to describe the elements of the Eucharistic Prayer are derived from Greek words – a sign of the antiquity of the form. Epiclesis expresses the calling down of the Holy Spirit so that what is presented may be transformed.

This is not just a form of words, but is accompanied by a gesture of outstretched hands which is integral to the prayer. In the first Epiclesis, at the beginning of the Eucharistic Prayer, the Spirit is asked to transform the gifts of bread and wine so that they become for those present the Body and Blood of Christ.

Institution narrative and consecration

The priest recounts the story (narrative) of the first time (institution) that bread and wine were made holy (consecration) by Jesus. The text is drawn from the Gospel accounts of the Last Supper. The words of Christ are used over the bread and the chalice and are accompanied by gestures: for example, after each text the consecrated host, and then the chalice, is shown to the people. However, the actions performed do not follow the exact sequence of the words – the breaking of bread does not take place until a later point in the Mass. The interweaving of narrative and gesture can be seen in the following extract from Eucharistic Prayer II:

At the time he was betrayed and entered willingly into his Passion,
He takes the bread and, holding it slightly raised above the altar, continues:
he took bread and, giving thanks, broke it, and gave it to his disciples, saying:
He bows slightly.
TAKE THIS, ALL OF YOU, AND EAT OF IT, FOR THIS IS MY BODY, WHICH WILL BE GIVEN UP FOR YOU.
He shows the consecrated host to the people, places it again on the paten, and genuflects in adoration.
After this, he continues:
In a similar way, when supper was ended,
He takes the chalice and, holding it slightly raised above the altar, continues:
he took the chalice and, once more giving thanks, he gave it to his disciples, saying:
He bows slightly.
TAKE THIS, ALL OF YOU, AND DRINK FROM IT, FOR THIS IS THE CHALICE OF MY BLOOD, THE BLOOD OF THE NEW AND ETERNAL COVENANT, WHICH WILL BE POURED OUT FOR YOU AND FOR MANY FOR THE FORGIVENESS OF SINS.

DO THIS IN MEMORY OF ME.

He shows the chalice to the people, places it on the corporal, and genuflects in adoration.

Memorial Acclamation

This acclamation by the people was an innovation in the Roman Rite after the Second Vatican Council. The acclamation is one of the ways in which the people make the prayer their own; the texts of the acclamations point towards the complexity of what is happening. They are not texts in praise of the Eucharistic elements, but focus on the Paschal Mystery:

> *[The priest says]* The mystery of faith.
> *And the people continue, acclaiming:*
> We proclaim your Death, O Lord,
> and profess your Resurrection
> until you come again.
> *Or:*
> When we eat this Bread and drink this Cup,
> we proclaim your Death, O Lord,
> until you come again.
> *Or:*
> Save us, Saviour of the world,
> for by your Cross and Resurrection
> you have set us free.

Anamnesis and Offering

The Greek word 'anamnesis' is related to the more familiar 'amnesia', but it means the opposite of 'forgetting'. Anamnesis means to remember or recall past events, in such a way that the past is made present. As the saving death and resurrection of Christ are called to mind in the liturgy, they are made present and salvific (or effective).[17]

Epiclesis II and intercessions

The second calling down of the Holy Spirit is upon the whole Church. This is followed by a series of intercessions for the living and the dead that end with a plea for the faithful to be called to join Mary and the saints in heaven.

Doxology

Having begun in thanksgiving the Eucharistic Prayer ends in praise. Each Eucharistic Prayer concludes with the same text, which is a concise expression of the Trinitarian dynamic of the whole liturgy – through Christ in the power of the Holy Spirit glory is offered to the Father. This accompanies the raising of the gifts symbolically to the Father. The people give their assent in the Amen.

> Through him, and with him, and in him,
> O God, almighty Father,
> in the unity of the Holy Spirit,
> all glory and honour is yours,
> for ever and ever.
> *The people acclaim*:
> Amen.

Music in the Eucharistic Prayer

Singing can be a powerful way of participating and giving assent in the Eucharistic Prayer. The Prayer contains three acclamations that are intended to be sung by all: the Sanctus, the Memorial Acclamation and the Amen. Musical settings should be chosen with a sensitivity to the context of the whole prayer: a structural imbalance can be created, for example, if the singing of the Sanctus takes longer to complete than does the next part of the Eucharistic Prayer. A parish might have a number of different settings that reflect the different times of the liturgical year – a subdued setting might be appropriate for Lent, an exuberant one for Easter.

> **Question for Reflection**
>
> The examples given above have been taken from Eucharistic Prayer II.
>
> • Look at the text of another Eucharistic Prayer; can you identify the various elements?

Communion Rite

The Communion Rite is made up of a series of prayers and actions that reflect the unity of the Church and therefore prepare the assembly to receive Holy Communion.

The Lord's Prayer

The 'Our Father' – or, the Lord's Prayer – is the common prayer of the baptized, handed over to catechumens during Lent in preparation for the initiation at Easter.[18] The text is taken from Matthew's Gospel (6.9–13) as Jesus' response to the request 'Lord, teach us to pray'. It offers a model of praise followed by petition. From the early Church, there has been a tradition that the Lord's Prayer should be prayed three times a day: at Mass and at Morning and Evening Prayer. The doxology 'For the kingdom . . .' is found in some early Gospel manuscripts, though not in the earliest. In the Communion Rite it is separated by an embolism, an inserted text – as in the Sanctus. The embolism here continues the prayer for protection from sin and distress and adds an eschatological dimension, 'as we await the blessed hope and coming of our Saviour, Jesus Christ'.

The Sign of Peace

The next act of communion is the sharing of a Sign of Peace. This is introduced by a prayer for the peace and unity of the Church that is said by the priest alone, and is based on Jesus' own promise of peace from John's Gospel, 'Peace I leave you, my peace I give you' (John 20.26). This is followed by the short dialogue

'The peace of the Lord be always with you' and followed by, 'And with your spirit', which points to the significance of the action that the rubric describes as expressing 'peace, communion and charity'.[19]

Pope Benedict XVI considered moving the Sign of Peace to before the Preparation of Gifts (where it is found in Anglican rites). When placed there, the sign takes on a different meaning. Instead of the promise of peace given in John's Gospel, the scriptural image becomes Jesus' requirement in Matthew's Gospel that before offering gifts at the altar one should make peace with one's brother.[20] Exchanging the Sign of Peace at this position, therefore, suggests an understanding of peace as reconciliation. Placed, instead, before Communion, the Sign represents a sharing in the peace that flows from Christ through the baptized.

The Fraction or Breaking of Bread

The accounts of the Last Supper speak of Jesus breaking the bread before speaking the words, 'Take, eat . . .' In the Emmaus story, it is only when the stranger breaks bread for the disciples that they recognize that he is Jesus. Both stories attest to the importance of this action, which served as a name for the whole of the celebration of the Eucharist in the Acts of the Apostles. Historically, it has served a number of purposes: it recalls the actions of Jesus himself, it serves a practical function, and it has a symbolic value. This last has a paradoxical twist: the breaking of the bread into smaller pieces is a further sign of communion. St Paul wrote to the Corinthians: 'The bread that we break, is it not a participation in the body of Christ? Because there is one bread, we who are many are one body, for we all partake of the one bread' (1 Cor. 10.16–17).

The action's symbolic theme of unity was picked up in one of the earliest non-scriptural texts to discuss the Eucharist: 'As grain once scattered on the hillside was brought together and made one bread, so may the Church be gathered together from the ends of the earth, by partaking in this bread broken and shared by all.'[21] As the bread is broken, the 'Agnus Dei' is sung:

> Lamb of God who takes away the sins of the world, have mercy on us. (x 2)
> Lamb of God who takes away the sins of the world, grant us peace.

Further repetitions of the first line may be introduced to extend the singing if the breaking is prolonged. This text introduces a further set of related scriptural allusions. The most obvious is to John 2.29, which is directly quoted: it is the designation by which John the Baptist points out Jesus to his disciples. It also evokes the heavenly banquet described in the Book of Revelation. The text, therefore, underscores the Eucharistic themes of Christ's presence, sacrifice, and the orientation of the celebration towards the future. The apparently simple action of breaking bread, therefore, operates on a number of levels.[22] Given the symbolic richness of the action, however, its relatively low profile in most cele-brations of Mass can come as a surprise; the singing of the Agnus Dei usually takes rather longer to complete than does the actual breaking.

The distribution of Communion

The reception of Communion is the final act of communion within the rite. It balances the personal devotion of the individual seeking to be nourished and the more communal aspects where to say 'Amen' is a sign of communion with the Church and also a commitment to carry on the work of building communion.

The communal elements are also found strengthened by the Communion Procession. *Celebrating the Mass* describes this as 'the humble patience of the poor moving forward to be fed, the alert expectancy of God's people sharing the Paschal meal in readiness for their journey, the joyful confidence of God's people on the march toward the promised land' (*CTM*, 210). The procession is accompanied by the Communion Antiphon or another suitable song. The text of the antiphon can take a phrase from the Gospel and draw out new dimensions by placing it in the context of Communion.

In many parishes Communion will be distributed under both kinds from both the paten and the chalice and the priest will be assisted by commissioned lay ministers. The reception of Communion is followed by a period of silent prayer and thanksgiving. Though there can be tasks to be done directly after the distribution, it is desirable that all present share in a time of silence. This may be followed by a hymn of thanksgiving.

Prayer after Communion

The final part of the Communion Rite is the short prayer following the Collect pattern, said by the priest. The text usually brings together a number of themes such as thanksgiving for Communion, desire to live out what has been received, and hope of salvation. For example,

Grant, we pray, almighty God,
that our reception of this paschal Sacrament
may have a continuing effect in our minds and hearts.
Through Christ our Lord.[23]

Question for Reflection

• What differences might there be between musical settings chosen for the Communion Procession and for a hymn following Communion? (Consider the themes, the style and any practical issues that might need to be factored in.)

Concluding Rites

The Mass takes its name from its ending. The word 'Mass' is derived from the final command given to the congregation in Latin: '*Ite, missa est*', which is difficult to translate, but a good approximation might be, 'Go, be sent'. The expression shares the same linguistic root as the English word 'dismissal'. To celebrate the Eucharist is for the Christian community to come together so that, like the disciples, its members today can be sent out. The rites that take place at the end of the Mass are brief – almost perfunctory – as though no time should be wasted in getting on with sharing the fruits of what has been received. The purpose of the Concluding Rite 'is to send the people forth to put into effect in their daily lives the Paschal Mystery and the unity in Christ which they have celebrated. They are given a sense of abiding witness to Christ in the world and to bring that Gospel to the poor.'[24]

Concluding Rites: Structure

Notices
Blessing
Dismissal
(Procession, Hymn)

Notices

This is the place for any announcements about the life of the community in the coming week.

Blessing

To bring the celebration to a conclusion the priest blesses the congregation. For the last time they engage together in the dialogue, 'The Lord be with you'/'And with your spirit'. Then the priest pronounces a blessing in the name of the Trinity, echoing the Sign of the Cross that was made at the start of the Mass. On some occasions, such as Easter, a more solemn formula of blessing can be used. This follows a three-part structure; the priest invites the congregation to bow their heads for God's blessing, and pronounces three short formulas of blessing over them, to each of which the people respond, 'Amen'. It concludes with the usual Trinitarian blessing.

Dismissal

Four brief phrases of dismissal are provided for use at the end of Mass. If a deacon is present, it is he who announces these phrases. Two of them are simple instructions: 'Go forth, the Mass is ended' and 'Go in peace'. Two others, that were added at the initiative of Pope Benedict, elaborate a little on the mission with which the Church sends its members out from the Eucharist into the world: 'Go, and announce the Gospel of the Lord', 'Go in peace, glorifying the Lord by your life'. Whichever of the four is used, the people make the same response, 'Thanks be to God'.

Adaptation

When Mass is followed by another rite the Concluding Rites are curtailed and the blessing and dismissal omitted. Such instances include funerals where the body is taken to its final place of rest, or Exposition of the Blessed Sacrament, where a host consecrated at the Mass is placed on the altar for a time of Adoration.

Masses with children

In 1973 the Vatican issued two texts about children and Mass: *The Directory for Masses with Children*[25] and the three *Eucharistic Prayers for Masses with Children*.[26] Both take a progressive approach to children's development – for example, the three Eucharistic Prayers are intended for use with different age ranges. Although the Eucharistic Prayers for Children contain all the elements described on pages 144–9, both the language in which they are framed and the imagery they draw upon have been simplified. A feature of the prayers is the use of additional acclamations such as 'Glory and praise' which punctuate the prayer and draw out the themes of praise and petition. As acclamations, these short phrases can be learned by heart – especially if they are sung.

The purpose of the *Directory* was two-fold: to enable and encourage children's participation in the celebration of Mass in ways suitable to their age and development, and the gradual deepening of their engagement in the liturgy that would facilitate their full participation at Sunday Mass. This second aspect is often given less attention than the first. The *Directory* draws a distinction between Masses celebrated with children at which only a few adults participate, and Masses celebrated with a primarily adult congregation but at which children also participate. For the first instance, a range of adaptations is suggested. For example, the Introductory Rites may be simplified to include only one element after the opening Sign of the Cross and Greeting, or the use of only one reading from the Scriptures. Even when only a few children are present at Mass, some adaptation is suggested.

One development that flowed from the *Directory for Masses with Children* is the celebration of a discrete Liturgy of the Word with Children in a place apart from the main assembly on Sundays:

Sometimes, moreover, if the place itself and the nature of the individuals permit, it possibly will be appropriate to celebrate the liturgy of the word, including a homily, with the children in a separate, but not too distant, location. Then, before the eucharistic liturgy begins, the children are led to the place where the adults have meanwhile celebrated their own liturgy of the word.[27]

Though the *Directory* describes this as an exceptional practice, it has become an embedded feature of many parishes. Children are led out during the Introductory Rites and typically will engage with one reading – usually the Gospel. This is followed by a reflection on that text through discussion, some activity and prayer. The children return to the church at the Preparation of Gifts. It can be a challenge to maintain a liturgical – rather than a catechetical – focus. In large parishes, it is possible to divide the children into age-related cohorts. The challenge to which the practice in each parish needs to respond relates to the second purpose of the *Directory* – how does this celebration prepare children for participation in the Liturgy of the Word with the 'adult' congregation?

Worship of the Eucharist outside Mass

Consecrated hosts are primarily reserved to be taken to the sick and to the dying. As the Church's understanding of the Eucharist developed – particularly with regard to the presence of Christ in the Sacrament – the reserved host itself came to be an object of particular veneration. Two very popular devotional practices developed: the offering of silent prayer by the individual before the Blessed Sacrament reserved in the tabernacle, and the communal practice Exposition of the Blessed Sacrament (the 'showing' of the host in an elaborate holder known as a monstrance) followed by a blessing of the people by the priest as he held the monstrance – Benediction. The combination of Exposition and Benediction became a popular form of communal prayer.

The renewal of the liturgy after the Second Vatican Council emphasized the connection between the celebration of Exposition and Benediction and the Mass, stressing that the central theme of time of exposition is Christ. The revised rite of Exposition is made up four stages: Exposition – the placing of the host on the altar; Adoration – an extended time of prayer which includes periods of silence and also readings, music, prayers and even Morning or Evening Prayer;

Benediction – the blessing with the host which may be made only by a priest or deacon; Reposition – the returning of the host to the tabernacle.

Celebrations in the absence of a priest

By the mid twentieth century, Mass would have been celebrated more or less every day in most Catholic churches. However, by the start of the twenty-first century a marked reduction in the number of priests across the English-speaking world has made the meeting of that previous custom increasingly difficult. A popular response has been that on those weekdays when Mass cannot be celebrated, a Service of the Word and Communion is held. The service is led by a deacon or layperson, and Holy Communion is distributed from the tabernacle. The practice is not without its problems, especially when it becomes established as a regularly recurring practice, as this appears to establish as normative that which is, properly speaking, exceptional.

In parishes where Sunday Mass is still celebrated regularly, the community may do better to explore what other possibilities the liturgy provides for a week-day gathering for prayer, rather than by replacing a weekday Mass with a Service of Word and Communion. Such possibilities could include Services of the Word, the celebration of the Liturgy of the Hours, or Exposition of the Blessed Sacrament and various devotions. More challenging pastorally are those situations where the provision of Sunday Mass itself has become difficult, and for which the Services of Word and Communion have an evident role.

Liturgical Space

Most churches contain at least two discrete liturgical spaces: a larger space in which the congregation gather, and the sanctuary towards which much of the liturgical action is directed. The congregational section should incorporate a good processional route and ideally the sanctuary should be clearly visible.

The sanctuary contains three sites for the celebration of Mass: the chair, the ambo and the altar. The priest presides from the *chair*, and conducts there the Introductory and Concluding Rites. He should have a clear sight line with the assembly from the chair, but also be able to be seen to listen to the word of God. The Scriptures are proclaimed from the *ambo*. Given the importance the liturgy places on the Scriptures, the ambo is reserved for the readings and the intercessions. The *altar* is where the Liturgy of the Eucharist takes place: where the gifts are prepared; the sacrifice of praise is offered and from which the fruits of Communion are given.

Conclusion

> If you are the body and members of Christ, then it is your sacrament that is placed on the table of the Lord; it is your sacrament that you receive. To that which you are you respond 'Amen' and by responding to it you assent to it. For you hear the words, 'the Body of Christ' and respond 'Amen.' Be then a member of the Body of Christ that your Amen may be true . . . O sacrament of devotion! O sign of unity! O bond of charity![28]

The reception of Holy Communion carries consequences. The 'Amen' spoken by each communicant immediately before receiving is not only an assent to Christ's Eucharistic presence, an agreement that this is the Body of Christ, but also a re-commitment to active membership of the Body of Christ. The dismissal that follows so closely after reception of Holy Communion is a sending out of the members of that Body to their mission in the world. In his 2018 Apostolic Exhortation on the Call to Holiness, *Gaudete et Exultate*, Pope Francis calls on the teaching of St Thomas Aquinas to draw out the link between Christian worship and Christian mission, especially the mission of service:

> Here I think of Saint Thomas Aquinas, who asked which actions of ours are noblest, which external works best show our love for God. Thomas answered unhesitatingly that they are the works of mercy towards our neighbour, even more than our acts of worship: 'We worship God by outward sacrifices and gifts, not for his own benefit, but for that of ourselves and our neighbour. For he does not need our sacrifices, but wishes them to be offered to him, in order to stir our devotion and to profit our neighbour. Hence mercy, whereby we supply others' defects, is a sacrifice more acceptable to him, as conducing more directly to our neighbour's well-being.'[29]

Roman Missal

History	Contents
Missale Romanum	Apostolic Constitution
• Editio typical, 1969	General Instruction on the Roman Missal
• Editio typica altera, 1975	Universal Norms on the Liturgical Year and Calendar
	Proper of Time: Advent–Ordinary Time
• Editio typica tertia, 2002, 2008	Order of Mass
	Proper of Saints: January–December
Roman Missal	Commons
• First edition, 1973	Ritual Masses
• Third edition, 2010	Masses for Various Needs and Occasions
(London: Catholic	Votive Masses
Truth Society)	Masses for the Dead

Notes

1 Dogmatic Constitution on the Church, *Lumen Gentium* (henceforth *LG*), 11.

2 1 Cor. 11.23–26.

3 Justin, *First Apology*, 67, text from http://www.earlychristianwritings.com/text/justinmartyr-firstapology.html.

4 Justin, *First Apology*, 66.

5 For more on the textual sources of the liturgy, see Chapter 3.

6 OM 1.

7 *GIRM* 46 and 47.

8 Cf. Luke 4.16–21; cf. Isa. 61.1–2.

9 Cf. *CTM*, 166.

10 *GIRM*, 65.

11 See Chapters 6 and 10.

12 See *GIRM*, 69.

13 Dix, Gregory, *The Shape of the Liturgy*, revised 2nd edition (London: Bloomsbury, 2015).

14 *RM*, Nativity of the Lord, Mass during the Night.

15 *GIRM*, 78.

16 Isa. 6.3; Matt. 21.9.

17 A more detailed discussion of this complex idea is given in Chapter 8.

18 See Chapter 5.

19 OM, 138.

20 Matt. 5.23–24.

21 *The Didache*, 9.

22 *CTM*, 206.

23 *RM*, Second Sunday of Easter.

24 *CTM*, 217.

25 Sacred Congregation for Divine Worship, 1973, *Directory for Masses with Children* (*DMC*).

26 *Eucharistic Prayers for Masses with Children* (London: Catholic Truth Society 1973, modified translation 2013).

27 *DMC*, 17.

28 St Augustine, *Sermon 272*, cited in Catechism of the Catholic Church, 1396, 1398.

29 *Gaudete et Exultate*, 106, referring to *Summa Theologiae*, II-II, q. 30, a. 4., ad 1.

8

The Theology of the Holy Eucharist

RICHARD CONRAD, OP

Introduction and Overview

> The Eucharist is 'the source and summit of the Christian life'.
>
> (Catechism of the Catholic Church 1324, quoting *Lumen Gentium* 11, itself referring to Pius XII, *Mediator Dei*)

The Eucharist holds a unique place in Catholic and Eastern Orthodox life and liturgy, theology and spirituality. It is the service most regularly attended by Catholics; indeed, participation in the Sunday Eucharist is prescribed for them. Its daily celebration is at the heart of parish as well as monastic communities, and at the heart of the whole liturgy. Although he saw Baptism as the most *necessary* sacrament, St Thomas Aquinas saw the Eucharist as the *greatest*,[1] since, while all the sacraments symbolize Christ's saving work, and channel its power to the Church in every age, the Eucharist actually *contains* Christ. It is a uniquely precious act of Jesus' friendship; it is Sacrifice as well as Sacrament. Not surprisingly, therefore, a particularly rich Catholic theology of the Eucharist has developed across the centuries, together with a very specialized vocabulary for speaking about it. This chapter introduces readers to both theology and terminology. In particular, the chapter will examine two key Catholic doctrines concerning the Eucharist:

- Christ's real presence: this is the belief that the bread and wine truly become Christ's Body and Blood, at the deepest level. The Western Church developed the term 'transubstantiation' to express this. A related doctrine is that the *whole* Christ, Body, Blood, Soul and Divinity, is present and received under either form.
- The Eucharist is a true Sacrifice – not in addition to Christ's one and all-sufficient Sacrifice, but as a kind of perpetuation of it.

Both doctrines are common to East and West; both have been the subject of controversy in the West. This chapter lays the ground for an exploration of these two key themes by examining the broader anthropological context for the celebration of the Eucharist and the specifically Jewish background of its institution. It concludes by exploring other important aspects of the Holy Eucharist, especially the power of this sacrament to build up the Church as Christ's Body, and to prepare its members for the coming Kingdom.

Eucharistic Terminology

The celebration of the Holy Eucharist is called by several names,[2] including:

- 'The Holy Eucharist', from the Greek word for 'thanksgiving', since at its heart is a prayer of thanksgiving and praise for God's saving work, accomplished through Jesus' passion and resurrection.
- 'The Holy Sacrifice', since Catholics believe that as the Eucharist is celebrated Jesus' saving Sacrifice becomes present in the here and now. This affects those who take part in two ways: the power of Christ's Sacrifice is applied to them (it becomes real and effective in their lives), and they offer themselves to God in union with Christ.
- 'The Holy Mysteries', since it communicates all Jesus' saving deeds and sufferings, including his incarnation, his Sacrifice, his giving of the Holy Spirit, and his return in glory.
- 'The Mass', from the words (*Ite, missa est* in the Latin) by which the congregation is sent out at the end.

- In the New Testament, 'the Breaking of the Bread', from the ritual Jesus used at the Last Supper.
- And, in the Eastern Churches, 'The Holy Liturgy'.

The central aspect of the celebration is the consecration of bread and wine to become Christ's Body and Blood, after which we speak of:

- 'The sacred Host', from a Latin word (*hostia*) for a sacrifice: this refers to Christ's Body present beneath the form of bread.
- 'The precious Blood', referring to Christ's Blood present beneath the form of wine.
- 'The Holy Eucharist', referring to both.
- 'The Blessed Sacrament', referring to both, but especially to the sacred Host as it is reserved for Communion of the sick and for adoration.
- 'Holy Communion': this phrase is most often used when we speak of eating and drinking the Holy Eucharist, as in 'giving Holy Communion' or 'receiving Holy Communion'.

Contexts of the Eucharist

'You will not change me into yourself, as happens with what feeds your flesh; rather, you will be changed into me.' (St Augustine, *Confessions* VII, x, 16)

'No one feeds guests with himself as food, but this is exactly what the Lord Christ does: he himself is the host who invites; he himself is the food and the drink.' (St Augustine, *Sermon 329*)

Some twentieth- and twenty-first-century theology encourages us to locate the Holy Eucharist within:

1 The world of nature and the human world, to see how it affirms, purifies and blesses all that is good.
2 The Jewish context of its institution: it fulfils many types and earlier rites and draws upon them.

This reveals some of the resonances the Eucharist evokes for those who participate in it, and so helps explain something of its manifold impact and meaning. To some extent the human and Jewish context helps one understand the Eucharist. Many Catholic theologians, mystics, artists and poets see the Eucharist as a key to understanding human life and history, and the sacred history of the Old Testament: it helps the Christian recognize them for what they truly are in God's providence. Arguably, many devout Catholics instinctively share the same perspective.

The Eucharist within the human world and the world of nature

Common meal or sacrificial banquet?

From around 1970, shared meals have often been seen as an obvious context for understanding the Eucharist. Meals often do celebrate and cement community. Giving hospitality, and feeding people, are precious acts of service. The Eucharist takes this to a new level on two fronts. First, it is an act of extraordinary friendship: the host at this banquet feeds his guests with his own self. Second, and flowing from this: those who receive Christ in the Eucharist do not remain isolated individuals but are drawn into deeper union both with Christ and with the Church. In that sense, the ultimate grace and purpose of the Eucharist is the building up of the Mystical Body of Christ. Those who eat this Food do not turn it into their own selves; the opposite takes place, and Christ transforms them into his own self. As a consequence, the Eucharist has never been a shared meal in any straightforward sense. Luke 22.17–20 and 1 Corinthians 11.23–25 make it clear that at the Last Supper Jesus employed the ritual blessing over wine that took place after the meal, a blessing laden with significance. It is likely that the blessing over the bread that he employed was the densely symbolic blessing that was spoken before the meal itself was served. The earliest Christians did celebrate the Eucharist in connection with a shared meal, but fairly quickly let this meal drop out.

A related context in which to locate the Eucharist is the human instinct to offer sacrifice. By engaging this instinct, the Eucharist enables participants to express devotion to God in a way that suits their bodily and social nature.

But (like Jesus' Sacrifice on the cross, which it re-presents) it affirms, but also critiques and purifies, this instinct in three ways:

1   A sacrifice can be a ritual banquet that recognizes and gives thanks for food and other divine gifts. The Eucharist is such a banquet, but chiefly gives thanks for salvation.
2   A sacrifice can be a ritual present to honour God (or the 'gods'). The Eucharist is this, but it turns on its head the fancy that God 'greedily' demands that his followers should give up what is most precious to them. Ultimately, we receive more than we give, and what is received is the gift of Christ himself, and of his Sacrifice.
3   Human beings have sometimes attempted to use sacrifices to placate angry gods or buy divine favour. The language of 'placation' is found occasionally in both Scripture and liturgy,[3] but, like much religious language, must be taken carefully by recalling, for example, the frequent Old Testament condemnation of hypocritical or self-interested sacrifices.

Question for Reflection

- How helpful is it to explain to children that the Eucharist is a bit like a shared meal, or a kind of sacrifice, when many children do not experience family meals, or are impatient with them, and in a culture where ritual sacrifices (apart from the Eucharist!) are not performed?

Shedding a blessing on the whole of creation

At Mass, bread and wine are brought to the altar, and the prayers spoken as they are presented speak of them as 'fruit of the earth and work of human hands'. They are not discarded, but become Christ's Body and Blood: God uses symbols of human life and labour so as to give himself in a 'glorious exchange'.[4] Natural, created material is thereby proclaimed good; human work and skill are validated. In the early Church, after the consecration of the Eucharist, other foodstuffs were also blessed during Mass. This blessing can still be glimpsed in the prayer at the end of Eucharistic Prayer I (commonly known as the 'Roman Canon') which originally referred to such items that had just been blessed, 'Through [Christ] you continue to make all these good things, O Lord; you sanctify them . . . and bestow them upon us.' As an extension of Jesus' incarnation, Sacrifice and resurrection, the Eucharist sheds a blessing on nature and life.

The Eucharist's Old Testament and Jewish context

Typology

From the authors of the New Testament onwards, Christians have looked back to the Hebrew Scriptures to identify events and rituals that prophetically foreshadowed the Eucharist. The technical term to refer to such foreshadowings is to call them 'Types'. Two of the most frequently recurring Old Testament types in Scripture and liturgy are the manna that sustained Israel on its journey to the Promised Land, and the Passover. Thus, for example, after feeding the 5,000, Jesus in John presented himself as the True Manna, and spoke of how his flesh would have to be eaten, and his blood drunk, so that his followers might journey to eternal life (John 6.27–58). That theme of journeying becomes linked to that of liberation by the second type, the Passover. The first Passover is presented by the Book of Exodus as being celebrated on the eve of the Israelites' escape from slavery in Egypt. The Eucharist fulfils this dynamic, enabling its participants to enter into Christ's Passing Over, and to be filled afresh with the liberating Spirit won by his Sacrifice.

Useful Research: Types of the Eucharist appear in Christian art, such as mosaics in Ravenna, and can be seen on the Internet. The hymns for the Divine Office for Corpus Christi, composed by Thomas Aquinas, assembles a wide range of scriptural texts relevant to the Eucharist.

The meal blessings

At the Last Supper, Jesus seems to have employed existing rituals that preceded and followed any important meal. Although it is difficult to reconstruct first-century Jewish practice, the blessing over bread would have run something like: 'Blessed art thou, O LORD, King of the cosmos, who bringest forth bread from the earth.' The prayer over the 'cup of blessing' was probably introduced by 'Let us give thanks to the Lord our God', and praised God both for the fruit of the vine, and for saving his people (the choice vine he had planted; see Ps. 80, Isa. 5.1–7); it then made intercession for the people. God's gifts brought home to the participants what they represent: creation, grace, and the hope of further salvation. We can propose: (a) by making the Eucharistic Bread into the Body sacrificed and raised so as to establish the *New* Creation, Jesus brings home to his followers the New Creation, enabling those who eat his flesh to have eternal life; and (b) by making the wine into his Blood poured out as the New and Eternal Covenant, Jesus brings home to his followers the salvation won on the cross, so as to make them into God's people. As the shared meal that took place between these two blessings dropped out of use, they were run together into one Eucharistic Prayer in which, on behalf of the community, the presiding bishop or priest prays that the bread and wine may become the gifts of Christ's Body and Blood, and his Sacrifice may renew the gift of the re-creating Spirit, strengthening the hope of full redemption.

The synagogue service

The synagogue services, too, may well have contributed to the liturgy. Like pagan temples, the Jewish Temple in Jerusalem was a fairly small 'house'; the worshippers and the altar of sacrifice stood in the courts *outside* it. Away from the Temple, Jews of Jesus' time gathered in local synagogues, which could be quite large structures intended to contain an assembly of people. Christian churches are like Jewish synagogues; they enclose all the worshippers, who themselves are God's true Temple. Synagogue worship typically comprised services of readings and intercessions. In the early Church, this worship pattern may well have been conflated with the Eucharistic Blessings over the Bread and the Cup, giving rise to the pattern that has been observed ever since, in which the Liturgy of the Word precedes the Liturgy of the Eucharist.[5]

Christ's Real Presence in the Eucharist

> Because it is a very typical feature of friendship that friends live together . . . [Christ] promised us his bodily presence as our reward [i.e. in Heaven] . . . But meanwhile, he has not deprived us of his bodily presence while we are on pilgrimage, but has joined us to himself in this Sacrament through the reality of his Body and Blood . . . Hence because of so homely a joining of Christ to us, this Sacrament is a sign of [his] immense love, and uplifts our hope. (St Thomas Aquinas, *Summa Theologiae*, 3a 75, 1)

'This is my body' – the faith of the Universal Church

The Catholic Church's faith in Christ's real presence in the Eucharist is based on the conviction that Jesus meant and effected what he said at the Last Supper: 'This is my body . . . this is my blood of the covenant' (Matt. 26.26–28; Mark 14.22–24; Luke 22.19–20; 1 Cor. 11.24–25).[6] St Paul taught that eating and drinking unworthily profanes the Lord's Body and Blood (1 Cor. 11.27). In John 6.48–58, Jesus says that his followers need to eat his flesh and drink his blood. Catholic theology understands that its interpretation of such texts stands in a long line of continuity to the earliest generations of Christians. For example, around AD 110 St Ignatius criticized heretics who 'abstain from the Eucharist and from prayer, because they do not confess the Eucharist to be [the] flesh of our Saviour Jesus Christ, which suffered for our sins, and which the Father, of his goodness, raised up again' (*Epistle to the Smyrnaeans*, Ch. 7).

Transubstantiation

The development of the term 'transubstantiation'

Although the Catholic and Orthodox Churches have always firmly held that in the celebration of the Eucharist the bread and wine truly become Christ's Body and Blood, theologians have wrestled with how to defend and express the reality of this change. Some accounts struck other theologians as too 'physical', and some as too 'spiritual'. When a theologian called Berengar of Tours suggested that Christ's presence did not require a material change in the bread and wine, a Council held at Rome in 1079 required him to acknowledge that they *are* changed 'substantially', so that Christ's Body and Blood are present 'not just as signified and by a sacramental power, but in their true nature and the reality of their substance'. Such arguments led theologians to coin the term 'transubstantiation', which received official sanction at the Fourth Lateran Council in 1215.[7] The equivalent Greek term has been used by some Eastern theologians since the fifteenth century.

The theologians who coined the term 'transubstantiation' relied on the distinction drawn by the ancient Greek philosopher Aristotle between substance and accidents. Substance means something's inner being or basic nature, while the accidents are everything else about it, such as its qualities, size, position, and action on other things. So, when the bread and wine become Christ's Body and Blood, their inner being and nature are changed. But the accidents do not change, so we say that Christ is present under the appearance, or beneath the accidents, of bread and wine. The size, shape, colour and taste of the Host are the size, shape, colour and taste of the bread that used to be there. If someone drank a large quantity from the chalice, they would experience the intoxicating ability of the wine that had been there.

Attempts to explain the eucharistic change have limited value

It does not go against logic to say that the substance of the bread and wine are changed, while the accidents do not change. After all, when an animal dies, the size, colour and position of the corpse do not change at once, even though a corpse is a very different thing from a living body. Conversely, accidents can change while basic nature does not, so that the same cat can become fatter, or more placid. Nor are accidents always a good indication of substance; two seedlings that look similar may belong to different species. But simply to point out that accidents are not always a good guide to substance, risks implying that the appearances of bread and wine are a kind of disguise for Jesus; this reduces their rich symbolic value, since they are meant to *reveal* Jesus as our strength and joy, our peace and unity. Likewise, if we suppose that the terms 'substance' and 'accidents' explain the Eucharistic change we diminish the mystery of the Eucharist. Hence the Council of Trent (1545–63) recognized that human beings can hardly find words to express Christ's true and real presence in the Holy Eucharist, though this change is possible for God, and was taught by Christ. Trent affirmed that the term 'transubstantiation' is fitting,[8] but, by speaking of 'substance' and 'appearances' rather than 'substance' and 'accidents', the Council avoided imposing any one technical account of the Eucharistic change.

The Second Vatican Council reaffirmed Christ's unique form of presence in the Blessed Sacrament, which surpasses, but does not belittle, his other forms of presence in liturgy and sacraments.[9] Yet, around the time of the Second Vatican Council, some theologians worried that the term 'transubstantiation' was not only a misguided attempt to explain a mystery, but was also too closely tied to an outmoded theory of the natural world. They proposed a number of other ways of expressing Christ's presence, of which the most frequently used were 'transfinalization' – the consecration changes the use and purpose of the bread and wine; and 'transignification' – the consecration changes the meaning of the bread and wine for the community. Fairly obviously, these accounts also look like explanations that explain away the mystery! In 1965, Pope Paul VI entered into the debate with his Encyclical *Mysterium Fidei*. The Pope reaffirmed Christ's 'par excellence' presence in the Holy Eucharist and the value of the term 'transubstantiation'. He saw transfinalization and transignification as inadequate accounts of Christ's Eucharistic presence, and rejected some other accounts such as relying on a special quality of Christ's Risen Body that would allow it to be everywhere. Although the Eucharist is an efficacious sign of Christ's spiritual presence and intimate union with his faithful, to say no more than this loses the sense in which it surpasses other sacraments.

Thomas Aquinas on the Eucharistic change

St Thomas is known as a great defender of 'transubstantiation'; it is not always realized that he does not see it as explaining Christ's presence. He points out that creatures have limited power: human beings cannot bring things into being out of nothing, but can only alter existing things, using the range of natural possibilities (or 'potentialities') presented by those things. I can convert flour into bread by means of yeast and baking because flour has a natural potentiality to become bread. But a piece of bread has no natural potentiality to become the whole Body of Christ. God alone has power to bring things into being, without using anything already there, and his power extends into the depths of things. Hence God can and does change the whole being of the bread into the whole Body of Christ, and the whole being of the wine into his whole Blood. In the Eucharistic change, God works at the deepest level, where he alone can work. So this change is unique, and does not fit into any of the kinds of change that happen in the natural world. Therefore we cannot understand it, for to understand something is to fit it into what is familiar. It is not the change of one substance into another that Aristotle wrote about.[10] No powers of sense, no experiment, no angel, can tell that God has changed the bread and wine into Christ's Body and Blood. By faith alone can we tell that Jesus' words, 'This is my body', have had their effect.

But, as the sacrament of Jesus' friendship towards humanity, as his most home-ly way of being with his followers while they cannot see him as he is, Christ's presence in the Eucharist makes deep sense: it fits with everything else we believe about the divine self-giving, which always goes beyond what humanity strictly needs so as to give all God can give. The Eucharist recalls how, in the incarnation, God gave himself into the human family, rather than simply raising up a great prophet, and how, in the crucifixion, he gave himself to die for us, rather than simply living for us. Likewise, in the Eucharist, he gives himself, rather than simply employing a powerful symbol. Thereby he pledges that he will give him-self to his members to be seen and known when they share his glory.

Question for Reflection

- How helpful is it to speak of God 'changing the whole being of the bread and wine' or 'changing them at the deepest level'? Are there any viable alternatives?

Aspects of the Eucharistic Presence

It is useful to summarize several points in the Catholic understanding of Christ's presence in the Eucharist:

1 Bread and wine are not annihilated, to be replaced by Jesus' Body and Blood; they become them. Hence the stuff of this world, and the fruits of our labour, are not discarded, but ennobled.
2 The whole of Christ is present in each part of the sacrament. There is not a bit of Christ's Body in one Host, and another in another, but the whole of Christ's Body is present beneath each part of each Host.
3 Therefore breaking the Host does not mean Christ's Body is itself broken.
4 By the power of the sacrament, the bread becomes Christ's Body and the wine becomes his Blood; but because of the union of divinity and humanity in Christ, Christ-as-God is received in the Eucharist, as well as Christ-as-man. Further, the risen Jesus is beyond death, hence when his Body is received, so too are his Blood and Soul, and when his Blood is received, so too are his Body and Soul.
5 If you received many hosts, you would put on weight; if you drained a full chalice, you would get drunk. The nourishing power of bread, and the intoxicating power of wine, are among the accidents that remain.
6 Jesus' presence beneath the appearances of bread and wine remains while those appearances remain.

Holy Communion under one or both signs

During the Middle Ages it became usual for people other than the presiding bishop or priest to receive Holy Communion only under the form of bread. Since the 1960s the chalice has been offered more and more widely. The Order of Mass requires the consecration of both bread and wine, and the reception of the Eucharist under both forms by the bishop or priest who consecrates. This symbolizes Christ's giving of his Body and Blood on the cross, and the application of the power of this Sacrifice to the whole human being for the sake of eternal life and joy for body and soul. But it follows from points (2) and (4) above that if the congregation receive only under the form of bread, or a coeliac receives only under the form of wine, they receive the whole Christ. However, if it can be done safely and reverently, the richness of the Eucharist's symbolism is brought home more powerfully if the communicants receive under both forms.

Question for Reflection

- How widely should the chalice be offered? What reasons (of convenience, or health, etc.) might lead to people not receiving from the chalice?

Eucharistic reservation, adoration and Communion outside Mass

It follows from (6) in the text above that the Blessed Sacrament can be reverently reserved after Mass, usually in a special safe called a tabernacle, for the following purposes:

1 Communion of the sick who cannot attend Mass, and for the dying (this practice dates back to the very early Church). When the sick receive Holy Communion at home or in hospital, a short expression of repentance, a Scripture reading, and the Lord's Prayer, typically precede the reception, and a short prayer and blessing follow. Communion for the dying is called 'Viaticum', 'Food for the journey'. In this case the recipient is invited to renew his/her baptismal vows.

2 Communion in the church building, outside Mass. This takes several forms:
   - The 'Liturgy of the Presanctified Gifts' is celebrated by the Eastern Churches on Wednesdays and Fridays of Lent, so that Holy Communion may be received on days when the Eucharist is not consecrated. This ritual, of Scripture readings, intercessions and the giving of Holy Communion, is celebrated in the West only on Good Friday, with the addition of the solemn veneration of the cross.
   - A very simple ritual of a short expression of repentance, the Lord's Prayer, the reception of Holy Communion, and a short prayer and blessing, so that the faithful who want Communion but cannot attend Mass may receive it. This service was frequent into the 1960s.

- A 'Liturgy of the Word and Holy Communion' equivalent to the 'Liturgy of the Presanctified Gifts', used by a deacon or an authorized lay minister in places or on days when a priest is not available.

3 Adoration. Forms of adoration of the Sacred Host developed in the Middle Ages:

- Exposition, in which the Host is placed in a transparent small shrine called a 'monstrance' (i.e. a vessel for showing), so that people may see and adore it.
- Processions in which the Host is carried in a monstrance.
- Benediction, in which a bishop, priest or deacon raises the Host above the people in blessing.
- Private prayer in front of the tabernacle.

Such acts of Eucharistic adoration are an extension of the contemplative aspect of the Holy Eucharist: they allow worshippers to enter into the presence of the divine and to contemplate the drama of salvation. The adoration of the Host is not a substitute for receiving Holy Communion, but can foster a more reverent participation in the Eucharistic Sacrifice and a more fruitful reception of the sacrament.

Questions for Reflection

- If it is, as suggested, true that Eucharistic adoration is becoming widespread again, what does this phenomenon suggest?
- What might account for its reported popularity among some young people?

The Eucharistic Sacrifice

At the Last Supper, on the night he was betrayed, our Saviour instituted the **Eucharistic Sacrifice** of his Body and Blood. This he did in order to **perpetuate the Sacrifice of the Cross** throughout the ages until he should come again, and so as to entrust to his beloved Spouse, the Church, a **memorial of his Death and Resurrection**: 'a sacrament of love, a sign of unity, a bond of charity', a Paschal banquet . . . (Vatican II, *Sacrosanctum Concilium* 47, quoting Augustine, *Tractate 26 on John*, vi, 13)

An essential link between the events of Jesus' life, death and resurrection, the Liturgy, and the theme of sacrifice was drawn out in Chapter 1 of this book. As the above-quoted text from the Second Vatican Council draws out, that link becomes particularly intense in the Catholic understanding of the Eucharist. As the Council put it, the Catholic Church understands that linkage to permit one to speak of the Eucharist as a Sacrifice that does not add to, but somehow perpetuates, the Sacrifice offered on the cross. This immediately takes us into complex terrain that became a source of particular contention during the Reformation. It is, nonetheless, essential to a Catholic understanding of the Eucharist, and forms the second key theological theme explored by this chapter.

The sacrificial understanding of the Eucharist

Scriptural data

The Old Testament does not contain a single over-arching concept of 'sacrifice'. It does not describe a 'mechanism' by which sacrifices work; it does not, for example, say that someone's sin was transferred to the animal he offered, which then suffered the death due to him.[11] It very rarely uses the image of 'propitiating an angry God'. The Old Testament does describe a range of rituals, which are known by different names, none of which covers all of them. They comprise cereal and incense offerings as well as animal sacrifices; 'shared meals' in which God symbolically got the blood and fat, and the priests and worshippers other portions; symbolic gifts of whole animals; rituals to undo sin, guilt, or ritual uncleanness. The 'shared meals' spoke of joy, thanks, and community of life; sometimes they forged covenants. The Passover enabled the Jews to enter into the Exodus experience.

The New Testament presents Jesus' self-giving as achieving all that the Old Testament rituals sought but could not deliver: spiritual nourishment, peace and communion with God and one another, liberation from slavery to sin and death, access to God. The question arises at this stage what the link is between that self-giving of Jesus and the Eucharist; the answer would provide the foundation of a sacrificial understanding of the Eucharist. A Catholic response would begin by asking what Jesus understood himself to be doing at the Last Supper. The New Testament accounts present Jesus as using the language of self-giving and sacrifice, declaring the bread to be 'my body which is for you', and identifying the cup over which he gave thanks with 'my blood of the covenant'.[12] 'Blood of the covenant' alludes to the covenant-sacrifice in Exodus 24.3–8.

In John's account, towards the end of the Last Supper Jesus consecrates himself so that his followers, too, may be consecrated – in that Supper he dedicated himself as a Sacrifice so that others could be caught up in his Sacrifice. This reflects what happened at the beginning of the Supper: Jesus washed his disciples' feet as an exemplar of self-giving, and even as a commitment to the kind of death meted out to slaves. John does not recount the institution of the Eucharist; perhaps he felt something so precious and so mysterious should not be committed to writing and made available to just anyone.[13] But assuming he expected any Christian readers to know that Jesus did institute the Eucharist at the Last Supper, his account suggests that what Jesus did and said at the Last Supper, including the celebration of the Eucharist, was a commitment to his passion, which would establish his followers as the New Vine.

St Paul also draws an essential connection between the Eucharist and the sacrificial death of Christ when he writes, 'as often as you eat this bread and drink the cup, you proclaim the Lord's death' (1 Cor. 11.26). The letter to the Hebrews (13.10, 15–16) says we have an altar from which those who serve the Tabernacle have no right to eat, and urges the readers to offer up a sacrifice of praise by acknowledging God's Name and living sacrificially. Both texts suggest that the Eucharistic Sacrifice must inspire a pattern of life modelled on Jesus' Sacrifice.

Early liturgy and theology

Sacrificial themes appear in very early Christian liturgy. Thus, the Roman Canon (Eucharistic Prayer I) uses sacrificial language throughout, and one of its oldest sections refers to the Old Testament sacrifices of Abel, Abraham and Melchizedek as types of the Eucharistic sacrifice of the Church. The sacrificial themes that gradually came together to underpin the Catholic understanding of the Eucharist as sacrifice include:

1 The offering of the Christian's whole life in union with Christ (cf. Rom. 12.1; Heb. 13.15–16).
2 Worship as a sacrifice of praise and thanksgiving.
3 The offering of bread and wine as first-fruits of creation.
4 The anamnesis (commemoration) of Christ's Sacrifice and (usually) of his resurrection.
5 The offering of Christ to God the Father by the Church or bishop.
6 Propitiation and intercession.[14]

For St Augustine, Christ is the Priest who offers the Sacrifice as well as the sacrifice that is offered. The Eucharist is the sacrament of Christ's Sacrifice on the cross, and the Church's Sacrifice; it teaches us, and somehow incorporates our self-offering into Christ's:

> The true Mediator, the man Christ Jesus, became the Mediator between God and men insofar as he took the form of a slave . . . in the form of a slave he preferred to be Sacrifice rather than to receive sacrifice . . . Therefore he is also Priest; he is the offerer, and he is the offering. He willed the Church's Sacrifice to be the daily sacrament of this reality; since she is one body with her Head, she learns to offer herself through him. (*City of God*, X, xxi)

Anamnesis

Of the themes in the text above, (4) is the most important for a liturgical theology. To gain some sense of what 'commemoration' is, one has to move beyond concepts of 'nostalgia' and 'reminiscing' and notice how even at the human level people bear absent loved ones in mind and heart. People publicly commemorate events that have formed and – with the help of these ceremonies – continue to form their societies. In the Old Testament the commemoration of the Exodus events kept them alive even more powerfully, chiefly because the Covenants forged between the people and their timeless, ever-living God were an enduring reality that nurtured them. Those Covenants were affirmed, fulfilled and surpassed by Jesus' Sacrifice as the New and Eternal Covenant; and in his risen humanity Jesus is ever-living and ever-filling his Body, the Church, with the Spirit, while he bears his people in his heart. The celebration of the Eucharist is not a 'Passion Play' (emotionally powerful though a good Passion Play is). Nor is it a distant re-enactment of a past meal. It makes Christ's Sacrifice present to the participants – both the Sacrifice of Calvary, and Christ's ongoing heavenly intercession and thanksgiving. This is done in a way that can be felt in faith, but is difficult to express in words. Time and space collapse, and at Mass the assembly stand by Jesus' cross, and with the disciples in the upper room, and in heaven, and at the Last Judgement. All this makes sense, if the role of the Holy Spirit discussed in Chapter 2 is taken into consideration.

Reaffirmation

The teaching that the Mass is a Sacrifice was rejected by Luther, probably in reaction to some strands of late medieval theology and devotion rather than in reaction to, say, Aquinas' theology. That rejection was shared by all the Protestant Reformers. In response, the Council of Trent reaffirmed the traditional Catholic position that the Mass is a sacrifice:

> It was fitting for God, the Father of mercies, to ordain that another priest should arise according to the order of Melchizedek, Our Lord Jesus Christ . . . True, he was to offer himself once to God the Father on the altar of the Cross . . . But since his priesthood was not to be extinguished by his death, at the Last Supper . . . he left his beloved bride, the Church, a visible sacrifice such as human nature needs. This was to represent that sacrifice, accomplished once on the Cross, in which he shed his Blood; so that its memory should endure to the end of the age; and so that its saving power might be applied to the remission of those sins we commit daily . . . he offered his Body and Blood to God the Father beneath the appearances of bread and wine . . . and commanded [the Apostles] and their successors in the priesthood to offer them

... This therefore is that offering which the types prefigured ... In this divine sacrifice which is enacted in the Mass, the same Christ is contained, and is offered without the shedding of blood, who offered himself once on the altar of the cross with the shedding of blood. Hence the holy Synod teaches that this sacrifice is truly propitiatory ... For the sacrifice is one and the same: the one who now offers himself by the ministry of priests, is the same who then offered himself on the Cross – only the manner of offering differs.[15]

Trent made it clear that the Eucharistic Sacrifice does not diminish the efficacy of Christ's Sacrifice on the cross; on the contrary, it is an effect of its immense efficacy, a consequence of the permanence of Jesus' own Priesthood and the enduring power of his Sacrifice. Trent also carefully steered clear of the theological opinion Luther was chiefly afraid of – namely, that the Church or the priest offers Christ to God the Father independently of, or alongside, Christ's self-offering. Trent, and authentic Catholic theology, see the Sacrifice of the Mass as Christ's own self-offering, somehow performed through the ministry of priests. As in many of its documents, Trent left room for all legitimate schools of theology, and so did not give a definition of 'sacrifice', nor lay down a 'mechanism' by which the Mass fulfils this definition. Trent's teaching was reaffirmed in the mid twentieth century by Pope Pius XII, who also brought out the participation in the Sacrifice of all the faithful:

All the faithful should be aware that to participate in the Eucharistic sacrifice is their chief duty and supreme dignity ... 'the priests offer the sacrifice, but also all the faithful: for what the priest does personally by virtue of his ministry, the faithful do collectively by virtue of their intention'.[16]

The conviction that in the Mass Jesus' Sacrifice is truly offered, and its power applied to particular people, led to the practice of asking a priest to offer Mass for a particular intention, and of making an offering on that occasion – not to purchase the Mass, but to enable the ongoing provision of Masses. This custom has endured from the early Middle Ages to the present day.

How is the Eucharist a sacrifice?

Aquinas' account

When showing that Christ is sacrificed in the Eucharist (*Tertia Pars* 83, 1), Aquinas took for granted his idea that sacrifice is a formal present given to God, which expresses repentance, prayer and praise, and enables us to live sacrificially. He focused on how the Eucharist relates to *Jesus'* Sacrifice by:

1 Symbolic representation: the Eucharist represents Christ's Sacrifice.
2 Application: the celebration of the Eucharist channels the fruits of Christ's Sacrifice to us.

Of these, (1) is not unique to the Eucharist. The Old Testament sacrifices prophetically represented Christ's Sacrifice, and each sacrament symbolizes it (and the whole Paschal Mystery) in some way or other. However, (2) is indeed unique to the Eucharist. While all the Christian sacraments channel the power of Christ's Sacrifice to those who receive them, the Eucharist also channels it to those for whom the Mass is offered, whether present or not, whether living or dead. This is an immense claim: the consecration of the Eucharist applies the saving power of Christ's Sacrifice to those participating, to those mentioned in the Eucharistic Prayer, and, with special intensity, to those for whom each priest consecrating the Eucharist intends to offer the Sacrifice. The Prayer over the Gifts for the second Sunday of Ordinary Time says: 'Whenever the memorial of this sacrifice is celebrated the work of our redemption is accomplished.'

In summary, we can say:

- Christ's self-giving in his passion is the central saving event which gives meaning to all valid religious activity, and shows up all idolatry and all false attempts to manipulate the true God.
- The Eucharist brings Jesus' Sacrifice home to us, by a rich and dense symbolism.
- The Eucharist channels the saving power of Christ's Sacrifice to the participants and to all those for whom it is offered, living and dead.
- Jesus' Sacrifice on the cross is somehow perpetuated in the Eucharist through his ministers.
- The Eucharist inspires, empowers and incorporates the Church's and the Christian's self-offering.
- Jesus' Sacrifice, and its prolongation in the Eucharist, fulfil and surpass all valid sacrifices that God had inspired or commanded. The cross and the Eucharist achieve all that those sacrifices yearned for.

The Trinitarian dynamic of the Eucharistic Sacrifice

The Eucharist gives the Spirit

If we compare John 7.37–39 and 16.7 with 19.30, 34–37 we see that when Jesus 'bowed his head and handed over the Spirit', he fulfilled his promise to send the Paraclete. This gift was symbolized by the Blood-and-Water – that is, Living Water– that flowed when he was pierced. By revealing the Father's love, Jesus' passion and death were the perfect channel for the Holy Spirit, the Divine Love in person, to come into the world. This important effect of Jesus' Sacrifice is perpetuated in the Eucharist. Hence Eucharistic Prayers II, III and IV pray that participating in Christ's Body and Blood we may be gathered into unity by the Holy Spirit; that being refreshed by Christ's Body and Blood we may be filled with his Holy Spirit; that those who partake of the one Bread and one Chalice may be gathered into one body by the Holy Spirit and so perfected in Christ into a living sacrifice.

The Spirit gives the Eucharist

Early theologians, Eastern and Western, attributed the change of bread and wine into Christ's Body and Blood to the power of his words. As the Eternal Word, Jesus brought all things into being; therefore the words he uttered in the flesh have the power to change the being of things. His words, 'This is my body' have the power to be true.

Early Eucharistic Prayers often invoked the Spirit on the participants after they commemorated Christ's passion, death, resurrection and ascension, since Pentecost was the outcome of Jesus' Sacrifice. The Catholic Eucharistic Prayers II, III and IV do the same today. In the fourth century, in the East, this invocation of the Spirit was enlarged, in order to emphasize the Holy Spirit's Divinity, which had become a matter of controversy, with the result that the Spirit was called on to effect the Eucharistic Change – but after the Words of Institution had been spoken. Eucharistic Prayers II, III and IV call on the Holy Spirit to effect the Eucharistic Change before the Words of Institution. This matches the historical order of the saving events, since Christ's conception took place by the power of the Holy Spirit: the Spirit who overshadowed Mary so that Christ's Body would be formed in her, overshadows the altar so that the same Body becomes present. Jesus' humanity is both the gift of the Spirit, and the channel by which the Spirit overflows to us.

Question for Reflection

- How useful is it to bring out that in the celebration of the Eucharist we receive not only Jesus, but also the Holy Spirit?

Holy Communion augments our union with Christ. The principal fruit of receiving the Eucharist in Holy Communion is an intimate union with Christ Jesus. Indeed, the Lord said: 'He who eats my flesh and drinks my blood abides in me, and I in him.' Life in Christ has its foundation in the Eucharistic banquet: 'As the living Father sent me, and I live because of the Father, so he who eats me will live because of me' (Catechism of the Catholic Church 1391, quoting John 6.56–57).

The Eucharist makes the Church

The ultimate grace and purpose of this sacrament is to make those who participate in it into the Body of Christ – Christians receive his Body so as to be his Body, which implies sharing his mission in some way. Hence the Eucharist is the third of the Sacraments of Initiation: receiving it for the first time brings one fully into Christ's Body.

At a visible level, it is the hierarchically structured Church that performs the Eucharist. In a deeper sense, however, and as explored in Chapter 1, Jesus himself performs it through his ministers, in and for his Body. So, the best 'icon' of the Church is found when the bishop, representing Christ, celebrates Mass, assisted by clergy and faithful. This ceremony manifests the Church, gathered into one by the power of the sacrificed and risen Christ, and animated by the Holy Spirit, whose coming is the fruit of Jesus' Sacrifice. Within a fragmented and divided humanity, that vision takes on a broader and more urgent relevancy. Jesus' Sacrifice has made our peace (Eph. 2.13–16), and is the New and Eternal Covenant, the great act of God's love and loyalty. Since this is made present and active in the Eucharist, St Augustine hails it: 'O sacrament of devotion! O sign of unity! O bond of charity!'[17] The Church's unity must be preserved in charity – that is, in the Holy Spirit (cf. Eph. 4.1–6) – for the Spirit can be seen as the Divine Love in Person. Moreover, the unity of the Church, expressed above all in the Eucharist, should be a sign to humanity of its own hope, its own destiny.

The importance of visibility and the impulse towards unity also inform the Catholic Church's broad position of not admitting people from other branches of the Christian family to the Eucharist. To some, the Catholic Church's position may appear counterintuitive. After all, if the Eucharist is understood as bringing about unity, it can surely seem desirable for Christians who are not fully united to celebrate it together, as a means of becoming united. Yet, the Catholic Church's constant practice has been to resist this conclusion. If people come together to receive Holy Communion, while intending to go away remaining members of different Churches or bodies of Christians, then can we say that their intention here and now is truly to receive the full unity in faith, hope and charity that the Sacrament is intended to effect? From a Catholic perspective, it is only when that visible, tangible unity is in place that there can be common participation in the Eucharist. (It should be noted that in cases of serious personal need the Church relaxes her rule on this matter. See, for example, the Catechism of the Catholic Church 1398–1401.)

Questions for Reflection

- Is this the best way to defend the Church's discipline concerning intercommunion?
- Can you suggest others?

The Eucharist is a sacrament both of unity and of mission. This finds expression in the abrupt manner in which the Roman Rite of Mass traditionally ends. After the reception of Holy Communion, a brief prayer is recited by the priest, a blessing is given, and the congregation is told to go: '*Ite, missa est.*' Receiving Christ's Body sends them out to be Christ's Body in and for the world.

The Eucharist and the Christian's Journey

The Church encourages her members to receive the Eucharist frequently, even daily. It strengthens them as members of Christ, building them up in faith, hope and love, so that they may fulfil their calling to be Christ's members, and imitate his self-giving. It forms them as peace-makers. Hence it is both grace and challenge.

The Eucharist should be received with reverence and an openness to its grace. Hence those who are in 'a state of mortal sin' should not receive it until they have received the Sacrament of Reconciliation. That is, those guilty of some major act or omission that is incompatible with charity are not understood to be open to the grace of the Eucharist until they have formally repented and been reconciled to the community. This is analogous to the way human relationships work. We regularly let each other down in small ways that do not imply we do not love one another. We do not need to apologize on each of these occasions; the many ways in which we *do* express love and care are a daily antidote to such failures. Likewise, Catholics need not refrain from receiving Holy Communion if they are guilty only of what are called 'venial sins' – on the contrary, the Eucharist is an antidote to such sins. But if someone seriously betrays a friend or spouse, he or she cannot carry on as if nothing much had happened. A formal apology and reconciliation is needed. Likewise, after a sin that counts as a serious betrayal of God's love, one cannot pretend that nothing much has happened. Catholics guilty of such sins are urged to use the process of formal apology and reconciliation that God has provided, namely the Sacrament of Reconciliation, and in that way return to the reception of Holy Communion.

As a sign of reverence, the Church requires its members to fast from ordinary food for a period before receiving Holy Communion. Currently, given the demands of contemporary life, this period is only one hour. But turning from ordinary food before receiving the supernatural food that is a pledge of future glory reminds us that the Eucharist is not 'the food that perishes, but for the food that endures to eternal life'; it is 'the bread that comes down from heaven, so that one may eat of it and not die' (John 6.27, 50). The Eucharist is the New Manna, food for the journey. It sustains the Church while it is on pilgrimage, and empowers its members to lay hold off the goal of our pilgrimage. That is why the Church desires that those who are dying receive Holy Communion as Viaticum, as Food for the Journey. The life-giving flesh of Jesus enables his members to rise from the dead and live for ever. For the moment, the appearances of bread and wine both reveal and veil the risen Jesus, but in the Kingdom he shall be seen as he is. He who feeds his followers now with his Body and Blood will then feed us – make us live – with the clear vision of his Father, in the unity of the Holy Spirit, the personal divine love and joy.

Notes

1　*Summa Theologiae, Tertia Pars*, Q. 65, art. 3.

2　See the Catechism of the Catholic Church, 1328–1332, and *Tertia Pars*, 73, 4.

3　E.g. the Prayer over the Gifts for the Saturday after Ash Wednesday speaks of *sacrificium placationis et laudis*, 'the sacrifice of conciliation and praise'.

4　Prayer over the Gifts for the twentieth Sunday of Ordinary Time.

5　A detailed theory of the development of patterns of Eucharistic celebration on the basis of Jewish liturgy was proposed by Louis Bouyer (*Eucharist: Theology and Spirituality of the Eucharistic Prayer*, Notre Dame, IN: 1968). More recent scholarship has been more reticent about reconstructing such processes, but has tended to reaffirm the influence of Jewish cycles of scriptural readings.

6 In Catholic Eucharistic doctrine, a version of Jesus' words is the 'form', the essential spoken element of the Sacrament. Bread and wine are its 'matter'; a validly ordained bishop or priest is the minister.

7 Heinrich Denzinger, 2012, *Compendium of Creeds, Definitions, and Declarations on Matters of Faith and Morals* (hereafter DS) (San Francisco, CA: Ignatius Press), 700 and 802 for the texts of these Councils.

8 Session 13 (1551), Decree on the Most Holy Eucharist, chapter 4 (DS 1642).

9 *SC*, 7.

10 For all this, see *Tertia Pars* Qu. 75, articles 4 and 8.

11 The only Old Testament ritual in which sin is transferred is the scapegoat (Lev. 16.10, 20–22). This is not a sacrifice, nor is it killed, nor is it referred to in the New Testament as a type of Christ.

12 1 Cor. 11.24; Luke 22.19; Mark 14.24; Matt. 26.28.

13 John 13—17. John 20.31 seems to imply he was writing for those who were not yet Christians.

14 For a succinct account, with quotations, see Paul Bradshaw, *Early Christian Worship: A Basic Introduction to Ideas and Practice* (second edition, London: SPCK, 2010), specifically chapters 7 and 9, 'Anamnesis and Epiclesis' and 'The Bloodless Sacrifice'.

15 *Doctrine concerning the Most Holy Sacrifice of the Mass*, Session 22, 1562.

16 *MD*, 86, quoting Innocent III, *De Sacro Altaris Mysterio*, 3.6.

17 St Augustine, Sermon 272, cited in Catechism of the Catholic Church 1396, 1398.

9

Sacraments at the Service of Communion

MARTIN FOSTER AND PETER MCGRAIL

Introduction

Having explored the three Sacraments of Christian Initiation, we now consider two sacraments that support the organic unity of the Body of Christ, and consequently are described by the Catholic Church as being 'at the service of Communion'. The dimension of unity is clearly evident in the case of the first, which is Marriage; in the midst of a human family that all too frequently is marked by division and fragmentation, this sacrament celebrates the gift that two people make of themselves to each other, and their unity of life. Not only is this a very practical action that draws two lives together; it is also a symbolic action that offers a powerful image of the unity of Christ with his Church, and indeed of God's plan for the unity of the whole of creation. The second sacrament 'at the service of communion' is that of Orders; what will be studied here are the rites of the Ordination of Bishops, Presbyters (commonly spoken of as 'priests') and Deacons. These ordained ministers serve the communion of the Church by celebrating its sacraments, guiding its life and mission, and fostering above all a spirit of charity within it. The chapter will first consider the sacrament of Marriage and then will move to Ordination.

Marriage

Introduction

And they lived happily ever after. The end of many a fairytale is the wedding of the prince and princess. It brings the story to completion and order has been restored. These stories express human aspirations that in marriage the true partner is found, that love can flourish, that the good order of society is built up and its continuation, through the potential children of the marriage, is assured. Society has always had a stake in marriage which has evolved over the centuries. Though the romantic image of the true love would now be the norm, historically and across different classes and cultures the reality has been very different with marriage often being seen as a dynastic or business contract between families.

Consenting to a new contract is at the heart of both the Church's and the state's understanding of marriage. Two parties, freely and without outside interference, agree to make a new life together. 'I, John Smith, take thee Mary Brown to be my wedded wife.' In this statement of giving oneself to another the Church sees an image of the relationship of Christ to the Church, often described in the close intimate terms of being like that of a bride and bridegroom. The experience of love is a glimpse into the eternal love that is the foundation of the Trinity. This image is also one of the Covenant between God and the people he has chosen to remain faithful and so the bond of marriage is a lifelong commitment. Marriage is found in the story of creation where Eve is formed of Adam – they are of one flesh. The purpose of marriage is two-fold: the deepening love and companionship of the couple, and the openness to human life in the procreation of children.

The Catholic Church's understanding of marriage as a lifelong commitment between a man and woman that is open to the gift of children has for centuries shaped social attitudes and been shared by civil society. Over the last century, however, Western societies have in various ways moved away from this understanding, and a very different understanding of commitment and of family formation has become widely diffused. Yet, there are still many people who seek to be married in church. Whether or not they easily may articulate it (and Marriage Preparation plays an important part here), by requesting a marriage in church, a couple are seeking God's blessing on their new beginning, and at least implicitly stating that in their hopes and aspirations for the future God has a part to play. This last point reminds us that when focusing on the celebration of the sacraments there is a danger in regarding them as endpoints and goals rather than as an outpouring of God's grace for a new beginning.

The Rite

Order of Celebrating Matrimony

History
Ordo Celebrandi Matrimonium
- Editio typica, 1969
- Editio typica altera, 1991

Rite of Marriage
- 1969

Order of Celebrating Matrimony
- 2015 (Catholic Truth Society)

Contents
Introduction
1   The Order of Celebrating Matrimony within Mass
2   The Order of Celebrating Matrimony without Mass
3   The Order of Celebrating Matrimony in the Presence of an Assisting Layperson
4   The Order of Celebrating Matrimony between a Catholic and a Catechumen or a Non-Christian
5   Various Texts to be used in the Rite of Marriage and in the Mass for the Celebration of Marriage

Appendices
1   Examples of the Universal Prayer
2   The Order of Blessing of an Engaged Couple
3   The Order of Blessing of a Married Couple within Mass on the Anniversary of Marriage
4   Order of Celebrating Marriage: Form for Use at Convalidation

---

The *Order of Celebrating Matrimony* (henceforth, *OCM*) was published in England and Wales in 2016. It is the English translation of the second edition of the post-conciliar rite. The first edition was published in England and Wales in 1969 and marked an adoption of the Roman Rite for marriage that hitherto had not been used. Among the various sacramental rites Marriage is unique in allowing for a completely local rite to be drawn up. Until 1969 this country had continued with the medieval Sarum Use. Though in broad structural terms there were substantial differences, what Sarum had offered was a highly influential language of Marriage. The Sarum words of consent (see below) are the basis of the texts of most English-speaking denominations and, more than that, provided a text for the revisers of the post-conciliar rite and so entered the Roman Rite in Latin. (It is worth noting that the words spoken by the couple were always in the vernacular.) Though, despite some previous efforts, there has not been a restored local rite for England and Wales, the 2016 text does include some further texts from the Sarum heritage.

Who celebrates?

Before looking at some specific aspects of the text it may be interesting to consider the range of people who are involved in the liturgy.

The couple

Weddings involve a couple: a bride and a groom. The wedding represents a significant point, indeed a turning point, in their relationship. It marks a beginning and an ending, and therefore one of the ways of approaching the texts of the rite is to view the relationship of the couple according to past, present and future perspectives. The couple will have, in old-fashioned terms, courted, become engaged and then in marriage they are committing to a lifelong service to each other.

The presumed starting point for the rite is that the parties are both Catholics. However, the different chapters of the *OCM* recognize that this is not the only possible case, and so the rite presents a range of adaptations that take into account a breadth of different circumstances – especially providing for when a Catholic is marrying another baptized Christian or someone who is unbaptized.

The spouse in this last case might be someone of another faith, of no faith or even a catechumen awaiting Baptism. Anyone with experience of weddings in the Catholic Church will know that all these liturgical variations are necessary to meet the needs of the variety of couples seeking Marriage in a Catholic church.

In the Roman Rite the couple are the ministers of the sacrament. The Catechism expands on this concept by stating that 'the spouses as ministers of Christ's grace mutually confer upon each other the sacrament of Matrimony by expressing their consent before the Church'.[1] The sacrament is 'mutually conferred' by the couple – and for marriage to be valid both bride and groom are required freely to give their consent to it: within the rite they enjoy complete equality. In the Eastern Christian traditions the same emphasis on consent is to be found, but the blessing of the priest is also necessary.

The Presider

A priest or a deacon is the liturgical minister at a Catholic wedding in England and Wales; a deacon may preside at a wedding without Mass. The role of the presider is to witness and receive the consent of the couple on behalf of the Church. That is to describe the priest's or deacon's role at a minimal level. They will not only preside over the liturgy but usually through the time of preparation will have got to know the couple and helped them articulate and deepen their faith and love for each other.

OCM includes a chapter 'The Order of Celebrating Matrimony in the presence of an Assisting Layperson' (Chapter III). This is the provision for when neither a priest nor a deacon is available. This is currently not an option in England and Wales, as there is no pressing pastoral need, in part due to the fact that weddings are planned months in advance. Indeed, if it were to be implemented it would require specific permission from the Holy See. However, the text has a wider interest, as the first text in the liturgical books which sets out the liturgical adaptations required when a layperson presides. For example, the dialogue that normally precedes the Gospel, of 'The Lord be with you . . . A reading from . . ', is replaced by the exhortation, 'Listen, brothers and sisters, to the words of the Holy Gospel according to N.' It is useful also to compare the different terms used to describe the person who presides at the liturgy in the various chapters of *OCM*:

I   priest

II minister (i.e. priest or deacon)

III assisting layperson

IV the one who presides (i.e. priest or deacon, but also a layperson where permitted)

The assembly

The spectrum of possible couples marrying in church ranges from two committed Catholics to a Catholic who does not attend church marrying someone of no faith at all. Not surprisingly, this same spectrum will be reflected and amplified in those who attend the wedding. The assembly will usually comprise family and friends and so the relationship with the Church and the familiarity with its worship can be extraordinarily varied. It will be increasingly the case that for some people present this may be their first time in a church. Nonetheless, the rite regards this unusual assembly as having a four-fold liturgical role:

- To join the couple in giving thanks to God.
- To pray for the couple and their future life together.
- To be witnesses to the marriage.
- To offer support for the couple both through their participation in the liturgy and over the years to come.

Taking into account the varied backgrounds from which members of the assembly will be drawn, while also respecting the expectations of the formal rite, can create a challenge for the minister who has to welcome those present and facilitate their appropriate participation in the liturgy. The challenge that this can present is exemplified by one of the additions in the new edition of the Marriage rite, an acclamation that the assembly is invited to make after the minister has received the consent of the couple. The acclamation takes the form of a dialogue, 'Let us bless the Lord', 'Thanks be to God'. It is fair to suggest that even to a regular Sunday Mass-goer this would be an unfamiliar response, at least in this context. Although the rite allows for 'another acclamation to be sung or said', what will happen at many celebrations is a round of applause, a custom that entered into practice before the publication of the new edition. In a liturgical context, this applause gives rise to a significant question: exactly who is being applauded? From the perspective of a contemporary Western culture that celebrates achievement, this applause could be understood as an affirmation of the couple for getting this far; however, within the liturgical context all praise and thanksgiving is addressed to God alone. The challenge for the presider who invites applause at this point, therefore, is to shift the focus from the couple to the Creator.

There is a related tension in understanding a wedding as an ecclesial act. This is not to doubt that those seeking to get married in church do wish to receive God's blessing upon their marriage. Rather, the dimension that can be missing from the celebration itself is that of the wider Church – even if by that just the local parish community is understood. How does a Saturday afternoon wedding relate to parish Mass on Sunday morning? Theologically, a range of responses can immediately spring to mind, most notably that the union of life represented in the wedding directly relates to the notion of communion at the heart of the Eucharist. But how that might be experienced by many couples – and regular Mass-goers – alike is debatable.

The registrar

The last person who plays a formal role in the marriage is the civil registrar, or the 'Authorized Person' who delegates for them. England and Wales enjoy a unique relationship between Church and state with regard to marriage. In other countries, either the state recognizes that what the Church does fulfils the civil requirements, or the civil and religious dimensions are completely separated – for example, in many places the couple are required to sign the civil register in the Town Hall before they go on to hold a church wedding. In England and Wales, on the other hand, the civil and religious requirements are intertwined, and civil texts provided by the state are incorporated within the marriage liturgy. There are two points where this occurs: in the last of the questions asked of the couple before the consent, 'Are you free lawfully to marry?' and in the initial phrase of the consent itself, 'I, John Smith, take you, Mary Jones, to be my wedded wife'.

Marriage within Mass

This is the first of the rites provided by *OCM*, and is intended to be used at the marriage of two baptized Catholics. It offers the normative form of the wedding rite, though its key elements are common to all celebrations. Following the general pattern found in the celebration of other sacraments, the celebration of Marriage itself follows the proclamation of the Word.

The Order of Celebrating Matrimony within Mass

The Introductory Rites
Entrance
Sign of the Cross and Greeting
Introduction
Penitential Act omitted
Gloria
Collect
The Liturgy of the Word
The Celebration of Marriage
Introduction
The Questions before the Consent
The Civil Declaration of Freedom
The Consent
The Reception of the Consent
Acclamation by All
The Blessing and Giving of Rings
Hymn
Universal Prayer
Liturgy of the Eucharist
Preparation of Gifts
Eucharistic Prayer
Including Commemoration for husband and wife
Communion Rite
Our Father
Nuptial Blessing
Sign of Peace
Communion

> **The Conclusion of the Celebration**
> Blessing
> Signing of Register

The entrance

The rite offers a number of options for how the liturgy can begin. The first set relate to the position of the priest at the start of the celebration: does he welcome the couple at the church door, or does he greet them when they have arrived at their places inside the church? The other option concerns who takes part in the procession. The tradition of the Roman Rite is that everyone, the bride and groom, attendants, family and friends, arrives at the door of the church together, and are welcomed there. In the English-speaking world, however, the expectation is that it should only be the bride who formally processes into church, accompanied by her father and attendants. In the rite the term 'bridal party' is intended to allow for both options.

> **Questions for Reflection**
>
> Imagine a wedding beginning with the entrance of the bride and another beginning with the entrance of bride and groom and families.
>
> - What differences would you notice?
> - How might it affect the beginning of the liturgy?
> - Why might you choose one over the other?

The place of custom

The question of the procession touches on a larger issue about the place of custom in marriage traditions and how it interacts with the liturgical rite. The image of weddings that people have can be shaped by a wide range of sources, and these can include ideas drawn from popular culture or the previous experience of the weddings of friends. It can come as a surprise that elements that many people regard as key are not to be found in the rite of Marriage – such as the wearing of a bridal veil, its formal lifting, or the invitation to the groom to kiss the bride. The Introduction to *OCM* recognizes that there are traditions that may be adopted, but cautions that they need to be the subject of careful and prudent consideration. Such a consideration might include the following questions:

- What are the meanings or significances of the custom?
- How do these reflect the meaning of Marriage presented by the Church?
- What is the significance of its proposed place within the rite?
- How does it affect the flow and focus of the liturgy?

The consent

At the heart of the wedding is the exchange of consent by the couple which 'makes the marriage'.

> I, A.B., take you (thee), C.D., to be my wedded wife/husband, to have and to hold from this day forward, for better, for worse, for richer, for poorer, in sickness and in health, to love and to cherish till death do us part.

As previously noted, the origin of this text is medieval England. It is worth considering this in a number of ways. First of all, as a 'cultural object'. Many people, whether married or not, will recognize these words and be able to complete each line if prompted. This is in part due to its longevity but also it is memorable because of its rhythm and the simplicity of its language – it is a crafted text. Not only have its phrases been taken up by popular culture, but it has shaped how marriage is understood.

Although it is not a prayer, and God is not mentioned, the consent is nonetheless a liturgical text. In the life of sacrificial love that it sets before the couple and in its explicit mention of death itself, it gives clear expression to their intention to model their lives together after Christ's Paschal Mystery. More, indeed, is going on here than a modelling – because of the liturgical context in which they speak it, the couple set their faces towards a progressive, lifelong participation in the Paschal Mystery. For other married couples in the assembly, the public declaration of this text will invite a dimension of anamnesis. This familiar text has the power to evoke not only a recollection of their wedding day, but also of all that has passed since then, inviting the recognition of how life in all its riches and complexities has been named in this text.

The consent is also a ritual text. It is a very clear example of a performative text – it does what it says it will do. In saying these words to each other John Smith and Mary Jones really do take each other as wedded husband and wife.

> These various aspects of the consent point to a liturgical principle often expressed in Latin as *Lex orandi, lex credendi* – this means the law (or rule) of prayer, the law of belief, or what we say in liturgy is an expression of the belief of the Church. Some liturgical theologians take this further and see the liturgy of the Church as its first or primary theology. Sometimes a further addition is made: *lex orandi, lex credendi, lex vivendi*. How we pray shapes what we believe and how we live. CCC, 1124

The consent once given is received by the priest who then invites the congregation to express their praise of God by a short acclamation (already discussed). This is followed by the illustrative or explanatory ritual of the Blessing and Giving of Rings.

The Nuptial Blessing

Holy Father, maker of the whole world,
who created man and woman in your own image
and willed that their union be crowned with your blessing,
we humbly beseech you for these your servants,
who are joined today in the Sacrament of Matrimony.

May your abundant blessing, Lord,
come down upon this bride, N.,
and upon N., her companion for life,
and may the power of your Holy Spirit
set their hearts aflame from on high,
so that, living out together the gift of Matrimony,
they may adorn their family with children
and enrich the Church.

In happiness may they praise you, O Lord,
in sorrow may they seek you out;
may they have the joy of your presence
to assist them in their toil,
and know that you are near
to comfort them in their need;
let them pray to you in the holy assembly
and bear witness to you in the world,
and after a happy old age,
together with the circle of friends that surrounds them,
may they come to the Kingdom of Heaven.
Through Christ our Lord.
R. Amen.

Question for Reflection

• Think of a married couple you know. How would you express the
ideas of this blessing for them in your own words?

Marriage without Mass

The structure of Marriage without Mass is very similar to Marriage with Mass up
to the end of the Celebration of Marriage. The Liturgy of Eucharist is omitted,
and the Nuptial Blessing follows on from the intercessions. The rite concludes
with the Lord's Prayer and blessing. Though the rite allows for Holy Communion to be distributed, this would be exceptional.

Marriage without Mass is intended to be used for a couple where one is a
Catholic and the other baptized into another Christian denomination. It can be
difficult for Catholics who are used to Sunday Mass as their principal liturgical experience to appreciate the reasons for choosing Marriage without Mass.
The reasons are based on the fundamental question of participation. Mass demands a more intense congregational participation than other liturgies, but at
play here is a more fundamental question than whether the people who come
to a wedding would be familiar with the Gloria or know when to stand or kneel

during the Eucharistic Prayer. For a Catholic, participation in the Mass leads to the reception of Holy Communion. If the majority of those present are not able to participate in Holy Communion, then Marriage without Mass is the proper option. Otherwise, what should be a moment of unity – literally, communion – highlights instead the incomplete nature of communion among Christians, as one spouse only and their family and friends are able to receive the Body and Blood of Christ, while the other spouse can not.

Marriage preparation

Those who are getting married are encouraged to participate in a preparation course. Such preparation programmes will present the Church's theology of marriage and will also seek to help couples to understand and appreciate their relationship – so that they will be able to make connections between their marriage and the life and mission of the wider Church.

Couples will also be involved in the preparation of their wedding liturgy. This can involve choosing the form, considering the readings, reflecting on the marriage texts and identifying possible music. Choosing from the readings proposed by the Church for the celebration of Marriage can itself prove to be an important aspect of the overall preparation. As the couple look at the various options presented to them, they may not only discover how differently they respond to them, but the encounter with this focused body of scriptural passages can also give rise to questions that can help them explore their relationship.

Help in preparing the wedding liturgy will often be given by the celebrant and also by the musicians. Both celebrant and musicians can frequently face the pastoral challenge of balancing the wishes of the couple and the requirements of the liturgy. The inclusion of some songs, for example, may cut across the flow of the liturgy. The often-delicate task of celebrants and musicians is to find a way of engaging with the couple's preferred choices that is positive yet faithful to the tradition of the Church. For musicians a further difficulty can be that of helping the couple to identify a selection of music that a widely diverse congregation will be familiar with. It can prove taxing to identify a hymn that everyone could sing with the gusto that itself might be a sign of love and support for the couple; but an additional challenge, or even a primary one, is how to facilitate the singing of the liturgy itself – not least in its psalms and acclamations.

Questions for Reflection

- Identify a song or a piece of music that you would consider suitable for inclusion in a wedding in a Catholic church. What aspects of it make it suitable?
- Identify a song or a piece of music that you would consider **not** suitable for inclusion in a wedding in a Catholic church. What aspects of it make it unsuitable?

Conclusion: blessings

The Appendix to *OCM* includes two blessings:

- The Order of Blessing an Engaged Couple.
- The Order of Blessing a Married Couple within Mass on the Anniversary of Marriage.

These are both excerpts from the *Book of Blessings* and, with texts such as the blessing of a new home, offer ways in which the parish can make connections with those seeking and celebrating Marriage.

Book of Blessings

This is a book of the Roman Rite that gathers together blessings of people and objects. People can be blessed according to their state of life: a blessing for a pregnant mother, or someone who is ill, or for a position: a blessing of a catechist. Both sacred and secular objects can be blessed: a religious statue or a school building. Some blessings are related to the time of year, such as the blessing of the crib at Christmas. Blessings can occur either within or outside Mass. The common liturgical features are Scripture, intercessions and a blessing prayer. The blessing is addressed in thanksgiving to God so that he will pour down blessing on the person or activity.

The blessings offered to engaged and married couples are a reminder that sacraments happen in a context or within time. They imply a before and an after, they are prepared for, celebrated and are lived out. The inclusion of these blessings is a reminder that the wedding liturgy is not an end point in itself, but a beginning that requires support and prayer to flourish.

The Sacrament of Orders

A characteristic feature of the Catholic Church is that it is hierarchical. It might easily be tempting to regard the hierarchical dimension of the Catholic Church as being in some way analogous to the internal organization of a large multinational corporation, with its 'Head Office' in Rome, and local 'branches' in the dioceses of the world. Such a perspective, however, misses the theological understanding that the Church has of its own hierarchical nature – and it especially misses the keynote of service that underpins the whole. The Catholic Church does not regard the hierarchical structure purely as a functional or administrative aspect of its life. Instead, it perceives its hierarchical structure as directly flowing from the mission of Christ and his Apostles; it is essential to its constitution and to its unity in faith and mission. For that reason, the entry into one of the three 'Orders' of the hierarchy is not an act of human commissioning. One becomes a bishop, a priest or a deacon through the reception of a dedicated sacrament that 'confers a gift of the Holy Spirit that permits the exercise of a "sacred power" which can come only from Christ himself through his Church'.[2]

Participation in the Priesthood of Christ

The foundation from which the Catholic understanding springs is the priesthood of Christ that was discussed in Chapter 2. If we look at the earthly life of the incarnate Christ, then we can see that his priesthood entailed the exercise of three 'offices': prophetic (proclaiming the Good News of the Kingdom), priestly (offering worship to the Father) and kingly. This last point calls for a little explanation: Christ explicitly 'came not to be served but to serve, and to give his life a ransom for many' (Mark 10.45). Christ's gift of himself on the cross inverts all 'normal' notions of power: the kingly service of that office that forms part of his priesthood is perhaps best described as 'shepherding'.

As was noted in Chapter 6, all the baptized share in Christ's three-fold priesthood. This sharing is frequently described as the 'Common Priesthood of the Faithful' ('Common' in the sense of 'shared' – not commonplace or ordinary!). But in order to serve the faithful, to bring focus and direction to their efforts, and to ensure the unity of the whole, some men are called from among the priestly people to the ministerial or hierarchical priesthood. The Second Vatican Council insisted that these two priesthoods are very much ordered to each other, and both share – each in its proper way – in the one priesthood of Christ.[3] There is, however, an essential difference between them:

> While the common priesthood of the faithful is exercised by the unfolding of baptismal grace – a life of faith, hope and charity, a life according to the Spirit, the ministerial priesthood is at the service of the common priesthood. It is directed at the unfolding of the baptismal grace of all Christians. The ministerial priesthood is a *means* by which Christ unceasingly builds upon and leads his Church. For this reason it is transmitted by its own sacrament, the Sacrament of Holy Orders.[4]

From College of Apostle to College of Bishops

The Catholic Church finds the roots of the ministerial or hierarchical priesthood in the relationship between Jesus and his Apostles. Vatican II draws a parallel between the mission of the Son and the mission of the Apostles – the Father sent Jesus, who in turn sent out the Apostles.[5] The Apostles formed a discrete group – or 'College' – at the head of which Jesus placed Peter (John 21.15–17). The Catholic Church understands that the pattern of relationships represented by the College of Apostles established a paradigm that extended beyond the lifetime of the Apostles themselves. Thus, their successors, the bishops, similarly form a College, whose head is the Bishop of Rome as the successor of Peter. As such, the Pope is the 'perpetual and visible source and foundation of the unity both of the bishops and of the faithful'.[6]

Bishops and their dioceses

Bishops are understood, therefore, as successors to the Apostles. As members of the Episcopal (Bishops') College, they share in concern for the whole Church, but they have particular responsibility for a local church – or 'diocese'. Within this local church, the individual bishop is 'the visible source and foundation of unity'.[7] In an 'eminent and visible manner, [bishops] take the place of Christ himself, teacher, shepherd and priest, and act as his representative'.[8] This finds its clearest expression when the bishop presides at the Eucharist – 'an expression of the Church gathered around the altar, with the one who represents Christ, the Good Shepherd and Head of the Church presiding'.[9]

The 'fullness of the sacrament of Orders' is conferred upon bishops.[10] Not surprisingly, therefore, the liturgy for their ordination is particularly dramatic. For example, the Book of the Gospels is held open over the head of a bishop-elect throughout the (lengthy) Prayer of Ordination as a sign that the pre-eminent obligation of his office is to preach the word of God.

Priests: Co-workers of the bishops

While the bishop, nonetheless, is ultimately responsible for the pastoral life of his diocese, he cannot exercise that role without close collaborators. That role is performed by the second hierarchical order, which is the presbyterate. Priests are co-workers with the bishops, and they take part in the bishop's priesthood and mission. Just as the bishops collectively form a College, so too the priests of a local church together constitute a priestly College, or 'presbyterate'. Priests are most usually assigned responsibility for one or more parish communities. There, they make present the ministry of the bishop, presiding with his authority at the Eucharist, and at all the other sacraments except that of Ordination. Priests would not normally confirm, but they can be delegated by the bishop to do so in specified circumstances – for example, at the Baptism of an adult, or in an emergency.

Deacons

The third Order is that of the diaconate. For many centuries Ordination to the Diaconate has been little more than a stepping stone on the road to priesthood, but since the Second Vatican Council the notion that it is a distinct Order in its own right has taken root. The Council opened the way for the restoration of the diaconal ministry in its own right, opening the Order to married men as well as single.[11] Deacons are not ordained to priesthood, but for a three-fold ministry of service – in the liturgy, in proclaiming the Gospel and in the exercise of charitable service. It is the third of these that the Church regards as the most characteristic ministry of the deacon.[12] This reflects the biblical origins of the ministry in the appointment by the Apostles of seven men who were charged with the care of the most needy in the community.[13] They engage with – and, where appropriate, take a leading role in – the Church's charitable outreach. The fact that they also play a visible role in the liturgy makes clear the link between the Church's worship and its call to serve. Even the deacon's liturgical roles underline the deacon's orientation towards the pastoral care of others: he will frequently baptize, bless marriages, preside at funerals and burial rites, and administer Holy Communion and Viaticum to the housebound and dying. He also serves the proclamation of the word by acting as minister of the Gospel in the liturgy and also exercising a catechetical role.

Rites of Ordination

History
De Ordinatione Episcopi, Presbyterorum et Diaconorum
- Editio typica, 1968
- Editio typica altera, 1990

The Ordination of Deacons, Priests, and Bishops
- First edition, 1975 (out of print)
- Second edition, forthcoming, *Ordination of a Bishop, of Priests, and of Deacons*

Contents

The Celebration of Ordination

The Ordination Rites for all three Orders take place within a celebration of the Eucharist, immediately after the proclamation of the Gospel. The ordaining minister is always a bishop. The three rites follow a common structure:

- Preparatory Rites.
- Laying on of Hands and Prayer of Ordination (the 'essential element' of the Ordination).[14]
- Explanatory Rites.

The rites, of course, differ on many details. For example, all the bishops present lay their hands on the head of the candidate at the Ordination of a Bishop; at Ordination to the Priesthood the ordaining bishop and all priests present do so. When a deacon is ordained, however, the ordaining bishop alone lays on hands. The explanatory rites also differ considerably across the three Orders. The overall structure, nonetheless, is constant.

To illustrate how this works in practice, we present here a walk-through of the ritual that is the most likely to have been seen because it is frequently celebrated in parish churches rather than cathedrals. This is Ordination to the Priesthood. One or more priests can be ordained during the same ceremony – for our purposes here we will presume that it is one individual, which reflects the most common experience.

Ordination of a Priest: Structure

Introductory Rites
Liturgy of the Word
Ordination of a Priest
    Calling of the Candidate
    Presentation of the Candidate
    Election by the Bishop and Consent of the People
    Homily
    Examination of the Candidate
    Promise of Obedience
    Invitation to Prayer
    Litany of the Saints
    Laying on of Hands
    Prayer of Consecration
    Investiture with Stole and Chasuble
    Anointing of Hands
    Presentation of the Gifts
    Kiss of Peace
Liturgy of the Eucharist
Concluding Rites

The Preparatory Rites

The Preparatory Rites are fundamentally identical for all three Orders: the candidates are formally 'elected', a homily is preached, and a series of solemn promises is made.

The calling of the candidate

This section of the rite parallels the central action of the 'Rite of Election' of the *RCIA*. The candidate for Ordination to the Priesthood is called forward by name. A priest designated by the bishop – usually a person who has been responsible for their formation for ordination – presents him to the bishop:

Most Reverend Father, holy Mother Church asks you to ordain this man, our brother, for service of priest.
The bishop asks him:
Do you judge him to be worthy?
He replies:
After inquiry among the people of Christ and upon recommendation of those concerned with his training, I testify that he has been found worthy.
Bishop:
We rely on the help of the Lord God and our Saviour Jesus Christ, and we choose this man, our brother, for priesthood in the presbyteral order.
All present say: Thanks be to God, *or give their assent to the choice in some other way, according to local custom.*[15]

The homily follows. A text for the bishop's homily is provided (paralleling the Rite of Confirmation), but he may use his own words. The homily begins by addressing the congregation, offering a succinct summary of the role of priests as co-workers of the bishops. The candidate is then spoken to as 'my son', and the homily outlines how his priestly ministry will be played out as a particular participation in the three-fold priesthood of Christ: as teacher of the gospel, celebrant of the liturgy – above all, of the Eucharist – and as pastor of Christ's flock. The homily underlines the need for an ongoing conversion on the part of the priest in each of these three dimensions of his ministry:

- As teacher: 'Meditate on the law of God, believe what you read, teach what you believe, and put into practice what you teach.'
- As celebrant of the liturgy: 'Know what you are doing and imitate the mystery you celebrate. In the memorial of the Lord's death and resurrection, make every effort to die to sin and to walk in the new life of Christ.'
- As pastor: 'Always remember the example of the Good Shepherd who came not to be served but to serve, and to seek out and rescue those who were lost.'

The rite provides corresponding homilies for the Ordinations for Bishops and Deacons.

Examination of the candidate

At the end of the homily the candidate steps forward to stand in front of the bishop. There, he makes four solemn promises that establish the contours of the life that lies ahead of him. Like the baptismal promises, these Ordination promises take a question and answer form: the bishop asks four questions, each of which opens with the words, 'Are you resolved . . .?' To the first three questions the candidate makes the reply, 'I am'. In these first three questions he is asked to state his resolution to care for the 'Lord's flock', to celebrate the liturgical mysteries 'faithfully and religiously as the Church has handed them down', and to preach the gospel and teach the Catholic faith. Finally, the bishop asks him:

> Are you resolved to consecrate your life to God for the salvation of his people, and to unite yourself more closely every day to Christ the High Priest, who offered himself for us to the Father as a perfect sacrifice?

To this final question the candidate replies, 'I am, with the help of God.'

Questions for Reflection

- How does this fourth promise relate to the theme of the Paschal Mystery?
- What understanding of the ordained priesthood emerges from this text?

The promise of obedience

The candidate kneels in front of the bishop, places his hands between those of the bishop, and promises obedience and respect to him and his successors. If he is ordained by a bishop who is not the bishop of his own diocese, he promises respect and obedience to 'his Ordinary', that is, his own bishop. Similarly, members of religious Orders promise respect and obedience to the diocesan bishop and also to their legitimate superior.[16]

This ritual is also carried out at the Ordination of Deacons. A particularity of the promises made at Ordination to the Diaconate is that they normally include the promise to live a life of celibacy. However, this promise is not required of the many married candidates for the diaconate.

Litany of the Saints

Before moving to the core rituals of the Ordination, the assembly embarks on an intense intercession for the Elect, using the Litany of the Saints to ask the saints to add their prayers for the Elect and for God's people to the prayers of the Church on earth. Throughout the Litany the Elect prostrates himself, face down.

The Litany follows a responsorial structure: a series of short invocations are sung by cantors, to each of which the congregation makes a brief sung response. The Litany falls into five clear sections:

1 'Lord have mercy – Christ have mercy – Lord have Mercy' – each invocation repeated by the congregation.
2 The invocation of the Saints. This takes the form of a list of names, beginning with 'Holy Mary, Mother of God', and concluding 'All holy men and women'. As each saint is named, the congregation responds, 'Pray for us'. A basic core of saints to be invoked is provided by the rite, but other names may be inserted – for example, that of a diocesan or parish patron saint.
3 A sequence of intercessions, invoking God's mercy and protection. The congregational response changes to 'Lord, save your people'.
4 Three invocations that cumulatively request God's blessing on the candidate himself:

Bless this chosen man	Lord, hear our prayer
Bless this chosen man and make him holy	Lord, hear our prayer
Bless this chosen man, make him holy, and consecrate him for his sacred duties.	Lord, hear our prayer

5 Three final invocations of Christ:

Jesus, Son of the living God	Lord, hear our prayer
Christ, hear us	Christ, hear us
Lord Jesus, hear our prayer	Lord Jesus, hear our prayer

The laying on of hands and the Prayer of Ordination

The laying on of hands and the Prayer of Ordination form 'the centre of an Ordination'.[17] The laying on of hands is carried out in complete silence: nothing is spoken and, unusually, a rather complex piece of liturgical choreography is carried out without musical accompaniment. The Elect kneels before the bishop, who lays hands on his head. When this has been done, all the priests present come forward and one by one they, too, lay their hands on the head of the Elect; this signifies that ordination incorporates the Elect into a body, into the presbyterate. All this should be done in a manner that makes the action clearly visible to the congregation. At the end of the laying on of hands, the Elect is left kneeling in front of the bishop, who is surrounded by his co-workers, the presbyterate. If we factor in the deacons who will be assisting the bishop and the faithful gathered in the congregation, then the extent to which the Ordination rites provide a powerful image of the local church becomes evident.

The silence is broken by the voice of the bishop as he, alone, prays the Prayer of Ordination. This is a very ancient Roman prayer, and (unlike the Prayers for Bishops and Deacons) was barely changed in the revision of the rites that followed the Second Vatican Council. It is very lengthy, but it can be broken down into a number of clear sections. An opening invocation of God is followed by a two-part anamnesis. This Greek term refers to the way that the Church recalls God's actions in the past when it celebrates the liturgy. This 'remembering', however, has a dynamic edge – as the Church remembers God's saving actions, the Holy Spirit makes present in the here and now the core thrust of those actions. In this case, the Prayer of Ordination recalls the assistants given to Moses and to his brother, the High Priest Aaron, and the Apostles and their companions given to Jesus – and the bishop prays that through the action of the Holy Spirit the Elect will, now, become a similar helper to him. After the anamnesis comes the core of the prayer in which the bishop prays that the Elect will be given the dignity of the priesthood. Then follows a series of intercessions for the newly ordained priest(s), and the whole concludes with a typical Roman 'doxology', or final act of Praise of the Trinity.

1   *Opening Invocation*
Come to our help,
Lord, holy Father, almighty and eternal God;
You are the source of every honour and dignity,
Of all progress and stability.
You watch over the growing family of man
By your gift of wisdom and your pattern of order.

2a   *Anamnesis: Old Testament Typology*
When you had appointed high priests to rule your people,
you chose other men next to them in rank and dignity
to be with them and to help them in their task;
And so there grew up
The ranks of priests and the offices of levites,
established by sacred rites.
In the desert
You extended the spirit of Moses to seventy wise men
who helped him rule the great company of his people.
you shared among the sons of Aaron
the fullness of their father's power,
to provide worthy priests in sufficient number
for the increasing rites of sacrifice and worship.

2b   *Anamnesis: Christ*
With the same loving care
you gave companions to your Son's apostles
to help in teaching the faith:
they preached the Gospel to the whole world.
Lord, grant also to us such fellow workers,
for we are weak and our need is greater.

3   *The Essential Core of the Prayer*
Almighty Father,
Grant to this servant of yours
The dignity of the priesthood.
Renew within him the Spirit of holiness.

As co-worker with the order of bishops
May he be faithful to the ministry
That he receives from you, Lord God,
And be to others a model of right conduct.

4   *Intercessions for the Ordained*
     May he be faithful in working with the order of bishops,
     So that the words of the gospel may reach the ends of the earth,
     And the family of nations,
     made one in Christ,
     may become God's one, holy people.

5   *Concluding Doxology*
     We ask this through our Lord Jesus Christ your Son,
     Who lives and reigns with you and the Holy Spirit,
     One God, for ever and ever.
     All: Amen.[18]

Questions for Reflection

• What do the ideas expressed in both parts of the anamnesis tell us about the role of priests in the Church today?
• What do the Essential Core of the Prayer and the Intercessions tell us about the ministry of priests in the Church?
• What does the prayer as a whole tell us about the relationship between the bishop and his priests?

The explanatory rites

With the laying on of hands and the Prayer of Ordination, the Elect has now become a priest. The significance of this is drawn out by a series of explanatory rites that give symbolic expression to what has happened and how the life of the new priest will be shaped from this point on. Again, there are other liturgical parallels – most notably, the explanatory rites that follow Baptism (see Chapter 5).

Investiture with chasuble and stole

The newly ordained priest has thus far been vested very simply in an alb and a deacon's stole. The alb is a white, full-length, long-sleeved and quite close-fitting garment that is worn by all ordained ministers underneath other vestments; very frequently it is also worn by some non-ordained ministers, such as altar-servers. The stole is a narrow strip of material that is only ever worn by ordained ministers. The new priest had at some earlier point been ordained deacon, and so he had arrived at his priestly Ordination wearing the stole in a deacon's fashion – that is, over the left shoulder and across the body. Immediately after the Prayer of Ordination, his outer vesture is changed as a sign of his new role in the Church. Some of the priests who are present move his stole from its deacon's configuration to the simpler priestly way of wearing it: hanging down his body from his neck. Then, they place a chasuble over his alb and stole; the chasuble is the vestment worn by bishops and priests when celebrating the Eucharist. The liturgical ministry of the new priest is thus expressed in an immediately visible manner.

Anointing of hands

The newly ordained priest then kneels before the bishop, who anoints the palms of his hands with the oil of Chrism as a sign that the priest participates in the Priesthood of Christ. As he anoints, the bishop says:

> The Father anointed our Lord Jesus Christ
> Through the power of the Holy Spirit.
> May Jesus preserve you to sanctify the Christian people
> And to offer sacrifice to God.[19]

Presentation of the gifts

Members of the congregation bring forward the bread and a chalice of wine mixed with water. These are passed to the bishop, who places them into the hands of the new priest, saying,

> Accept from the holy people of God the gifts to be offered to him.
> Know what you are doing, and imitate the mystery you celebrate:
> model your life on the mystery of the Lord's cross.[20]

The words and action have a double edge. On the one hand, they point to the action of the priest in presiding at the Eucharist. However, the last line of the bishop's text also directs the new priest to the inner meaning of the Eucharist: to follow the crucified one, to participate in (let alone, preside at) the celebration of his Supper, is to be open to modelling one's own life upon Christ's – with all the possible consequences.

Kiss of peace

Finally, the newly ordained priest exchanges the kiss of peace with the bishop and with the other priests present. This sets a kind of seal on admission of the priest into his new status – as co-worker with the bishop and as a member of the Order of priests. He then joins the other priests around the altar for the celebration of the Liturgy of the Eucharist, at which, for the first time, he is present as concelebrant.

Question for Discussion

- What understanding of priesthood emerges from the four explanatory rites?

Notes

1 CCC, 1623.

2 CCC, 1538.

3 *LG*, 10.

4 CCC, 1547.

5 *LG*, 19; *Decree on the Pastoral Office of Bishops in the Church, Christus Dominus*, 4.

6 *LG*, 23.

7 *LG*, 23.

8 *LG*, 21.

9 CCC, 1561; see also *SC*, 41.

10 *LG*, 21.

11 *LG*, 29.

12 Congregation for Catholic Education, *Basic Norms for the Formation of Permanent Deacons* (Rome, 1998), 9. http://www.vatican.va/roman_curia/congregations/ccatheduc/documents/rc_con_ccatheduc_doc_31031998_directorium-diaconi_en.html.

13 Acts 6.1–6.

14 *ODPB*, General Introduction, 7.

15 *ODPB*, Chapter III, 9–13.

16 *ODPB*, Chapter III, 16.

17 *ODPB*, General Introduction, 7.

18 *ODPB*, Chapter III, 22.

19 *ODPB*, Chapter III, 24.

20 *ODPB*, Chapter III, 26.

10

Sacraments of Healing

MARTIN FOSTER AND PETER MCGRAIL

Introduction

The final pair of sacraments are Penance and Anointing of the Sick. These engage with two fundamental human realities. The first reality is the extraordinary capacity that each living person possesses to hurt themself and others – in spite of what they may think or want to do at the deepest level. In other words, everybody sometimes can have the experience of being 'divided' – caught in a mismatch between the person we would like to be and what we actually do. When we speak of 'sin' in the life of the baptized Christian it is fundamentally this mismatch that is at play. It is a mismatch between the expectations of the Christian life set out in Baptism and the realities of life on the ground. Negotiating the complexities of the contemporary world brings its own stresses and demands constant choices; sometimes those stresses can fog the moral judgement, sometimes the choices made are not the best. The second human reality is that of sickness – not least when it brings death into focus.

In a Christian context these two aspects of human frailty – the first operating at a moral level, the second at the physical – generate particular resonances. When Christians damage their relationship with one another, they weaken the bonds of unity within the Church – which touches on its very nature as a communion of life. At the same time, and especially when Christians sin against others outside the Church, they blunt the Church's mission to the world. Sin introduces a fundamental sign of contradiction both of the Church's identity and of its capacity to proclaim its message. Similarly, for the Christian who has been baptized in Christ and therefore become particularly closely associated with Christ's death and resurrection, the realities of sickness and of death bring that alignment to Christ into sharper relief. That does not mean that the Christian's engagement with physical weakness, suffering and death is any easier or less complex than that of any other person: having faith does not offer a 'get out' card from the human physical and psychological processes that sickness and dying present.

All of the above helps to explain the description of these two rites as 'Sacraments of Healing'. The reality of sin affects a Christian's relationship not only with God, but also with others. All sin, therefore, has an inter-personal dimension. The Sacrament of Penance (Reconciliation) offers a framework for a restoration of relationships with both God and with others in a way that unites a respect for the individual person's dignity with a community dimension. The Constitution on the Church of the Second Vatican Council drew tightly together the horizontal and vertical dimensions of forgiveness and of reconciliation that are at play in the sacrament:

> Those who approach the Sacrament of Penance obtain pardon from God's mercy for the offence committed against him, and are, at the same time, reconciled with the Church which they have wounded by their sins and which by charity, by example and by prayer labours for their conversion.[1]

That communal dimension is also significant as regards sickness – not least because the experience of becoming weak, or elderly, can lead to a sense of increasing isolation. The narrowing of the circle of people with whom one engages regularly, diminishing opportunities to step outside one's home or room, and the fear that accompanies pain, weakness and the approach of death can all intensify a sense of isolation. The Sacrament of the Anointing of the Sick is a formal support that the Catholic Church offers to its members as they go through the processes of sickness, of ageing and of dying. It expresses the support of the community and the mercy of God, and encapsulates the Christian's participation in the Paschal Mystery that lies at the heart of the Catholic understanding of the liturgy.

In all of this, the question that was asked in Chapter 2 of this book, as to who is the primary actor in the liturgy, becomes visible. Ultimately, it is God who forgives sins, as it is God who heals. In both sacraments, the priest acts as the minister of Christ, and as a constant reference point in the rites of both Penance and Anointing is to the Paschal Mystery of Christ.

Scripture

Two characteristics of Jesus' ministry were that he showed a particular kindness towards those who were the subject of the moral judgement of others. He forgave sinners, and healed the sick and showed compassion to those who loved them. Sometimes, in Jesus' ministry, healing and forgiveness even went hand-in-hand. In a sense, therefore, these two sacraments are rooted in the fundamental attitudes of Jesus himself. He also passed on to his Apostles the same ministries. The Catholic Church believes that the authority that Jesus gave to his disciples to forgive sins establish the basis for the Sacrament of Penance.[2] In recognizing the scriptural foundation for the Sacrament of the Anointing of the Sick, the Catholic Church looks not only to Jesus' own example and his commissioning of the Apostles, but also to the practice of the early Church, and especially to that outlined in the Letter of James:

> Is anyone among you sick? Let him call for the elders of the church, and let them pray over him, anointing him with oil in the name of the Lord. And the prayer of faith will save the one who is sick, and the Lord will raise him up. And if he has committed sins, he will be forgiven. Therefore, confess your sins to one another and pray for one another, that you may be healed. (James 5.14–16a)

As we shall see, these actions of praying over someone and anointing them are very closely reflected in today's rites.

History

The history of the Sacrament of Penance is particularly complex. During the first Christian centuries the sense that Baptism represented a total break with sin was so powerful that there was a broad reluctance to readmit back to the fold any Christians who had been guilty of public and serious sin, such as adultery or apostasy. Gradually (and in the face of some opposition) bishops began to allow such people a once-in-a-lifetime opportunity to be reconciled to the Church. A sort of parallel Catechumenate developed, in which extended periods of penitential life led to an act of public reconciliation. This in turn gave way to a more private process in which the confession of sins to a priest led both to reconciliation and the undertaking of a penitential response.

The history of the Sacrament of Anointing of the Sick includes fewer dramatic twists and turns than that of Penance. A key factor that unites the various rites of East and West is that the oil used is blessed by a Bishop – it comes, therefore, from the heart of the local church. There is evidence of people taking that oil from the bishop and administering it themselves to their loved ones, but as the pattern of ministry stabilized across East and West the term 'presbyteroi' in the Epistle of James became identified with the 'presbyters' of the Church, the name given to those who make the bishop's ministry present in a particular area – the ordained priests.

In the West, this sacrament gradually underwent a change of focus – from being understood as a sacrament of healing to one that was administered to a person when they were on the point of death – hence its common name for a long time of 'Extreme Unction' ('Final Anointing'). The Constitution on the Liturgy, *Sacrosanctum Concilium*, broadened that perspective, insisting that it should more properly be called 'Anointing of the Sick', and that it should have a more extended use than had been the case across most of the second millennium.[3]

The Rite of Penance

History
Ordo Paenitentiae
- Editio typica, 1974
Rite of Penance
- 1976 (London: Collins)
Order of Penance
- new translation, forthcoming

Contents
Introduction
1 Rite for Reconciliation of Individual Penitents
2 Rite for the Reconciliation of Several Penitents with Individual Confession and Absolution
3 Rite for the Reconciliation of Several Penitents with General Confession and Absolution

4 Various texts
Appendix I: Absolution from Censures; Dispensation from Irregularity
Appendix II: Sample Penitential Services
Appendix III: Form of Examination of Conscience

Overview of Contents

The Rite of Penance gives three models for the celebration of the sacrament: for use with individual penitents; for a congregational celebration that incorporates individual confession and absolution; for a congregation with a general, non-individual confession and absolution. The first has been the familiar form for centuries – the penitent engages individually with the priest, usually, but not always, in the confessional. The penitent states how long it has been since their last confession, recalls their sins, receives absolution and makes an act of penance in the form of a prayer in which they express their sorrow for the sin committed and their resolution to amend their lives. The priest for his part welcomes the penitent and leads them through the rite. He might begin by reading a passage of Scripture,[4] he offers counsel to the penitent and imposes an act of penance or satisfaction, which may take the form of prayer, self-denial, or an act of service to others.[5] This act of penance should be

> suited to the personal condition of each penitent so that each one may restore the order which has been disturbed and be cured of the sickness from which he has suffered. Therefore, it is necessary that the act of penance really be a remedy for sin and a help to renewal of life.[6]

Finally, the priest pronounces the formula of absolution, which will be considered below.

The second form involves the people gathering for a common liturgical celebration. During that celebration they go forward individually to make their confession to a priest who may be seated in a side-chapel, or in a confessional, or on the sanctuary. This form of the rite will be examined in detail below.

The third form differs from the second in that penitents do not confess their sins individually to a priest, but together make a shared acknowledgement of sin and receive absolution together. This third form of the rite is intended for extraordinary circumstances where, for example, there is a danger of death.

The rite also provides for a non-sacramental liturgy, which it describes as 'Penitential Services'.[7] These are Services of the Word without the Sacrament of Penance but focus, through Scripture and prayers, on sinfulness, penance and reconciliation. An appendix to the rite offers six sample services for use during Advent and Lent, and for various groups such as children or the sick.[8] The intention of these liturgies is to prepare people for a subsequent reception of the sacrament and to 'foster a spirit of virtue and penance'.[9] This second intention points to a potential broader use of such liturgies – for example, they may have a role when a community wishes to acknowledge the wrong and the damage it has done and to seek God's mercy and healing.

Rite for the Reconciliation of Several Penitents with Individual Confession and Absolution

This liturgical celebration often occurs in parishes during Advent and Lent as a preparation for Christmas and Easter. It may be arranged in conjunction with other local parishes, as it requires a number of priests to be available to hear confessions.

Rite for the Reconciliation of Several Penitents with Individual Confession and Absolution

Introductory Rites
Song
Sign of the Cross
Greeting
Opening Prayer
Liturgy of the Word
Readings
Homily

Examination of Conscience
Liturgy of Reconciliation
General Confession of Sins
Individual Confession and Absolution
Proclamation of Praise for God's Mercy
Concluding Prayer of Thanksgiving
Concluding Rite
Blessing
Dismissal

Introductory Rites

The liturgy begins in a familiar way with an Entrance Song and procession, Sign of the Cross and Greeting. The priest offers a brief introduction to the service, which is followed by the Opening Prayer. This prayer brings to the fore two of the particular characteristics of this rite. The first is the range of options that it presents: in this instance, the celebrant is invited to choose between six very contrasting Opening Prayers provided. Here – as in other rites, most notably the *Order of Christian Funerals* – the provision of a broad range of texts is intended to resource appropriate responses to a range of pastoral needs. The second particularity highlighted by the Opening Prayers is the compositional freedom of the rite. The presidential prayers of the rite do not always reflect the constrained and compact style typical of the Roman tradition. For example, one of the Opening Prayers reads:

Almighty and merciful God,
you have brought us together in the name of your Son
to receive your mercy and grace in our time of need.
Open our eyes to see the evil we have done.
Touch our hearts and convert us to yourself.
Where sin has divided and scattered,
may your love make one again;
where sin has brought weakness,
may your power heal and strengthen;

where sin has brought death,
may your Spirit raise to new life.
Give us a new heart to love you,
so that our lives may reflect the image of your Son.
May the world see the glory of Christ
revealed in your Church,
and come to know
that he is the one whom you have sent
Jesus Christ, your Son, our Lord.
Amen.[10]

Liturgy of the Word

The Scripture readings usually follow the Sunday Lectionary pattern of an Old Testament reading, Psalm, New Testament reading, Acclamation and Gospel. However, here again the rite incorporates flexibility – it is possible to use a single reading, preferably a Gospel. The readings and psalms that the Lectionary provides for the Rite of Penance are notable for their length. For example, some of the responsorial psalms have ten or more verses – in contrast to the more usual four or five. The use of silence is encouraged.

A homily invites the congregation to reflect on the readings and apply them to the lives of the community. This should lead seamlessly into the Examination of Conscience. Model texts of different lengths are provided in the rite, but texts can also be written for the particular occasion.

Liturgy of Reconciliation

This begins with a General Confession of Sins by all. It has three components: a general formula of confession (e.g. 'I confess'), intercessions or song, the Lord's Prayer. The intercessions take the form of a litany:

You brought back the lost sheep on your shoulders,
– pity us and lead us home.
R. Christ, graciously hear us.[11]

The individual confession and absolution follow. The priests present go to various parts of the church to hear confessions. Members of the congregation approach a priest, confess their sins, accept a 'fitting act of satisfaction' and receive absolution. The formula of absolution is identical across the first two forms of the rite, and is one of two options available for the third form. The formula was revised in response to a specific request of the Second Vatican Council,[12] and it succeeds in expressing a few, very tightly constructed phrases, the theology of the Rite. The formula is strongly Trinitarian: it opens by proclaiming the mercy of the Father, succinctly summarizes the Paschal Mystery of the Son, and identifies the role of the Holy Spirit in communicating God's forgiveness of sins. The role of the Church in the economy of forgiveness is then recognized: it is through the Church's ministry that God communicates forgiveness and peace. All that having been stated, the priest pronounces the essential words, 'I absolve you from your sins'.

> God, the Father of mercies,
> through the death and resurrection of his Son
> has reconciled the world to himself
> and sent the Holy Spirit among us
> for the forgiveness of sins;
> through the ministry of the Church
> may God give you pardon and peace
> and I absolve you from your sins
> in the name of the Father, and of the Son,
> and of the Holy Spirit.
> Amen.[13]

Question for Reflection

Read John 20.19–23 and 2 Corinthians 5.17–21.
- How are the ideas found in these passages expressed in the prayer of absolution?

Once all who have desired to confess their sins have done so, the whole congregation is invited to unite in a proclamation of praise for God's mercy as a response to the forgiveness that has been experienced. This can take the form of the Magnificat, a psalm or another song. After this the priest offers a concluding prayer of thanksgiving and the liturgy concludes with the blessing and dismissal.

Celebration

This liturgy presents a simple logistic challenge. Depending on the number of people present wishing to go to confession and the priests available, the individual confessions can take a long time to complete. Some have tried to address this by inviting people to name just one sin to the priest. However, this approach risks placing restrictions where there should be freedom and thereby might impede the healing process of the sacrament. A related adaptation in a number of places has been the introduction of a symbolic gesture into the rite. For example, in some celebrations penitents have been invited to light a candle after they have made their confession – and perhaps to place that candle alongside those of other penitents at a focal point in the church (for example, around a wooden cross). On the one hand, such a symbolic action might, as the number of lights builds up, serve as an eloquent reminder of the communal nature of this liturgy. After all, one of the motivations behind the development of this second form was to express the understanding that sin not only harms the relationship of the person with God but also harms the communion of life within the Body of Christ. However, symbols can be innately ambiguous – and any use of them risks opening up unintended fields of meaning. For example, if, instead of placing their lit candles together, penitents were invited to take them back to their places, then it would become immediately apparent who within the congregation had or had not been to confession, and the symbol could highlight distinction rather than unity.

A further challenge is that of managing the transition from the expression of penitence to the final proclamation of praise in a manner that ensures that there is the appropriate contrast between the two, but also holds respect for what is in many regards an act of considerable humility. This task can be rendered even more difficult in cases where the time taken to complete the confessions has resulted in substantial numbers of the congregation choosing to leave before the formal ending.

The Location of Reconciliation

Confessionals have been a feature of Catholic churches since the late sixteenth century. They provide a place for individual confession so that the penitent can kneel and speak to the priest through a grille as a way keeping anonymity. Since the Second Vatican Council some penitents have preferred to see the priest, and be seen. This has given rise to reconciliation chapels where the penitent has a choice of a screen or not. The need for confidentiality remains an important aspect of the rite and this will affect the design in terms of sound and visibility. Another factor will be safeguarding and the safety and security of both penitent and priest.[14]

Conclusion

In offering individual and communal forms of the Sacrament of Penance the rite intends to provide not a distinct choice of one or the other, but a liturgical economy where both have their place and the two complement each other.

The Anointing of the Sick

Pastoral Care of the Sick:
Rites of Anointing and Viaticum

History
Ordo Unctionis infirmorum eorumque pastoralis curae
- Editio typica, 1972
Pastoral Care of the Sick
- 1983 (London: Collins)

Contents
General Introduction

I Care of the Sick
1. Visits to the Sick
2. Visits to a Sick Child
3. Communion of the Sick
4. Anointing of the Sick

II Pastoral Care of the Dying
5. Celebration of Viaticum
6. Commendation of the Dying
7. Prayers for the Dead
8. Rites for Exceptional Circumstances
   - Continuous Rite of Penance, Anointing, and Viaticum
   - Rite for Emergencies
   - Christian Initiation for the Dying

III Readings, Responses and Verse from Sacred Scripture

The liturgical texts for the Anointing of the Sick are published in a comprehensive book of pastoral rites entitled *Pastoral Care of the Sick: Rites of Anointing and Viaticum*. This volume offers different prayers and rites to be used in supporting the sick, and accompanying the dying. As noted above, the sacrament is now offered to any Catholic whose health has become seriously impaired by sickness or by old age, or before surgery.[15] The sacrament can be given more than once during a person's lifetime. The thrust of the liturgy, therefore, is to give support and strength to a person as they face the isolation and fear that serious illness or old age can bring. The minister may be a bishop – for example, at celebrations of the sacrament during diocesan pilgrimages or during parish visitations – but is most usually a priest, and the rite tends to refer to the minister as such throughout. That convention, therefore, is followed here.

Forms of the rite

Several different ways of celebrating the sacrament are provided – reflecting the range of contexts in which it may be celebrated. The three major patterns are

Anointing outside Mass, Anointing within Mass and Anointing in a Hospital or Institution. The third of these presents the rite in a substantially abbreviated form – as appropriate to a hospital context. A further, emergency form of anointing is also provided, which strips the rite down to its barest essentials. This would be used at the scene of a disaster, or before a person is taken for emergency surgery.

Anointing outside Mass

Introductory Rites

Greeting
Sprinkling with Holy Water
Instruction

Penitential Rite
Liturgy of the Word
Reading
Response

Liturgy of Anointing
Litany
Laying on of hands
Prayer over the Oil
Anointing
Prayer after Anointing
The Lord's Prayer

[Liturgy of Holy Communion]
Communion
Silent Prayer
Prayer after Communion
Concluding Rite
Blessing

Though the structure of the rite may appear complex, in practice it is short, simple and flexible – all of which allow it to be adapted to the pastoral circumstances of the sick person. For example, the responses (such as, 'Lord, have mercy') are the same as those used at Mass, and therefore might be expected to be familiar to those present. It is assumed that alongside the sick person there will be others – frequently family members, friends or carers. Their presence can be a very tangible sign of the support of loved ones and the community for the sick person. However, the rite may also be celebrated with only the sick person and the priest present. The place of celebration could be in someone's home or in a church or chapel.

Introductory Rites

The priest begins the celebration of the sacrament by greeting those present. He then may optionally sprinkle them with holy water, as a reminder of Baptism. Then, either using his own words or the text provided by the ritual, the priest offers a brief introduction to the rite. The text provided quotes the passage from the Letter of James discussed at the start of this chapter. The Introduction leads into a Penitential Rite, using either the first or third forms from the Mass.

Liturgy of the Word

As with the other rites renewed after the Second Vatican Council, the sacramental action takes place after, and in some ways as a response to, the proclamation of the Word of God. The rite proposes that there should be a single reading. This is followed by a response that may take the form of a period of silence and/or a brief homily by the priest. While a broad range of readings is possible, the rite specifically directs attention to three Gospel passages:

- Matthew 11.25–30.
- Mark 2.1–12.
- Luke 7.18b–23.

Questions for Reflection

Read through the three Gospel passages given above.

- What does each tell us about Jesus' attitude towards sickness and suffering?
- What do the passages tell us about the Church's understanding of this sacrament?

Liturgy of Anointing

The anointing is preceded by a brief litany of intercession, containing expressions such as: 'Come and strengthen him/her through this holy anointing: Lord, have mercy. Lord, have mercy.'

That this is a sacrament of 'anointing' implies that at its heart is the use of oil – in continuation of the practice described in the Letter of James. The 'Oil of the Sick' that is used in this celebration consists of pure olive oil, and a fresh supply is blessed by the bishop once each year at the Chrism Mass, which takes place at the cathedral during Holy Week. It is then distributed to the various parishes of the diocese. The priest says a short prayer of thanksgiving over the oil – or, if he needs to replenish his stock, he may bless some new oil, using the same prayer as that used by the bishop at the Chrism Mass. Both the prayer of thanksgiving and the blessing speak of the role of the Holy Trinity in bringing strength to the sick or elderly person – and the prayer of thanksgiving invites the participants to draw a link between the situation of the person being anointed and the Paschal Mystery that is the heart of all liturgy:

> Praise to you, God the almighty Father.
> You sent your Son to live among us and bring us salvation.
> **Blessed be God who heals us in Christ.**
> Praise to you. God the only-begotten Son.
> You humbled yourself to share in our humanity
> And you heal our infirmities.
> **Blessed be God who heals us in Christ.**

Praise to you, God the Holy Spirit, the Consoler.
Your unfailing power gives us strength in our bodily weakness.
Blessed be God who heals us in Christ.[16]

The priest then lays hands on the sick person in silence, before anointing them with oil on the forehead and on the hands. Where it is possible, the priest may also anoint the area of pain or injury. As he anoints the body of the sick person, the priest says:

Through this holy anointing
may the Lord in his love and mercy help you
with the grace of the Holy Spirit.
Amen.
May the Lord who frees you from sin
save you and raise you up.
Amen.[17]

The anointing is followed by a prayer for the sick person, which follows the typical pattern of a Roman Collect. The rite presents a range of optional prayers for use at this point, including prayers for extreme or terminal illness, for those of advanced age, before surgery and for a child. Here we see the same concern to respond to diverse pastoral needs that was noted above with regard to the Opening Prayer of the Rite of Penance. The priest then invites all to pray the Lord's Prayer.

Liturgy of Holy Communion

In some circumstances, the priest then gives Holy Communion to the sick person and those present. This is a further reinforcement of the link between this sacrament and the Paschal Mystery: the participants, at a time when human frailty, sickness or even impending death are at the forefront of their minds, receive the sacrament of Christ's own death and resurrection. This link is even more poignant when there is an anticipation that this will be the last time that a person who is rapidly approaching death will receive the Eucharist. In such instances, Holy Communion takes on a special resonance as 'Viaticum' – food for the journey:

The celebration of the Eucharist as Viaticum, food for the passage through death to eternal life, is the sacrament proper to the dying Christian. It is the completion and crown of the Christian life on this earth, signifying that the Christian follows the Lord to eternal glory and the banquet of the heavenly kingdom.[18]

The dimension of 'food for the journey' is underscored by the words used by the priest at the administration of Viaticum, which differ subtly from those normally used in the distribution of the Eucharist. The normal words 'The body/the blood of Christ . . . Amen' are used, but the priest immediately adds, 'May the Lord Jesus Christ protect you and lead you to eternal life'.[19]

Concluding Rite

The liturgy ends with a blessing which, for example, asks God to bless, heal and enlighten the sick person.

Notes

1 Vatican II, Dogmatic Constitution on the Church, *Lumen Gentium*, 11. See also *RP*, 4.
2 See John 20.21–23; Matt. 16.19. See also CCC, 1440–45.
3 *SC*, 73.
4 *RP*, 17.
5 *RP*, 18.
6 *RP*, 6.
7 *RP*, 36.
8 *RP*, Appendix II, Sample Penitential Services.
9 *RP*, Appendix II, 1.
10 *RP*, 54.
11 *RP*, 58.
12 *SC*, 72.
13 *RP*, 59.
14 For further information, see *CFW*, 245–55.
15 *Pastoral Care of the Sick: Rites of Anointing and Viaticum* (PCS), *General Introduction*, nos. 8–11; see also CCC, 1514–15.
16 *PCS*, 123.
17 *PCS*, 124.

18 *PCS*, 8–11: see also CCC, 1524–5.
19 *PCS*, 193.

Part 3

Beyond the Sacraments

11

Funerals

ANDREW DOWNIE

Introduction

Death comes to everyone and, even in a secular age, the majority of families still turn to a Christian church to provide the appropriate formalities for their loved one – though this may be changing rapidly. A funeral is an event loaded with meaning, a meaning hinted at by words such as 'appropriate' and 'formalities'. It can be a powerful moment of evangelization – or a painful point of conflict between different sensibilities. The preparation and celebration of funerals is a significant part of the life of most Catholic parishes.

Care for the bodies of the dead, and the marking of their passing in ritual, is a universal fact of human culture. Recent research suggests that Neanderthal humans buried their dead. In ancient Rome, the aim of funerary rites was to satisfy the requirements of family honour, and to appease the spirits of the dead, who might otherwise take revenge on the living.[1] Jewish funeral practice, on the other hand, reflected a belief that the deceased would face God's judgement, but could hope for mercy and resurrection.[2] The funeral practices of the early Church reflected the cultural and religious environment in the midst of which Christians lived, but also, from the start, expressed a distinctively Christian eschatology (theology of the 'last things', from the Greek for 'last'). The first Christians adopted many of the rituals characteristic of the surrounding culture, except when these were believed to be contrary to faith. But the tone of the celebration was one of prayerful joy: a realistic expression of grief, combined with a firm hope that physical death would be followed by eternal life in Christ.[3]

And the communal dimension of the ritual was central. The Church grieved and prayed as one for its deceased member.

The optimistic and pessimistic attitudes to death – death as 'going to Christ', or as a summons to judgement and inevitable punishment for sin – have remained in tension in Christian funeral practice throughout the Church's history.[4] The modern funeral rite reflects this tension, holding both attitudes in a careful balance, reflecting the teaching of the Second Vatican Council that, 'The rite for the burial of the dead should express . . . the paschal character of Christian death.'[5] However, the cultural context in which the rite is prepared and celebrated has changed rapidly in recent years, and continues to do so. Very little can be assumed about common traditions or symbols. New layers of secular symbolism have become attached to death, in particular. Bouquets of flowers, or even homemade shrines, by the roadside at the sites of traffic accidents; silence at football matches for the victims of terrorist attacks; controversies over the wearing and colour of Remembrance poppies by public figures; all speak of a concern to 'do the right thing' in the face of death, without necessarily being certain what the right thing is. This cultural context – diverse and often fragmented – can make the minister's task challenging, but can also open up possibilities for fruitful dialogue and witness.

Theology and Practice

The Church's task when celebrating a funeral is to implore spiritual help for the dead, and to seek comforting hope for the living.[6] Prayer for the dead has deep roots in the Christian tradition, but was rejected by the Reformers (and by the modern heirs to their traditions) as presumptuous – for how could human intercession influence God's judgement of a human life? Nevertheless, the custom remains stubbornly persistent. Some writers trace the revival of prayers for the dead in the Anglican tradition to the aftermath of the First World War. Certainly, prayer for the dead forms part of the bedrock of traditional Catholic piety: requesting Masses at which deceased family members and friends are remembered, or for the Holy Souls; frequent repetition of 'Eternal rest grant unto them, O Lord . . .' and 'May the souls of the faithful departed . . .' For a younger generation of Catholics, however, such prayers do not come as such an instinctive response. The traditional piety was based on a clear geography of the afterlife.[7] The saints, and the exceptionally holy, died and went straight to heaven. Those who died in a state of mortal sin went straight to hell. The majority could expect to spend some time in Purgatory, where they would undergo a process of purification before being admitted to eternal life. The living could support the dead through prayers and especially through Masses, connecting the living with the dead in the communion of the Church.

The theology of Purgatory is a humane and necessary part of a Catholic understanding of judgement and redemption. However, such a geography of the afterlife unfortunately lends itself to simplistic misunderstanding. Modern believers, understandably, reject a mechanistic view of what happens after death, but will often retain a vague awareness of the language and customs that were familiar to their parents and grandparents. They are likely to express their hopes for their loved one by saying, for example, that the deceased has 'gone to a better place', and is already 'with God' or 'with the angels'. The funeral rite is more restrained. It asks God's mercy on the deceased, and speaks of a 'sure and certain hope' of eternal life. Here we see one of the tensions that have to be negotiated. The Reformers were right to warn against presuming on God's judgement, and the funeral minister should try to cast the language of liturgy and preaching in a way that carefully and sensitively balances hope and trust with a recognition of the need of sinful human beings for God's mercy.

Praying for the dead is relatively straightforward. Offering comfort and hope to the living is more complex, and it is here that both challenges and opportunities arise. The Tridentine funeral rite placed a heavy emphasis on wrath and judgement. In its words, music and gestures, it gave ample expression to the feelings of grief, fear and anger that often accompany death.[8] The post-Vatican II rite is, in many respects, more positive and optimistic, with an emphasis on the hope of resurrection and eternal life. However, this calls for careful judgement on the part of the minister preparing the funeral. The reality of bereavement is a complex mixture of sadness, guilt, anger, often relief, regret, faith, doubt and, sometimes, despair. A well-planned liturgy can allow these emotions to be expressed and acknowledged in a way that is healing and helpful. The human need for ritual goes deep. Burying the dead is traditionally seen as one of the corporal works of mercy. In the contemporary context, providing a good funeral can be a priceless service to those in need.

Ritual is made up of word, symbol and gesture. It expresses meaning. Both the meaning and its expression have become complex and contested in postmodern society, and these complications can become visible in the planning of a funeral. A traditional Catholic family will reach for the familiar symbols. But for many families today, such symbols are neither familiar, nor particularly meaningful. The outpouring of grief at the death of Princess Diana in 1997, and her dramatic, televised funeral, have had a huge impact on the British sense of what is an appropriate response to death. If asked what makes for a good funeral, many might reply that it should be personal, reflecting the uniqueness of their loved one's life and personality, and expressive of the family's grief. In practice, this may mean a request for music and symbols that seem alien to Christian liturgy. Any attempt by the funeral minister to resist such requests (or, sometimes, demands) is likely to be met with incomprehension at best, anger and hostility at worst. However, a discerning assessment of the needs of the bereaved family, and a sensitive approach to the planning of the funeral, make possible a liturgy that is at the same time human, holy and healing.

Order of Christian Funerals

History
Ordo Exsequiarum
- Editio typica, 1969

Order of Christian Funerals
- First edition, 1970 (Rite of Funerals)
- Second edition, 1990 (London: Geoffrey Chapman)

Contents

Part I: Funeral Rites

Vigil and Related Rites and Prayers
Prayers after Death
Vigil for the Deceased
Vigil for the Deceased with Reception at the Church

Funeral Liturgy
Funeral Mass
Funeral Liturgy outside Mass

The Rite

The *Order of Christian Funerals* (*OCF*) is the revised English version of the 1969 *Ordo Exsequiarum*. It has been in use in England and Wales, and also in Scotland, since 1990. It covers all of the various forms of funeral liturgy and associated rites, with an extensive selection of texts for each form. A smaller volume also exists, for use by the funeral minister at the committal of the deceased at the cemetery or crematorium, containing only the texts that are needed there.

The minister

A Requiem Mass must be celebrated by a priest. A funeral liturgy outside Mass can be celebrated by a deacon or a properly prepared layperson, and some dioceses in England and Wales have now commissioned lay funeral ministers. Sometimes, different parts of the liturgy will be led by different ministers. Normally, a professional funeral director will also play an important part. The term 'minister' is used hereafter to mean the priest/deacon/layperson.

The Form of the Liturgy

In the classical form of the funeral rite, the *OCF* speaks of three stages or 'stations', in the sense of 'stopping places', rather like the 'stations' on the Way of the Cross. These stations are the home of the deceased, the church and the cemetery.[9] Some celebrations only involve the latter two, or the last one: nowadays, the place of death will often be a hospital or institution, rather than the home of the deceased, and committal may happen at a crematorium rather than a cemetery. However, it is helpful to understand that the Church envisages the funeral, in some respects, as a single liturgy celebrated in three parts, even when some elements may be abbreviated or absent.

Question for Reflection

Prayer of Commendation

Into your hands, Father of mercies,
we commend our brother/sister N.
in the sure and certain hope
that, together with all who have died in Christ,
he/she will rise with him on the last day.

We give you thanks for the blessings
which you bestowed on N. in this life:
they are signs to us of your goodness
and of our friendship with the saints in Christ.

Merciful Lord,
turn towards us and listen to our prayers:
open the gates of paradise to your servant
and help us who remain
to comfort one another with assurance of faith,
until we all meet in Christ
and are with you and with our brother/sister for ever.
Amen.

- In what way does this prayer articulate the purposes of the funeral rites given on page 32?

At the place of death

The death of a Christian can occur in many different circumstances: suddenly and unexpectedly, or long anticipated; at home, or in a hospital, care home or hospice. *Pastoral Care of the Sick* provides rites to cover every eventuality. They reflect an understanding of the importance of the presence of the Church, represented by her minister; providing the sacraments to the dying person and expressing the solidarity of the community with the family in their moment of loss. The texts of the rites are also designed to express a continuity between the liturgy for the dying and that for the dead.[10] In ancient forms of the liturgy, prayers and texts were provided to accompany the washing and preparation of the dead body, reflecting a sacramental understanding of the human body, even in death – a thoroughly Catholic vision of the goodness of material creation and the physicality of the human person. Nowadays, however, the preparation of the body for the funeral would almost always be seen as a professional task, to be carried out by healthcare staff and the funeral director.

At the church

The body of the deceased will be brought to church at the beginning of the funeral liturgy, or the evening before. The vigil service at which the body is taken into the church on the evening before the funeral – usually referred to as 'Reception into Church' – has become less common. But this vigil can offer possibilities for lay leadership, and for creative use of the options available in the rite. On a practical level, it can allow mourners to attend who will be unable to take part in a funeral liturgy held during the working day.

The funeral liturgy itself is described by *OCF* as either a 'Funeral Mass' or a 'Funeral Liturgy outside Mass', though the latter will invariably be referred to in pastoral practice as a 'Funeral Service'.

At the place of committal

OCF provides rites for burial (including burial at sea) and cremation. If a funeral liturgy has taken place beforehand, the rite of committal will be brief, but sometimes this single 'station' will be the only one at which a liturgy is celebrated.

The assembly

The array of options offered by *OCF* adds up to a potentially bewildering set of decisions for a bereaved family to make, in the course of planning a funeral. It will be part of the minister's task to guide the mourners towards suitable and realistic choices: and this judgement will be shaped by a pastoral assessment of the family's situation and needs.

The deceased

The person at the centre of the funeral liturgy cannot take an active part in its preparation, though he or she may have left instructions – perhaps very detailed – about their wishes. Sometimes, the deceased person will be well known to the minister as a staunch parishioner. If this is not the case, a careful conversation will allow the minister to gain an impression. The deceased person may have been brought up a Catholic, but drifted away from regular involvement in the life of the community. Or, he or she may have lived for many years in a state of anger against the Church, for some real or perceived slight or hurt, but nevertheless have wished for a Catholic funeral.

The family

The situation of the bereaved family can be complex and delicate. There may be one or more former spouses or partners on the scene, and a mixture of children and stepchildren. A wide range of personal or family difficulties may be in play. The minister will need to be aware of these complications, while reassuring the family that it does not all need to be aired publicly at the funeral. More simply, and very commonly, the deceased person was a committed Catholic, but their children and grandchildren rarely set foot in church. In such a case, the language of liturgy will be foreign to them, and they may feel intimidated or defensive when faced with a minister of the Church. It will be the minister's task to offer reassurance, and open a space in which the family can share fully in planning the funeral. The simple process of choosing Scripture readings and hymns can allow the family to feel that they have done their part, and other possibilities, such as writing and reading suitable bidding prayers, should be explored.

The community

OCF speaks of the call of the faithful to a 'ministry of consolation to those who have suffered the loss of one whom they love'.[11] It is striking that this is described as a ministry belonging to the whole community. At the planning stage, this should prompt the minister to encourage the maximum participation by the parish community in the funeral liturgy.

Funeral Mass

Funeral Mass Followed by Rite of Committal: Structure

Introductory Rites
  Greeting
  Sprinkling with Holy Water
  Placing of Pall
  Entrance Procession
  Placing of Christian Symbols
  Opening Prayer
Liturgy of the Word
  Readings
  Homily
  Intercessions
Liturgy of the Eucharist
Final Commendation
  Invitation to Prayer
  Song of Farewell
  Prayer of Commendation

Procession to the Place of Committal
Rite of Committal
Invitation
  Scripture Verse
  Prayer over the Place of Committal
Committal
  Intercessions
  Lord's Prayer
  Concluding Prayer
Prayers over the People

The funeral Mass, or Requiem Mass, unites two themes which are hallmarks of Catholic ministry to the dead: the gathering of the community to pray for the deceased, and the belief that, in the Eucharist, the propitiatory sacrifice of Christ can be 'applied' for the benefit of a particular person. It is therefore the 'default option' offered by *OCF*. A funeral Mass represents a step outside normal liturgical time: the prayers, readings and colours proper to the day are replaced by those given for Christian death. To the normal structure of the Mass are added the rite of reception of the body, and that of final commendation, reflecting the structure described above, in which the church is one of the three 'stations' of the funeral liturgy.

Funeral Liturgy outside Mass

Although the Requiem Mass is the default option, it is not always the most appropriate liturgical form for the funeral. Sometimes the family of the deceased are not used to taking part in worship, and might find the Mass unfamiliar, over-long and even alienating. In such a case, the minister will usually suggest that a 'funeral service' is the appropriate choice. The rite of reception and Liturgy of the Word are essentially the same as for a funeral Mass: the Prayer of the Faithful concludes with the Lord's Prayer, and then the liturgy moves directly to the final commendation. (The option to distribute Holy Communion to the congregation from the tabernacle is offered by *OCF*, but is very rarely used.)

Rite of Committal for Cremation or Burial

This type of liturgy is usually described as 'straight to the crematorium' (or, less commonly, 'straight to the cemetery'). It is often seen as the minimal option, sometimes dictated by cost, or by difficult family circumstances. The structure is similar to that of the funeral liturgy outside Mass, but the celebration will be constrained by the venue (usually a crematorium chapel) and the time allowed for the celebration. Despite these constraints, the minister, by careful preparation and discussion with the family, can still celebrate a liturgy that will be meaningful and fitting.

Practicalities

Involvement of the parish community

The celebration of a funeral involves several lay ministries: musicians, servers, readers and welcomers. In a large and active parish, a well-prepared team will already exist to carry out these roles – a visible expression of the ministry of consolation to which all the faithful are called.[12] Ideally, members of the parish community will also take part in the celebration of the vigil before the funeral, praying the Rosary with the bereaved family, and visiting the family before and after the funeral liturgy. If the parish does not have such a team available, identifying and preparing suitable volunteers should be a pastoral priority.

The role of the funeral director

The funeral director (undertaker) will take charge of the practical arrangements for the funeral, including the removal and preparation of the body and fixing the time and place for burial or cremation. The relationship between the Church's minister and the funeral director has its potential pitfalls. Most funeral directors adopt a thoroughly professional approach to their work, and many have a strong sense of vocation and care for their clients. However, they are running a business, with the pressures that this entails. The minister should be aware of these tensions, and should show the funeral director appropriate respect, while insisting on similar respect for his/her own role and the community that he/she leads. As always, time allows relationships of trust and respect to be built up.

Customs and Choices

The General Introduction to the *Ordo Exsequiarum* stated, and *OCF* cited, that it is the role of the priest (and, by implication, any minister of the Church involved in preparing a funeral):

> to comfort the family of the deceased, to sustain them amid the anguish of their grief, to be as kind and helpful as possible, and, through the use of the resources provided and allowed in the ritual, to prepare with them a funeral celebration that has meaning for them.[13]

The instructions for the preparation and celebration of a funeral strike a careful balance between grief and hope, consciousness of sin and expectation of forgiveness, the sadness of loss and thanksgiving for the blessings of the deceased's life. *OCF*, in citing *Ordo Exsequiarum*, deprecated 'empty display',[14] but affirmed that Christians should not show contempt for the attitudes or practices of their own time and place.[15] The honours due to civil authorities according to liturgical law are to be respected, but no special honours are to be paid to any person or class of persons.[16]

The rites allow considerable scope for personalizing the funeral liturgy, through the choice of readings, hymns and prayers, the composition of prayers of intercession, and even an address in remembrance of the deceased at the end of the service.[17] However, in contemporary society, the family of the deceased will sometimes wish to introduce elements that are completely extraneous to Christian liturgy: a football shirt draped over the coffin, a secular reading or poem, a pop song to accompany the procession with the coffin. Such wishes will, on occasion, be presented not as requests, but as expectations or even demands. At this point, the minister may experience a tension between the desire to be as kind and helpful as possible and the obligation to celebrate the mysteries of Christ appropriately.

The most fruitful approach to such difficulties will always be one of dialogue. The minister should encourage the family to make the most of the options that this liturgy does allow, and to find other ways to include elements that have no place in the church – for example, at the gathering and refreshments after the funeral, a kind of additional 'station' of the celebration. It should be put to the family that the Church's liturgy has tremendous power for consolation and healing, but that this power depends on respecting its nature and meaning as an act of worship.

Questions for Reflection

OCF allows the options of black, violet (purple) or white vestments for a funeral liturgy.

- In what situations would each colour be appropriate? Would this be an option for discussion with the family?
- What if the deceased has left a list of 'last wishes' for the funeral, including items that seem inappropriate for a church funeral. How would you approach this issue with the bereaved family?

Notes

1 Rutherford, Richard, *The Death of a Christian* (Collegeville, PA: Pueblo, 1991), p. 4.
2 Rutherford, *The Death of a Christian*, pp. 4–5, and see 2 Maccabees 12.38–45.
3 Rutherford, *The Death of a Christian*, p. 11.
4 Rutherford, *The Death of a Christian*, p. 28.
5 *SC*, 81.
6 *GIRM*, 379.
7 Duffy, Eamon, *Faith of our Fathers* (London: Continuum, 2006), p. 126.
8 Duffy, 116–24.
9 *OCF*, 42.
10 Rutherford, pp. 43–7.
11 *OCF*, 8.
12 *OCF*, 8.
13 *Ordo Exsequiarum*, 25.3 (cited in *OCF*, 436).
14 *Ordo Exsequiarum*, 3 (*OCF*, 432).
15 *Ordo Exsequiarum*, 2 (*OCF*, 432).
16 *Ordo Exsequiarum*, 20 (*OCF*, 434).
17 *OCF*, 181, 212.

12

Times and Seasons

JONATHAN HOW AND MARTIN FOSTER

The Liturgy of the Hours:
The Sanctification of Time

Overview

Ritual action is one of the ways in which human beings cope with transitions. For example, we have what are often spoken of as 'rites of passage' that take place at birth, in adolescence, in forming a new household, and around death and dying. But there are also rituals around smaller but still fundamental human transitions, such as from night into day or day into night. (If you doubt this then consider what happens when you disturb a child's bedtime routine or when you deprive an adult of their first cup of tea or coffee in the morning.)

Waking up and going to bed for many people are times associated with prayer. The morning is a time of thanksgiving: for a good night's sleep, for the gifts of God's creation. It is associated with the resurrection. Night-time is for reflecting on the day that has passed, what has been good or ill, and entrusting oneself to God's care. Devotional prayers such as the Angelus are connected with particular times of day; through the words of the Annunciation the prayer recalls the mystery of the incarnation.

Origins

The origins of Christian prayer are to be found in the fact that prayer is natural to human beings. There is not much evidence for what the first Christians did in their regular prayer. However, inasmuch as the New Testament provides a picture of Jesus and the Church at prayer we may presume that it in some ways guided or reflected the patterns of prayer of the communities in which the Scriptures became canonical.

The *Didache*[1], a late first-century text, follows the Jewish custom of prayer three times a day with recitation of the Our Father thrice daily (8.2–3). Over the following centuries liturgical prayer developed in two ways. The first was associated with the development of monasticism in the deserts of Egypt. The individual monks who came together to pray sought to make their whole life prayer. This was characterized by the recitation of the psalter (the Book of Psalms in the Bible, with 150 psalms), and they did this in varying patterns over a day or a week. The other pattern was found in urban centres where celebrations of Morning and Evening Prayer were simpler and reflected the time of day. In the evening therefore was a lighting of lamps, which was practical but also symbolized the light of Christ; specific psalms were chosen such as Psalm 140 which refers to the evening. This form is usually referred to as the 'Cathedral Office' as it took place in the main city church. These two patterns have influenced the current Liturgy of the Hours where the whole psalter is recited over a period (four weeks) but the psalms are arranged according to their suitability to the hour.

Liturgy of the Hours

The Liturgy of the Hours is a liturgical way of marking the passing of time through the day. It complements this basic human need to structure the day and ease us through its transitions. It shares in the priestly work of Jesus, the man of prayer, and sanctifies the day and the Christian people. Sometimes also referred to as the Divine Office or the Prayer of the Church, it is made up of a number of 'hours' – forms of prayer for particular times of day. Each consists mostly of psalms and canticles, Scripture and hymns. The principal hours are Morning and Evening Prayer; they are the 'hinges' of the day.

Liturgy of the Hours

History

Liturgia Horarum
- Editio typica – 4 volumes, 1971

Liturgy of the Hours
- 3 volumes, 1974 (London: Collins)

Also published in a number of shorter editions, including *Morning and Evening Prayer*.

Contents

General Instruction of the Liturgy of the Hours
Proper of Seasons
Commonly used texts
4-week Psalter
Night Prayer
Proper of Saints
Commons

Hours

Morning Prayer (also called Lauds) – a major office celebrated in the morning, marking the coming of day.
Prayer during the day – a lesser office celebrated during the working day.
Evening Prayer (also called Vespers) – a major office celebrated in the evening, marking the passing of day and coming of night; the ending of the day.
Night Prayer – a short office celebrated just before bed.
Office of Readings – an office with more extended readings celebrated at any appropriate time.

Structure

Morning and Evening Prayer share a common structure; the other hours omit some elements. The basic structure is:

Introduction
Hymn
Psalms and canticle (Old Testament – Morning; New Testament – Evening)
Reading
Responsory
Gospel Canticle (Benedictus – Morning; Magnificat – Evening)
Intercessions
Our Father
Collect
Conclusion/Blessing

Theology of particular hours

Morning Prayer, or Lauds as it is often known, is celebrated as day dawns. It sanctifies the morning, consecrating the first movements of our hearts and minds to God. And in the morning hour our minds rightly turn also to that morning, on the first day of the week, when Jesus Christ, the morning star, rose from the dead bringing light and life. It has a character of praise, and for centuries it included what are known as the 'Laudate psalms' (the 'Praise' psalms, from which the name Lauds comes). These days those psalms are spread across a four-week cycle, but the psalms for Morning Prayer are still chosen from those with a strong sense of praise. The modern office concludes with a set of invocations which consecrate the day.

The theme of praise for the new day and for salvation can be seen, for example, in the Canticle of Zachariah – the *Benedictus* – which refers to the action of God who 'has raised up a mighty saviour' who 'visits us like the dawn from on high' and who 'will give light to those in darkness' (see Luke 1.68–79).

Evening Prayer, or Vespers, is celebrated as day draws to a close. As darkness falls we recall our salvation and look forward to the return of Christ. Drawing on Psalm 140, used in First Evening Prayer (Vespers) of Sunday Week 1 – 'Let my prayer arise before you like incense, the raising of my hands like an evening oblation' – it is sometimes considered as an evening sacrifice, a theme that comes out even more clearly when the altar is incensed in more solemn celebrations. Morning Prayer is more laudatory, Evening Prayer has a stronger character of thanksgiving and of petition. In the Magnificat, the Church takes up Mary's canticle of thanksgiving to God who has 'worked marvels'. The intercessions have a clearly petitionary character.

In some places Evening Prayer will include a 'lucernarium', the lighting of lamps, rather as the church is lit at the start of the Easter Vigil. This ritual draws out the theme of Christ the light.

Night Prayer (formally, Compline) is said just before bed. It includes a brief examination of conscience, and the canticle of Simeon, the Nunc dimittis. It concludes with a Marian anthem (such as *Salve Regina*), invoking the prayer and protection of Mary for the night ahead. As well as a prayer for protection during the night it also carries something of an eschatological character, looking forward to the Last Days.

Theology of the Liturgy of the Hours in general

'The public and communal prayer of the people of God is rightly considered among the first duties of the Church.'[2] This short statement at the start of the *General Instruction on the Liturgy of the Hours* (*GILH*) underlines the importance of the Liturgy of the Hours for the life of the Church. This work of prayer is liturgy because 'Christ is always present in His Church, especially in her liturgical celebrations . . . He is present . . . when the Church prays and sings, for He promised: "Where two or three are gathered together in my name, there am I in the midst of them"' (Matt. 18.20). It is, therefore, alongside all Liturgy, 'an action of Christ the priest and His Body which is the Church' and thereby 'a sacred action surpassing all others'.[3]

The fathers of the Second Vatican Council expressed it in this way:

Christ Jesus, high priest of the new and eternal covenant, taking human nature, introduced into this earthly exile that hymn which is sung throughout all ages in the halls of heaven. He joins the entire community of mankind to Himself, associating it with His own singing of this canticle of divine praise. For he continues His priestly work through the agency of His Church, which is ceaselessly engaged in praising the Lord and interceding for the salvation of the whole world. She does this, not only by celebrating the eucharist, but also in other ways, especially by praying the divine office.[4]

Like most General Instructions/Introductions, *GILH* provides a rich theological basis for the liturgy it describes, and in fact gives a much clearer account of the prayer of the Church than *Sacrosanctum Concilium*, which too often treats it simply as the prayer of clergy and religious.

The instruction points to the way in which the Gospels give a clear picture of the prayer of Jesus as an integral part of his ministry. For example: he prays at the multiplication of the loaves and the raising of Lazarus; he goes off to a lonely place to pray; he joins the communal prayer at the synagogue; and on the night before he died. The picture is confirmed by the Letter to the Hebrews, for whom Jesus was the one who 'offered up prayers and supplications, with loud cries and silent tears' (Heb. 5.7, *GILH*).[5] It reminds us that prayer is commanded by Jesus: he tells his disciples to 'pray', 'ask', and 'seek'. And St Paul urges his readers to 'pray without ceasing' (1 Thess. 5.17).[6] Drawing from the description of the early Church in the Acts of the Apostles, it argues for prayer as 'expressing the very essence of the Church as a community'.[7]

Question for Reflection

GILH records not only the many times that Jesus prays in the Gospels (*GILH*, 4) but also how he encouraged others to pray:

> What Jesus himself did, he also commands us to do. He often said, 'Pray', 'Ask', 'Seek' (Matt. 5.44; 7.7) 'in my name'. (John 14.13; 15.16). He gave us the Lord's Prayer to teach us how to pray (Matt. 6.9–13; Luke 11.2–4). He instructed us on the necessity of prayer (Luke 18.1), and told us to be humble (Luke 18.9–14), watchful, (Mark 13.33), persevering and confident in the goodness of the Father (Luke 11.5–13; 18.1–8), pure in intention and worthy of God (Matt. 6.5–8).

Look up some of these references.

- Can you use them to write a brief description of Christian prayer?

The Calendar: The Sacramentality of Time

General theology of liturgical time

> The unfolding of the liturgical year is not just a commemoration of the actions by which Jesus Christ, by dying, has brought about our salvation. Nor . . . is this unfolding merely a *commemoration of past events* so that the faithful, even the more simple, might be instructed and nourished by meditating on them. The celebration of the liturgical year 'enjoys a *sacramental* force and a particular efficaciousness to nourish the Christian life'. (Paul VI, *Mysterii Paschalis*, 1969)

> Recalling thus the mysteries of redemption, the Church opens to the faithful the riches of her Lord's powers and merits, so that these are in some way made **present for all time**, and the faithful are enabled to lay hold upon them and become filled with saving grace. (*Sacrosanctum Concilium*, 102)

Universal Norms for the Liturgical Year and Calendar

The Calendar was one of the first elements to be revised following the Second Vatican Council; other parts of the liturgy such as the *Missal* and the Lectionary are dependent on it. As with the various liturgical rites there is an Introduction, called the *Universal Norms for the Liturgical Year and Calendar* (*UNLYC*),[8] which is found after the General Instruction in the *Roman Missal*. The order in which it considers the parts of the liturgical year may initially come as a surprise: the liturgical day begins with Sunday, then the second section on the Cycle of the Year begins with the Paschal Triduum, followed by Easter and Lent, then Christmas and Advent, and finally Ordinary Time. It is a reminder of the principle given in Chapter 3 that the order of items in liturgical books can denote either importance or chronology. In *UNLYC*, where a chronology starting with Advent might appear the more obvious, the relative importance is given weight.

This order will shape the presentation of the liturgical year; the treatment of each season provides a theological summary and then technical points about the Calendar.

Sundays

The Gospels all record that Jesus rose again on the first day of the week. At some point the various early Christian communities shifted their time of communal worship from the Sabbath (Saturday) to Sunday and probably from evening to morning. However, as with all early liturgical history there is a lack of evidence for its initial developments and little definite knowledge of the contemporary Jewish practice.

Gathering on a Sunday became one of the defining features of the religion. It is how Justin begins his description of the Eucharist; martyrs in North Africa in the early fourth century proclaimed 'We cannot live without Sunday'. What was retained from Jewish practice was that the liturgical day began on the evening before, so Sunday starts on Saturday evening.

Sunday is not only the day of resurrection but also the first day of creation. Indeed it is the first day of the new creation, or the eighth day that is outside time. Every Sunday is a little Easter – as Easter is to the year, so Sunday is to the week. It is the Day of the Lord and the primordial feast day (cf. *UNLYC*, 4). It is this rich, interwoven theology that gives an importance to Sunday as a day when the Church gathers to celebrate the Paschal Mystery most fully expressed in the Mass. It is also the day for infant baptism to take place – though not necessarily at Sunday Mass.

Holydays of Obligation

The Code of Canon Law lists Holydays of Obligation in addition to Sundays. A local Bishops' Conference can decide which of these are to be kept in its territory. In England and Wales the Holydays of Obligation are as follows:

Nativity of the Lord – 25 December
Epiphany of the Lord – 6 January
Ascension of the Lord
St Peter and St Paul – 29 June
Assumption of the Blessed Virgin Mary – 15 August
All Saints – 1 November
All Sundays
   When the celebration falls on a Saturday or a Monday it is transferred to
   the adjacent Sunday.

On these days there is an obligation to go to Mass and refrain from work – the link between holydays and holidays is direct. The latter aspect can be difficult for many and many parishes will have Masses first thing in the morning and in the evening on these days so that people who work can fulfil their obligation. Obligation can have negative overtones to some people; a more positive way of looking at these days is to recognize the importance of what they celebrate. Each is significant in the life of Christ and of the Church. In some ways the Church is calling people to come to Mass so that they can give thanks for these feasts and enter into them more deeply – they can be seen as essential to being Church.

Cycle of the year or the liturgical year

In the Northern hemisphere the liturgical year is shaped by the passing of the seasons – the moving from darkness to light at Christmas; the signs of new life at Easter. The liturgy is moving with the turning of the earth and the lengthening of days. The connection with key points in the lunar and solar cycles is concrete, as will be noted below.

UNLYC describes the liturgical seasons and, as already stated, this is not chronological and does not start with Advent. It groups the seasons together and places them around a central event. The seasons are Advent – Christmas and Lent – Triduum – Easter. The centre point of the first is the Nativity; the second the Triduum. For each there is a time of preparation (Advent, Lent) and a time of reflection (Christmas Season, Easter). In one liturgical book the following image is used: 'The annual observance of Lent is the special season for the ascent to the holy mountain of Easter' (*Ceremonial of Bishops*, 249).[9] This is a helpful image to understand the dynamic of the liturgical seasons. Advent and Lent are leading somewhere; the seasons of Christmas and Easter are the journey down from the mountain-top.

Lent, Triduum and Eastertide

Triduum

> Since Christ accomplished his work of human redemption and of the perfect glorification of God principally through his Paschal Mystery, in which by dying he has destroyed our death, and by rising restored our life, the sacred Paschal Triduum of the Passion and Resurrection of the Lord shines forth as the high point of the entire liturgical year. Therefore the pre-eminence that Sunday has in the week, the Solemnity of Easter has in the liturgical year. (*UNLYC*, 18)

The word 'Triduum' derives from the Latin for three days. It begins on Maundy Thursday evening and ends on the afternoon of Easter Sunday. The Triduum is often called the Paschal Triduum; the word 'Paschal' being related to two concepts: Passover and Passion. It is the annual celebration of the passion, death and resurrection of Jesus. Though the Gospels differ in the exact chronology of these events they are connected with the Jewish celebration of Passover. There are two milestones in the historical development of the liturgical celebration: the establishment of how the date of Easter was to be calculated, and the gradual development of the other celebrations. The date of Easter is connected with the date of Passover and linked to the solar and lunar calendars. There were different traditions in the early Church about whether you should celebrate Easter at exactly the same time as the Passover (which can fall on any day of the week) or whether the Lord's resurrection on Sunday is the defining factor. Sunday celebration became the norm. The date of Easter is calculated as the Sunday after the first full moon (so, lunar) after the Spring Equinox (so, solar – when light and darkness are equal). The Spring Equinox is currently 21 March.

The second aspect of the historical development is that initially the sole celebration was the Easter Vigil, at which new believers were initiated. Following the conversion of the Emperor Constantine and the Christianization of the Roman Empire in the early fourth century, the sites in Jerusalem of Jesus' passion, death and resurrection were discovered and became places of pilgrimage. The liturgies that ritualized these events became influential as pilgrims took their experience home. There is a pilgrimage account by a fourth-century nun named Egeria who recorded her experience of the Jerusalem liturgies. First the Liturgy of Good Friday was imitated, particularly where there was a relic of the cross, and then the Mass of the Lord's Supper on Maundy Thursday.

At first the Easter Vigil was the one liturgical celebration, encapsulating both death and resurrection, passion and Passover. The gradual development of the Triduum shows a desire to map the liturgy on to the gospel events, but there is a potential tension here. The liturgy is not a re-enactment of past events, a dramatization of the story (the events of the passion are not recreated), but a ritualization that holds the whole picture. It is a ritualization; the events of the passion are not recreated. The core symbol of Good Friday is the Veneration of the Cross, an action that of itself is not found in the Gospel accounts. The cross is venerated because through Christ's death upon it sin and death have been conquered. From the Entrance Antiphon of Maundy Thursday the texts of the Triduum are concerned with the complete Paschal Mystery.

> We should glory in the Cross of our Lord Jesus Christ,
> in whom is our salvation, life and resurrection,
> through whom we are saved and delivered.
> Maundy Thursday Entrance Antiphon. (cf. Gal. 6.14)

The Paschal Triduum of the passion and resurrection of the Lord begins with the evening Mass of the Lord's Supper, has its centre in the Easter Vigil, and closes with Vespers (Evening Prayer) on the Sunday of the Resurrection (*UNLYC*, 19).

The principal liturgical celebrations are:

Maundy Thursday
Evening Mass of the Lord's Supper
– Washing of the Feet
– Commemoration of the Institution of the Eucharist

Good Friday
Celebration of the Lord's Passion
– Passion according to John
– Solemn Intercessions
– Veneration of the Cross

Holy Saturday

Easter Sunday
Easter Vigil
– Lighting of Paschal Candle and Exsultet
– Extended Liturgy of the Word
– Sacraments of Initiation
Mass of Easter Day

Easter Season

The Easter Season flows out of the Triduum. It is the time of Mystagogia (see Chapter 5). The length of the season is shaped by the New Testament narrative of the post-resurrection appearances, the ascension and Pentecost. Pentecost falls on the fiftieth day and the season can be seen as one Sunday, seven weeks long.

The Lectionary exercises a sleight of hand (as it often does through the liturgical year). Though the Gospels say 40 days they do not describe even what happens on the Sundays. The Sunday Lectionary is not giving the stories as they happen; indeed, if you map the events against the probable dates after Easter there are discrepancies from the beginning.

What the Lectionary draws together are the strands of post-baptismal catechesis and the development of how the presence of Jesus will continue in the Church through the coming of the Holy Spirit.

The end of the Easter Season is marked by two great feasts. The Ascension of the Lord is celebrated 40 days after Easter, on the Thursday in the sixth week of Easter. It is the completion of the Paschal Mystery – Christ's glorification at the right hand of the Father, which means that humankind can aspire to a place in heaven. Pentecost Sunday marks the outpouring of the Holy Spirit on the Church so that the mission and ministry of Jesus can be continued.

The Easter Season begins on Easter Sunday and ends on Pentecost Sunday. The liturgical colour is white (but red at Pentecost).

Principal Celebrations

Easter Sunday
Easter Octave
Second to Sixth Sunday of Easter
Ascension of the Lord
Seventh Sunday of Easter
Pentecost Sunday

Lent

Lent is a preparatory season for the celebration of the Triduum, with twin focuses of Baptism and Penance. Catechumens are preparing for the Sacraments of Initiation at the Easter Vigil; the rest of the Church is preparing to renew the promises made at Baptism. For the faithful the desire for reconciliation comes from the reflection on how these promises have not been fulfilled. A key purpose of Lent is that the Triduum can be celebrated 'worthily and well'.

The Lectionary begins on Ash Wednesday with three powerful readings about the call to prayer, fasting and almsgiving, and the reconciling power of Christ. On the First Sunday of Lent the Gospel is of Jesus' temptation after his 40 days in the desert at the beginning of his ministry. As in the Easter Season, there is a discrepancy between the '40 days' of Lent and the lack of anything in the Gospels that fills this out; the accounts suggest that the temptations come at the end of the 40 days. Forty is a significant number within the Bible: it is the length of the days when the waters flooded the earth, the number of years that it took to get to the promised land after the Exodus.

On the Second Sunday the Gospel is the Transfiguration which comes midway through Jesus' ministry just before he sets his path for Jerusalem. The Transfiguration is an image of Christ in glory, the opposite of the previous week; here he is the fulfilment of the Law and the Prophets.

The Sunday Gospels diverge in weeks 3, 4 and 5. Year A is shaped by the Catechumenate and the period of Purification and Enlightenment, with three substantial passages from the Gospel of John: the Samaritan woman at the well, the healing of the man born blind, the raising of Lazarus. These are the Sundays of the Scrutinies (as discussed in Chapter 5) and they are focused on the baptismal symbols of water, light and the passover from death to life. In Year B the passages are again from John and are about the salvation offered when Christ is lifted on the cross. In Year C the focus is reconciliation, with the Gospel being the prodigal son, and the woman caught in adultery. The Sixth Sunday is Palm Sunday, the Passion of the Lord, when the liturgy begins with the marking of Jesus' triumphal entry into Jerusalem. In the main Liturgy of the Word the Passion reading is proclaimed.

Devotions especially associated with Lent, such as the Stations of the Cross, have shaped popular piety and understanding of the season. It is also a time when parishes offers Services of Reconciliation. Lent begins on Ash Wednesday and ends before the evening of Maundy Thursday, the Thursday of Holy Week. The liturgical colour is violet or purple.

Lent: Principal Celebrations

Ash Wednesday
First Sunday of Lent
Rite of Election
Second to fifth Sunday of Lent
Palm Sunday, the Passion of the Lord (Sixth Sunday)
Holy Week

Advent and Christmastide

Christmas – the Nativity of the Lord

'After the annual celebration of the Paschal Mystery, the Church has no more ancient custom than celebrating the memorial of the Nativity of the Lord and of his first manifestations, and this takes place in Christmas Time' (*UNLYC*, 32).

There are four separate Masses given for Christmas Day. Each has its own character based on the time of day, the unfolding of the story and the theology. The Vigil Mass on the evening of 24 December has the genealogy of Jesus from Matthew's Gospel. It not only emphasizes his royal pedigree but also the generations who have been waiting for a Messiah. The first reading of the Mass during the night is taken from Isaiah: 'The people who walked in darkness have seen a great light'. The Gospel gives Luke's account of how Jesus was born and this news was proclaimed by angels to shepherds. The Mass at Dawn continues the story of the shepherds visiting the newborn and Mary pondering these things in her heart. Finally, at the Mass during the day the beginning of John's Gospel is proclaimed – a reflection on the mystery of the incarnation.

Christmas Season

After the Nativity of the Lord there are a series of Feasts and Solemnities. The Octave day of Christmas (the eighth day, 1 January) has been through various options and is now the Solemnity of Mary, Mother of God. On 6 January the Epiphany of the Lord is celebrated, marking how (in Matthew's Gospel) Jesus after his birth is visited by wise men who bring him gifts. The end of the Christmas Season is the Baptism of the Lord, which marks the beginning of his public ministry and is usually celebrated on the Sunday after Epiphany. There is one further feast in the Christmas cycle, the Presentation of the Lord on 2 February when Christ is presented in the Temple, as required by the Jewish law 40 days after his birth. One way of thinking about this, and it complements the earlier image of a mountain, is that the liturgical season can be seen as a pool of water. The central event, the Nativity of the Lord, is like a stone tossed in the centre of the pool. The ripples caused by the stone go out in both directions, to Advent and to the Christmas Season. Some of the water even breaks the banks, marking the end of the season. The Presentation of the Lord is like a final ripple of the Christmas Season.

The Christmas Season runs from the evening of 24 December until the Sunday after 6 January when the Baptism of the Lord is celebrated.

The liturgical colour is white.

Christmastide: Principal Celebrations

Nativity of the Lord (25 December)
Holy Family of Jesus, Mary and Joseph (Sunday after 25 December)
Mary, Mother of God (1 January)
Epiphany of the Lord (6 January, or, in England and Wales, transferred to Sunday when it falls on a Saturday or Monday)
Baptism of the Lord (Sunday after 6 January)

Advent

> Advent has a twofold character, for it is a time of preparation for the Solemnities of Christmas, in which the First Coming of the Son of God to humanity is remembered, and likewise a time when, by remembrance of this, minds and hearts are led to look forward to Christ's Second Coming at the end of time. For these two reasons, Advent is a period of devout and expectant delight. (*UNLYC*, 39)

Advent is a preparation for the coming of the Messiah. It begins with preparation for Christ's coming at the end of time. This focus is initially found on the Sundays of November at the end of Ordinary Time, as though they were further ripples of the pool; it also means there is a smooth transition from one liturgical year to the next. The second and third Sundays of Advent focus on John the Baptist, his ministry and his teaching. The figure of John the Baptist will bookend the whole season as he will appear again at the Baptism of the Lord. In Advent the Messiah that John the Baptist is preparing for is the adult Christ. The fourth Sunday presents Gospel passages from the first chapters of Matthew's and Luke's Gospels across the three years; these relate more directly to the events leading up to the birth of Christ.

As the eight days (the Octave) after Christmas are marked, so are the eight days before. On the weekdays from 17 December at Evening Prayer the 'O Antiphons' are recited. These are so named as they all share the same beginning 'O'; each continues with a prophetic title of Jesus, ending with 'O Emmanuel' on 24 December.

Advent begins with First Vespers (Evening Prayer I) of the Sunday that falls on or closest to 30 November and it ends before First Vespers (Evening Prayer I) of Christmas (*UNLYC*, 40). The liturgical colour is violet or purple.

Advent: Principal Celebrations

First Sunday of Advent
Second Sunday of Advent
   Immaculate Conception of the Blessed Virgin Mary – 8 December
Third Sunday of Advent
   17–24 December – Weekdays ('O Antiphons')
Fourth Sunday of Advent

Ordinary Time

Besides the times of year that have their own distinctive character, there remain in the yearly cycle thirty-three or thirty-four weeks in which no particular aspect of the mystery of Christ is celebrated, but rather the mystery of Christ itself is honoured in its fullness, especially on Sundays. This period is known as Ordinary Time. (*UNLYC*, 43)

The use of the word 'Ordinary' is connected with ordinal numbers, or being 'in order', rather than signifying the commonplace. This is the ordered time where the Sundays are counted. It comes in two parts. The first is between the end of Christmas and the beginning of Lent. Across the three-year cycle the Gospels are about the beginnings of Jesus' ministry, his initial teaching, healing and other miracles. The second part is the longer and is from Pentecost until the last Sunday of the Church's year, the feast of Christ the King at the end of November. Because Easter is movable Pentecost can fall within a range of about a month, therefore the Sundays of this period are numbered backwards from Christ the King which is the 34th. In each year the Gospel is followed through semi-continuously and the life and teaching of Jesus are recounted according to Matthew, Mark and Luke. In Year B there are a number of Sundays devoted to John 6 where Jesus teaches about the 'bread of life'.

Ordinary Time begins on the Monday following the Baptism of the Lord in January and continues until the Tuesday before Ash Wednesday. It returns on the Monday after Pentecost and continues through the Summer and Autumn until the beginning of Advent. The liturgical colour is green.

Ordinary Time: Principal Celebrations

Second and subsequent Sundays in Ordinary Time
After Pentecost
Trinity Sunday (Sunday after Pentecost)
The Body and Blood of the Lord (Corpus Christi; Sunday after Trinity in England and Wales)
The Sacred Heart of Jesus (Second Friday after Trinity)
Sundays in Ordinary Time (up to 33rd)
Our Lord Jesus Christ, Universal King (last Sunday of Ordinary Time)

Conclusion

In the last Sundays of Ordinary Time the Gospel readings turn to the Last Judgement and the Second Coming of Christ. These make a natural link with the following Season of Advent and are a reminder that it is a cycle that comes round again and again. Part of the purpose is that those who listen and participate are not static in their response to any particular Sunday or season. Each person has changed in the time since the liturgy was experienced previously and so their relationship to the texts has changed.

Proper of Saints

What has been considered so far is the Proper of Time or Temporal Cycle. This describes the Sundays and the Liturgical Seasons of Advent, Christmas, Lent, Triduum and Easter. The Proper of Saints exists separately to this and in some ways overlays the seasonal calendar. The Proper of Saints or Sanctoral Cycle is the yearly celebration of the saints. As a rule, a saint is celebrated on the day of his/her death, their 'birthday' into heaven. Not every saint who has been canonized (the process of declaring a saint) is found in the Calendar, which has a number of levels.

There is a Universal Calendar, shared by the whole Church, which includes saints of global significance. This includes the Apostles, and well-known saints such as Francis and Thérèse of Lisieux. As the origins of the liturgy are in the city of Rome, in the past there has been a preponderance of saints and early martyrs connected with the city. To make it more universal saints have been included from all regions of the globe such as St Josephine Bakhita and St Andrew Dung-Lac.

The next level is the National Calendar which marks saints such as St Thomas Becket and St David. A diocese will also have its own calendar for more local saints, associated with the particular area.

The celebrations of saints are ranked according to whether they are Solemnities, Feasts, or Memorials. This dictates how the saint is celebrated and which liturgical texts are used. A Solemnity is like a Sunday with three readings, a Gloria and a Creed and all the prayers connected with the particular day. An example of a Solemnity would be St Peter and St Paul on 29 June. On a Feast there are just two readings and the Creed is not said. On a Memorial not all the texts given for a saint have to be used. The same saint can be a different rank in the various calendars. The commemoration of St Thomas Becket is a Memorial in the Universal Calendar but in England it is a Feast, as he has greater significance in England and Wales.

For the majority of saints, particularly those who are commemorated as Memorials, there is not an individual, full set of prayers and readings. To accommodate this there are Commons according to the type of saints – for example, Apostle, Martyr, Pastor, Holy Man or Woman – in both the Lectionary and the *Missal*, and the same also applies in the Liturgy of the Hours. On the Memorial of St Cosmas and St Damian (26 September), martyrs, the Lectionary suggests a selection from the Common of Martyrs but other readings from the Common as well may be chosen; in the *Missal* there will be a Collect but the other texts might be taken from the Common as well.

The history of the Sanctoral Cycle is one of gradual additions and periodic clearings, as with the renewal of the Calendar after the Second Vatican Council. The various celebrations could be seen as encroaching on Sundays and the liturgical seasons – it can come as a surprise to many people that the majority of saints are displaced by the Sunday celebration. For example, if Our Lady of Lourdes (11 February) falls on a Sunday, the Sunday readings and prayers will take precedence and the celebration will not be marked that year. Important as the saints are as models of holiness, they are celebrated as images of the Christ to whom they point. 'The feasts of saints proclaim the wonderful works of Christ in his servants and offer the faithful fitting examples for their initiation' (cf. *SC*, 111). The principle of Sunday as the overriding feast day is therefore recognized, and the celebration of the Lord's Day comes first.

Notes

1 The text is available on-line at www.thedidache.com.

2 Divine Office, 1974, *General Instruction on the Liturgy of the Hours* (*GILH*) (London: Collins), 1.

3 *SC*, 7.

4 *SC*, 83.

5 *GILH*, 4, citing among others Matt. 14.19; John 11.41; Mark 1.35; Luke 4.16; Matt. 26.36–44.

6 *GILH*, 5.

7 *GILH*, 9.

8 Roman Missal, 2010, *Universal Norms for the Liturgical Year and Calendar* (*UNLYC*) (London: Catholic Truth Society).

9 Congregation for Divine Worship, 1989, *Ceremonial of Bishops* (Collegeville, MN: Liturgical Press).

Further Reading

General

Paul F. Bradshaw, 2010, *Early Christian Worship: A Basic Introduction to Ideas and Practice*, London: SPCK Publishing.

Paul F. Bradshaw, 2013, *New SCM Dictionary of Liturgy and Worship*, London: SCM Press.

Ascar Chupungco, 1997, *Handbook for Liturgical Studies, Volume I: Introduction to the Liturgy*, Collegeville, PA: Pueblo.

Ascar Chupungco, 1998. *Handbook for Liturgical Studies, Volume II: Fundamental Liturgy*, Collegeville, PA: Pueblo.

Juliette Day and Benjamin Gordon-Taylor, 2013, *The Study of Liturgy and Worship*, London: SPCK Publishing.

James F. White, 2001, *Introduction to Christian Worship*, Nashville, TN: Abingdon Press.

Roman Rite

Bernard Botte, 1989, *From Silence to Participation: Insider's View of Liturgical Renewal*, Portland, OR: Pastoral Press.

A. G. Martimort, 1987, *The Church at Prayer: Volume I: Principles of the Liturgy*, Collegeville, PA: Liturgical Press.

James F. White, 2003, *Roman Catholic Worship: Trent to Today*, Collegeville, PA: Pueblo.

Liturgy Theology

David W. Fagerberg, 2007, *Theologia Prima: What is Liturgical Theology?*, Chicago, IL: Liturgy Training Publications.

Rita Ferrone, 1997, *Liturgy: Sacrosanctum Concilium (Rediscovering Vatican II)*, Mahwah, NJ: Paulist Press.

Aidan Kavanagh, 1990, *On Liturgical Theology*, Collegeville, PA: Pueblo.

Joseph Ratzinger, 2014, *Collected Works – Theology of the Liturgy*, San Francisco, CA: Ignatius Press.

Fundamentals

Juliette Day, 2014, *Reading the Liturgy: An Exploration of Texts in Christian Worship*, London: Bloomsbury, T&T Clark.

Gabe Huck, 1998, *Liturgy with Style and Grace*, Chicago, IL: Liturgy Training Publications.

Aidan Kavanagh, 1994, *Elements of Rite: A Handbook of Liturgical Style*, Collegeville, PA: Pueblo.

Julie McCann, 2006, *Spiritual Garments: A Handbook for Preparing Liturgical Assemblies in Schools*, Brandon, FL: Decani.

Sacramental Theology

St Thomas Aquinas, *Summa Theologiae, Tertia Pars* Questions 60–65.

John F. Baldovin and David Farina Turnbloom, 2015, *Catholic Sacraments: A Rich Source of Blessings*, Mahwah, NJ: Paulist Press.

Ascar Chupungco, 1999, *Handbook for Liturgical Studies, Volume IV: Sacraments and Sacramentals*, Collegeville, PA: Pueblo.

Fergus Kerr, 2009, *Thomas Aquinas, A Very Short Introduction*, Oxford: Oxford University Press.

A. G. Martimort, 1987, *The Church at Prayer: Volume III: The Sacraments*, Collegeville, PA: Liturgical Press.

Herbert McCabe, 2010, *The New Creation*, London: Sheed & Ward.

Joseph Martos, 1981, *Doors to the Sacred: A Historical Introduction to the Sacraments in the Catholic Church*, London: SCM Press.

Dennis C. Smolarski, 1994, *Sacred Mysteries: Sacramental Principles and Liturgical Practice*, Mahwah, NJ: Paulist Press.

Initiation

Gerard Austin, 1985, *The Rite of Confirmation: Anointing with the Spirit*, Collegeville, PA: Pueblo.

Maxwell E. Johnson, 2007, *Rites of Christian Initiation: Their Evolution and Interpretation*, Collegeville, PA: Pueblo.

Aidan Kavanagh, 1992, *The Shape of Baptism: The Rite of Christian Initiation*, Collegeville, PA: Pueblo.

Peter McGrail, 2007, *First Communion: Ritual, Church and Popular Religious Identity*, Abingdon: Routledge.

Peter McGrail, 2016, *The Rite of Christian Initiation: Adult Rituals and Roman Catholic Ecclesiology*, Abingdon: Routledge.

Thomas Morris, 1997, *The RCIA, Transforming the Church: A Resource for Pastoral Implementation*, Mahwah, NJ: Paulist Press.

Paul Turner, 2000, *Hallelujah Highway, A History of the Catechumenate*, Chicago, IL: Liturgy Training Publications.

Paul Turner, 2007, *Confirmation: The Baby in Solomon's Court*, Chicago, IL: Hillenbrand Books.

Paul Turner, 2007, *When Other Christians Become Catholic*, Collegeville, PA: Pueblo.

Nick Wagner, 2008, *The Way of Faith: A Field Guide to the RCIA Process*, New London, CT: Twenty-Third Publications.

Theology of Eucharist

Paul F. Bradshaw and Maxwell E. Johnson, 2012, *Eucharistic Liturgies, Their Evolution and Interpretation*, London: SPCK Publishing.

Ascar Chupungco, 1999, *Handbook for Liturgical Studies, Volume III: The Eucharist*, Collegeville, PA: Pueblo.

Paul McPartlan, 1995, *Sacrament of Salvation: An Introduction to Eucharistic Ecclesiology.* Edinburgh: T&T Clark.

A. G. Martimort, 1986, *The Church at Prayer: Volume I: The Eucharist*, Collegeville, PA: Liturgical Press.

Nathan Mitchell, 2000, *Real Presence: The Work of Eucharist.* New, expanded edn. Chicago, IL: Liturgy Training Publications.

Pope Paul VI, Encyclical Letter *Mysterium Fidei* of 1965.

Pope John Paul II, Encyclical Letter *Ecclesia de Eucharistia* of 2003.

Joseph Ratzinger, 2003, *God Is Near Us: The Eucharist, the Heart of Life.* San Francisco, CA: Ignatius Press.

Celebrating Eucharist

John F. Baldovin, 2003, *Bread of Life, Cup of Salvation: Understanding the Mass*, Lanham, MD: Sheed & Ward.

Edward Foley, 2008, *A Commentary on the General Instruction of the Roman Missal*, Collegeville, PA: Pueblo.

Edward Foley, 2009, *From Age to Age: How Christians Have Celebrated the Eucharist*, Chicago, IL: Liturgy Training Publications.

Edward Foley, 2011, *A Commentary on the Order of Mass of the Roman Missal*, Collegeville, PA: Pueblo.

Paul Turner, 2012, *Let Us Pray: A Guide to the Rubrics of Sunday Mass*, Collegeville, PA: Pueblo.

Marriage

Kenneth Stevenson, 1987, *To Join Together: The Rite of Marriage*, Collegeville, PA: Pueblo.

Paul Turner, 2017, *Inseparable Love: A Commentary on the Order of Celebrating Matrimony in the Catholic Church*, Collegeville, PA: Pueblo.

Orders

Paul F. Bradshaw, 2014, *Rites of Ordination: Their History and Theology*, London: SPCK Publishing.

Randy Stice, 2016, *Understanding the Sacraments of Vocation, A Rite-Based Approach*, Chicago, IL: Liturgy Training Publications.

Penance/Anointing

James Dallen, 1991, *The Reconciling Community: The Rite of Penance*, Collegeville, PA: Pueblo.

Randy Stice, 2015, *Understanding the Sacraments of Healing, A Rite-Based Approach*, Chicago, IL: Liturgy Training Publications.

Funerals

Richard Rutherford with Tony Barr, 1991, *Death of a Christian: The Order of Christian Funerals*, Collegeville, PA: Pueblo.

Paul P. J. Sheppy, 2003, *Death Liturgy and Ritual: Volume I: A Pastoral and Liturgical Theology*, Abingdon: Routledge.

Hours and Time

Paul F. Bradshaw and Maxwell E. Johnson, 2011, *The Origins of Feasts, Fasts and Seasons in Early Christianity*, London: SPCK Publishing.

Stanilaus Campbell, 1995, *From Breviary to Liturgy of the Hours: The Structural Reform of the Roman Office, 1964–71*, Collegeville, PA: Pueblo.

Ascar Chupungco, 2000, *Handbook for Liturgical Studies, Volume V: Liturgical Time and Space*, Collegeville, PA: Pueblo.

George Guiver, 2000, *Company of Voices: Daily Prayer and the People of God*, Norwich: Canterbury Press.

A. G. Martimort, 1986, *The Church at Prayer: Volume IV: The Liturgy and Time*, Collegeville, PA: Liturgical Press.

Adrien Nocent, 2013, *The Liturgical Year: Advent, Christmas, Epiphany*, Collegeville, PA: Liturgical Press.

Adrien Nocent, 2013, *The Liturgical Year: Lent, the Sacred Paschal Triduum, Easter Time*, Collegeville, PA: Liturgical Press.

Adrien Nocent, 2013, *The Liturgical Year: Sundays Two to Thirty-Four in Ordinary Time*, Collegeville, PA: Liturgical Press.

Robert Taft, 1993, *Liturgy of the Hours in East and West: The Origin of the Divine Office and Its Meaning for Today*, Collegeville, PA: Liturgical Press.

Thomas Talley, 1991, *The Origins of the Liturgical Year*, Collegeville, PA: Pueblo.

Glossary

Ambo   The place, on the **Sanctuary**, where the Scriptures are read from at Mass and other liturgies. Often in the form of substantial lectern or reading desk made from wood or stone.

Anaphora   The Greek-derived name for the **Eucharistic Prayer**. It literally means to carry back or up but is used in Greek versions of the Old Testament for offering.

Antiphon   A short text taken from the Scriptures and intended to be sung. In the **Order of Mass** an antiphon is given for the Entrance and Communion procession. It is often used with verses from the Psalms. In the **Liturgy of the Hour**s antiphons are given with psalms and canticles, and with the Gospel Canticle (e.g. **Magnificat**). The text of the antiphon can add meaning to the accompanying psalm (etc.) and/or the place in the liturgy.

Benedictus   The **Canticle** of Zechariah taken from the Gospel of Luke (1.68–79). It is part of Morning Prayer.

Bishops' Conference   The formal coming together of bishops within a particular country or territory (such as England and Wales). It is the decision-making body for many matters relating to the liturgy in that area, such as the approval of translations.

Blessed Sacrament   One of the names for the consecrated Bread and Wine. It usually refers to the reserved consecrated hosts which are kept in the **tabernacle** and are a fruit of the celebration of Mass.

Breviary   A name for the book which contains the **Liturgy of the Hours**.

Canticle   An Old or New Testament text that is similar to a psalm, poetic and, in the liturgy, intended to be sung. Canticles can be found in the **Lectionary**, in place of the psalm, and in the **Liturgy of the Hours**. There are three Gospel Canticles sung at different hours: **Benedictus, Magnificat, Nunc dimittis.**

Catechumen   An unbaptized person who seeks to become a member of the Church through the sacraments of Baptism, Confirmation and Eucharist at the Easter Vigil through the *RCIA*. It can refer to the person during the whole process or just during the **Catechumenate** between the Rite of Acceptance and the Rite of Election.

Catechumenate   The period in the *RCIA* when the main passing-on of the Catholic faith, through doctrine, liturgy and the life of the Church, takes place. It begins after the Rite of Acceptance and concludes with the Rite of Election. The period can take as long as is needed, even a couple of years. The term can also refer to the whole of the *RCIA* process. It is also referred to in the 'catechumenal model' where the principles of liturgy and catechesis found in the Catechumenate are applied to other rites.

Chair   Will usually refer to the distinct chair on the **Sanctuary** used by the priest to lead the liturgy.

Chrism   Oil (usually olive) that is made fragrant with balsam or other perfume. The oil is consecrated by the bishop at the Chrism Mass (which takes place before the beginning of the **Triduum**). The oil is used for anointing in the Sacraments of Baptism, Confirmation and Ordination.

Coetus   The Latin word for a 'group'. It can refer to the number of small groups that were established to renew the individual liturgical rites after the **Second Vatican Council**.

Compline   Another name for Night Prayer, which is part of the **Liturgy of the Hours**.

Confirmation   The second Sacrament of **Initiation**, after Baptism, where the candidate is anointed with **Chrism** and sealed with the gift of the Holy Spirit.

Consecration (n.b. more than one sense)   To make holy or to set apart. The gifts of bread and wine are consecrated in the **Eucharist**; the oil of **Chrism** is consecrated. In the language used in some of the rites some things that were once spoken of as 'consecrated' are now 'ordained' (bishops) or 'dedicated' (church buildings and altars).

Consilium   The body of bishops, assisted by liturgical experts and scholars, that was set up to implement the reform of the liturgy mandated by *Sacrosanctum Concilium.*

Divine Office   See **Liturgy of the Hours**.

Doxology   An expression of praise.

Editio Typica   The first edition of a Latin liturgical text. It is the reference point for translations.

Editio Typica Altera   An amended or second edition of a Latin liturgical text. It can include changes to match other liturgical books or additional material.

(the) Elect   Those who are chosen. In both the Catechumenate and Ordination the individual is chosen by the bishop on behalf of the Church so that they may go forward to the next stage.

Embolism   A text inserted between two passages of text that were once continuous.

Encyclical Letter   A papal document with high authority. Usually an examination of a theological issue.

Epiclesis   The calling down of the Holy Spirit through text and gesture (both hands held out). The Holy Spirit is asked to transform the focus of the prayer. Bread and wine, and later the Church in the **Eucharistic Prayer,** or the water used for Baptism.

Eucharist   Derived from the Greek word 'to give thanks'. It can refer to the consecrated Bread and Wine, as well as the whole of Mass.

Eucharistic Prayer   A long prayer text made up of a number of elements at the centre of the Mass. It is prayer of thanksgiving during which the gifts of bread and wine are transformed into the Body and Blood of Christ. The *Missal* contains a number of Eucharistic Prayer texts (see Chapter 7).

Exposition of the Blessed Sacrament   A host consecrated at a previous Mass is placed on the altar within a monstrance (an object for displaying the Blessed Sacrament) for a time of communal prayer and adoration. At the end, a priest or deacon gives Benediction (a blessing) by lifting up the monstrance and making the sign of the cross with it.

Exsultet   Also referred to as the Easter Proclamation. A prayer of praise and thanksgiving for the light of the Paschal candle sung at the beginning of the Easter Vigil.

Feast   One of the ranks of liturgical days between a **Solemnity** and a **Memorial**. Many of the Apostles are celebrated as Feasts. On a Feast the Gloria is sung. Feasts of the Lord (e.g. the Baptism of the Lord) take precedence over the Sunday readings and prayers.

Font   The place for Baptism. At its simplest a bowl for water but in most churches it will be a substantial structure given its own distinct space (see Chapter 3).

Incipit   See **Lectionary**.

Lauds   Another name for Morning Prayer, which is part of the **Liturgy of the Hours**.

Lectionary   In the Roman liturgy the readings are not read directly from a Bible but from a distinct liturgical book. The **editio typica** of the Lectionary, *Ordo Lectionum Missae*, is just a series of liturgical days and Scripture references. The Lectionary gives the Scripture text which may have been edited at the beginning (*incipit*) so that it makes sense.

Limen   A threshold, the part of a doorway that is neither inside or outside. Used as a term in Rites of Passage to describe a period between two stages of life.

Liturgy of the Hours   The formal, liturgical prayer that marks the different hours of the day, such as Morning and Evening Prayer. It is also called the Divine Office, the Prayer of the Church or the Breviary.

Magnificat   The **Canticle** of Mary taken from the Gospel of Luke (1.46–55). It is part of Evening Prayer.

Memorial   One of the ranks of liturgical days below a **Solemnity** and a **Feast**. The majority of the saints included in the liturgical calendar are Memorials. For celebration of Mass the Memorial is Obligatory or Optional.

Mystagogy   The final period of *RCIA* following the celebrations of the Sacraments of Initiation at the Easter Vigil. It lasts for the Easter Season. The word means to 'go deeper' and is a reflection on the experience of the sacraments and from that a deeper understanding of faith.

Neophyte   The name for the newly initiated through the sacraments at the Easter Vigil.

Normative   The usual, model or principal form of a text or a rite.

Nunc dimittis   The **Canticle** of Simeon taken from the Gospel of Luke (2.29–32). It is part of Night Prayer.

Order of Mass   The liturgical text of the unchanging parts in a celebration of Mass. Found in the *Roman Missal*.

Ordinary   There are a number of meanings in the liturgical context.
     The diocesan bishop or the superior of a religious community who has authority in Church matters.
     The unchanging parts of the **Order of Mass** sung or said by the people (Kyrie, Gloria, Creed, Sanctus, Lamb of God).
     The Ordinary Form is a **normative** form of the liturgy comprising the liturgical rites renewed after the Second Vatican Council.

Paschal Mystery   The passion, death, resurrection and ascension of Christ – through these events the redemption of humanity is achieved.

Praenotanda   The Latin name for 'General Introduction' to a liturgical book, offering a theological overview of the rite it contains, and indications as to how it is to be celebrated.

Proper   The changeable texts of Mass and the Liturgy of the Hours that are particular to a day or a season. Proper texts include Antiphons, Collects, Readings.

Rubric   An instruction embedded in the liturgical text that indicates how the rite or text is performed. The name derives from the red ink that is still used to differentiate the rubric from the spoken text.

Sacramentals   Sacred signs that bear a resemblance to the sacraments: for example, Holy Water, which puts one in mind of Baptism.

Sacrosanctum Concilium   The major document on the liturgy from the **Second Vatican Council**.

Sanctuary   The part of a church building where the altar, **ambo** and **chair** are placed.

Second Vatican Council   Throughout its history the Catholic Church has convened major meetings (Councils) of all the bishops of the Church. The Second Vatican Council (1962–65) is the last Council. It was concerned with the renewal of the life and teaching of the Church in the light of the contemporary experience. Following the Council all the liturgical rites were renewed according to the principles laid out in *Sacrosanctum Concilium*.

Solemnity   One of the ranks of liturgical days above a **Feast** and a **Memorial**. Solemnities mark major festivals in the liturgical year (e.g. The Nativity of the Lord or St Peter and St Paul). On Solemnities the Gloria and the Creed are said. A Solemnity takes precedence over a Sunday in the seasons of Christmas and Ordinary Time.

Tabernacle   The fixture where the reserved, consecrated host is placed. In churches it will be placed in a separate Blessed Sacrament Chapel, allowing for prayer and devotions, or on the **sanctuary**.

Typical Edition   See *Editio Typica*.

Vespers   Another name for Evening Prayer, which is part of the **Liturgy of the Hours**.

Acknowledgements of Sources

ICEL texts

Divine Office

Scripture

Scripture quotations are from

Index